Splunk Operational Intelligence Cookbook

Over 70 practical recipes to gain operational data
intelligence with Splunk Enterprise

Josh Diakun

Paul R Johnson

Derek Mock

PUBLISHING

BIRMINGHAM - MUMBAI

Splunk Operational Intelligence Cookbook

First published: October 2014

Production reference: 1241014

Published by Packt Publishing Ltd.
Livery Place
35 Livery Street
Birmingham B3 2PB, UK.

ISBN 978-1-84969-784-2

www.packtpub.com

Cover image by Paul R Johnson (paul@discoveredintelligence.ca)

Credits

Authors

Josh Diakun

Paul R Johnson

Derek Mock

Reviewers

Mika Borner

Amit Mund

Jon Webster

Commissioning Editor

Kartikey Pandey

Acquisition Editor

Rebecca Youé

Content Development Editor

Anila Vincent

Technical Editor

Veronica Fernandes

Copy Editors

Janbal Dharmaraj

Sayanee Mukherjee

Karuna Narayanan

Project Coordinator

Neha Bhatnagar

Proofreaders

Simran Bhogal

Mario Cecere

Bernadette Watkins

Indexer

Monica Ajmera Mehta

Production Coordinators

Kyle Albuquerque

Arvindkumar Gupta

Conidon Miranda

Alwin Roy

Cover Work

Conidon Miranda

About the Authors

Josh Diakun is an IT operations and security specialist with a focus on creating data-driven operational processes. He has over 10 years of experience in managing and architecting enterprise grade IT environments. For the past 5 years, he was managing a Splunk deployment that saw Splunk used as the platform for security and operational intelligence. Most recently, Josh has partnered in setting up a business venture, Discovered Intelligence, which provides data intelligence solutions and services to the marketplace. He is also a cofounder of the Splunk Toronto User Group.

I would first like to thank my co-authors, Derek Mock and Paul R Johnson, for their support, endless efforts, and those many late nights that led to this book becoming a reality. To my partner, Rachel—an endless thank you for being my biggest supporter and making sure I always remembered to take a break. To my mother, Denyce, and sister, Jessika—thank you for being the two most amazing people in my life and cheering me on as I wrote this book. Finally, to my late father, John, who was always an inspiration and brought the best out of me; without him, I would not be where I am today.

Paul R Johnson has over 10 years of data intelligence experience in the areas of information security, operations, and compliance. He is a partner at Discovered Intelligence—a company that specializes in data intelligence services and solutions. He previously worked for a Fortune 10 company, leading IT risk intelligence initiatives and managing a global Splunk deployment. Paul cofounded the Splunk Toronto User Group and lives and works in Toronto, Canada.

I would like to thank my fellow authors, Josh Diakun and Derek Mock, for their support and collaborative efforts in writing this book. Thanks guys for giving up nights, days, and weekends to get it completed! I would also like to thank my wife, Stacey, for her continuous support, for keeping me focused, and for her great feedback and patience.

Derek Mock is a software developer and architect, specializing in unified communications and cloud technologies. Derek has over 15 years of experience in developing and operating large enterprise-grade deployments and SaaS applications. For the past 4 years, he has been leveraging Splunk as the core tool to deliver key operational intelligence. Derek is a cofounder of the Splunk Toronto User Group and lives and works in Toronto, Canada.

I could not have asked for better co-authors than Josh Diakun and Paul R Johnson, whose tireless efforts over many late nights brought this book into being. I would also like to thank my mentor, Dave Penny, for all his support in my professional life. Finally, thanks to my partner, Alison, and my children, Sarah and James, for cheering me on as I wrote this book and for always making sure I had enough coffee.

About the Reviewers

Mika Borner is a management consultant for data analytics at LC Systems based in Switzerland, Germany, and Austria.

Drawing on his years of experience, he provides Splunk consulting in the telecommunications/ISP, financial, retail, and other industries. During the course of his career, he has held numerous positions in systems engineering in IT, with service providers, telecommunications/ISP companies, and financial institutions.

Mika was one of the first Splunk users in Europe and was later running one of the largest Splunk environments worldwide. He is also a regular speaker at the Splunk User Conference.

Amit Mund has been working on Linux and other technologies on automation and infrastructure monitoring since 2004. He is currently associated with Akamai Technologies and has previously worked for the website-hosting teams at Amazon and Yahoo!.

I would like to thank my wife, Rajashree, for always supporting me and my colleagues for helping me in my learning and development throughout my professional career.

Jon Webster has been fascinated with computers since he met his first mainframe at Hewlett-Packard at the age of 11 and played chess and Qubic on it.

In his roles from an ERP Developer through APM Product Manager and Splunk Architect, Jon has always sought to apply the maximum leverage that technology offers for his customers' benefit.

I'd like to thank my parents for encouraging me to explore these strange things they didn't understand, David Kleber and Kennon Ward for helping me learn how to optimize my code and my career, PeopleSoft for the amazing playgrounds and opportunities, Alan Habib for dragging me into APM (just attend one meeting!), and finally, Splunk for the most amazing people, tools, and opportunities I've ever had the pleasure of working with. The "Aha!" moments keep coming!

www.PacktPub.com

Support files, eBooks, discount offers, and more

You might want to visit www.PacktPub.com for support files and downloads related to your book.

Did you know that Packt offers eBook versions of every book published, with PDF and ePub files available? You can upgrade to the eBook version at www.PacktPub.com and as a print book customer, you are entitled to a discount on the eBook copy. Get in touch with us at service@packtpub.com for more details.

At www.PacktPub.com, you can also read a collection of free technical articles, sign up for a range of free newsletters and receive exclusive discounts and offers on Packt books and eBooks.

http://PacktLib.PacktPub.com

Do you need instant solutions to your IT questions? PacktLib is Packt's online digital book library. Here, you can access, read and search across Packt's entire library of books.

Why subscribe?

- ► Fully searchable across every book published by Packt
- ► Copy and paste, print and bookmark content
- ► On demand and accessible via web browser

Free access for Packt account holders

If you have an account with Packt at www.PacktPub.com, you can use this to access PacktLib today and view nine entirely free books. Simply use your login credentials for immediate access.

Table of Contents

Preface

In a technology-centric world, where machines generate a vast amount of data at an incredibly high volume, Splunk has come up with its industry-leading big data intelligence platform—Splunk Enterprise. This powerful platform enables anyone to turn machine data into actionable and very valuable intelligence.

Splunk Operational Intelligence Cookbook is a collection of recipes that aim to provide you, the reader, with the guidance and practical knowledge to harness the endless features of Splunk Enterprise 6 for the purpose of deriving extremely powerful and valuable operational intelligence from your data.

Using easy-to-follow, step-by-step recipes, this book will teach you how to effectively gather, analyze, and create a report on the operational data available in your environment. The recipes provided will demonstrate methods to expedite the delivery of intelligent reports and empower you to present data in a meaningful way through dashboards and by applying many of the visualizations available in Splunk Enterprise. By the end of this book, you will have built a powerful Operational Intelligence application and applied many of the key features found in the Splunk Enterprise platform.

This book and its easy-to-follow recipes can also be extended to act as a teaching tool for you as you introduce others to the Splunk Enterprise platform and to your new found ability to provide promotion-worthy operational intelligence.

What this book covers

Chapter 1, Play Time – Getting Data In, introduces you to the many ways in which data can be put into Splunk, whether it is by collecting data locally from files and directories, through TCP/UDP port inputs, directly from a Universal Forwarder, or by simply utilizing scripted and modular inputs. You will also be introduced to the datasets that will be referenced throughout this book and learn how to generate samples that can be used to follow each of the recipes as they are written.

Chapter 2, Diving into Data – Search and Report, will provide an introduction to the first set of recipes in this book. Leveraging data now available as a result of the previous chapter, the information and recipes provided here will act as a guide, walking you through searching event data using Splunk's SPL (Search Processing Language); applying field extractions; grouping common events based on field values; and then building basic reports using the table, top, chart, and stats commands.

Chapter 3, Dashboards and Visualizations – Make Data Shine, acts as a guide to building visualizations based on reports that can now be created as a result of the information and recipes provided in the previous chapter. This chapter will empower you to take your data and reports and bring them to life through the powerful visualizations provided by Splunk. The visualizations that are introduced will include single values, charts (bar, pie, line, and area), scatter charts, and gauges.

Chapter 4, Building an Operational Intelligence Application, builds on the understanding of visualizations that you have gained as a result of the previous chapter and introduces the concept of dashboards. The information and recipes provided in this chapter will outline the purpose of dashboards and teach you how to properly utilize dashboards, use the dashboard editor to build a dashboard, build a form to search event data, and much more.

Chapter 5, Extending Intelligence – Data Models and Pivoting, will take you deeper into the data by introducing transactions, subsearching, concurrency, associations, and more advanced search commands. Through the information and recipes provided in this chapter, you will harness the ability to converge data from different sources and understand how to build relationships between differing event data.

Chapter 6, Diving Deeper – Advanced Searching, will introduce the concept of lookups and workflow actions for the purpose of augmenting the data being analyzed. The recipes provided will enable you to apply this core functionality to further enhance your understanding of the data being analyzed.

Chapter 7, Enriching Data – Lookups and Workflows, explains how scheduled or real-time alerts are a key asset to complete operational intelligence and awareness. This chapter will introduce you to the concepts and benefits of proactive alerts, and provide context for when these alerts are best applied. The recipes provided will guide you through creating alerts based on the knowledge gained from previous chapters.

Chapter 8, Being Proactive – Creating Alerts, explains the concept of summary indexing for the purposes of accelerating reports and speeding up the time it takes to unlock business insight. The recipes in this chapter will provide you with a short introduction to common situations where summary indexing can be leveraged to speed up reports or preserve focused statistics over long periods of time.

Chapter 9, Speed Up Intelligence – Data Summarization, introduces two of the newest and most powerful features released as part of Splunk Enterprise Version 6: data models and the Pivot tool. The recipes provided in this chapter will guide you through the concept of building data models and using the Pivot tool to quickly design intelligent reports based on the constructed models.

Chapter 10, Above and Beyond – Customization, Web Framework, REST API, and SDKs, is the final chapter of the book and will introduce you to four very powerful features of Splunk. These features provide the ability to create a very rich and powerful interactive experience with Splunk. The recipes provided will open you up to the possibilities beyond core Splunk Enterprise and a method to make your own Operational Intelligence application that includes powerful D3 visualizations. Beyond this, it will also provide a recipe to query Splunk's REST API and a basic Python application to leverage Splunk's SDK to execute a search.

What you need for this book

To follow along with the recipes provided in this book, you will need an installation of Splunk Enterprise 6 and the sample data that is made available with this book. The recipes are intended to be portable to all Splunk Enterprise environments, but for best results, we suggest that you use the samples provided with this book.

Splunk Enterprise 6 can be downloaded for free for most major platforms from `http://www.splunk.com/download`.

The samples provided with this book will also be packaged with the Splunk Event Generator tool so that the event data can be refreshed or events can be replayed as new as you work through the recipes.

Who this book is for

This book is intended for all users, beginner or advanced, who are looking to leverage the Splunk Enterprise platform as a valuable Operational Intelligence tool. The recipes provided in this book will appeal to individuals from all facets of a business—IT, security, product, marketing, and many more!

Although the book and its recipes are written so that anyone can follow along, it does progress at a steady pace into concepts or features that might not be common knowledge to a beginner. If there exists the necessity to understand more about a feature, Splunk has produced a vast amount of documentation on all Splunk Enterprise features available at `http://docs.splunk.com/Documentation/Splunk`.

There might also be sections that utilize regular expressions and introduce recipes that take advantage of the Python and XML languages. Experience with these concepts is not required but beneficial.

Conventions

In this book, you will find a number of styles of text that distinguish between different kinds of information. Here are some examples of these styles, and an explanation of their meaning.

Code words in text, database table names, folder names, filenames, file extensions, pathnames, dummy URLs, user input, and Twitter handles are shown as follows: "The field values are displayed in a table using the `table` command."

A block of code is set as follows:

```
<table>
 <searchString>
   index=opintel status=404 | stats count by src_ip
 </searchString>
 <title>Report - 404 Errors by Source IP</title>
```

When we wish to draw your attention to a particular part of a code block, the relevant lines or items are set in bold:

```
<table>
 <searchString>
   index=opintel status=404 | stats count by src_ip
 </searchString>
 <title>Report - 404 Errors by Source IP</title>
```

Any command-line input or output is written as follows:

```
./splunk add monitor /var/log/messages –sourcetype linux_messages
```

New terms and **important words** are shown in bold. Words that you see on the screen, in menus or dialog boxes for example, appear in the text like this: "Quickly create a report by navigating to **Save As | Report** above the search bar."

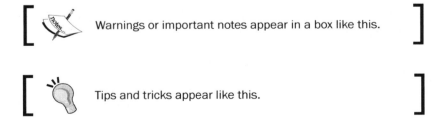

> Warnings or important notes appear in a box like this.

> Tips and tricks appear like this.

Reader feedback

Feedback from our readers is always welcome. Let us know what you think about this book—what you liked or may have disliked. Reader feedback is important for us to develop titles that you really get the most out of.

To send us general feedback, simply send an e-mail to `feedback@packtpub.com`, and mention the book title via the subject of your message.

If there is a topic that you have expertise in and you are interested in either writing or contributing to a book, see our author guide on `www.packtpub.com/authors`.

Customer support

Now that you are the proud owner of a Packt book, we have a number of things to help you to get the most from your purchase.

Downloading the example code

You can download the example code files for all Packt books you have purchased from your account at `http://www.packtpub.com`. If you purchased this book elsewhere, you can visit `http://www.packtpub.com/support` and register to have the files e-mailed directly to you.

Errata

Although we have taken every care to ensure the accuracy of our content, mistakes do happen. If you find a mistake in one of our books—maybe a mistake in the text or the code—we would be grateful if you would report this to us. By doing so, you can save other readers from frustration and help us improve subsequent versions of this book. If you find any errata, please report them by visiting `http://www.packtpub.com/submit-errata`, selecting your book, clicking on the **errata submission form** link, and entering the details of your errata. Once your errata are verified, your submission will be accepted and the errata will be uploaded on our website, or added to any list of existing errata, under the Errata section of that title. Any existing errata can be viewed by selecting your title from `http://www.packtpub.com/support`.

Piracy

Piracy of copyright material on the Internet is an ongoing problem across all media. At Packt, we take the protection of our copyright and licenses very seriously. If you come across any illegal copies of our works, in any form, on the Internet, please provide us with the location address or website name immediately so that we can pursue a remedy.

Please contact us at `copyright@packtpub.com` with a link to the suspected pirated material.

We appreciate your help in protecting our authors, and our ability to bring you valuable content.

Questions

You can contact us at `questions@packtpub.com` if you are having a problem with any aspect of the book, and we will do our best to address it.

1
Play Time – Getting Data In

In this chapter, we will cover the basic ways to get data into Splunk. You will learn about:

- ▸ Indexing files and directories
- ▸ Getting data through network ports
- ▸ Using scripted inputs
- ▸ Using modular inputs
- ▸ Using the Universal Forwarder to gather data
- ▸ Loading the sample data for this book
- ▸ Defining field extractions
- ▸ Defining event types and tags

Introduction

The machine data that facilitates operational intelligence comes in many different forms and from many different sources. Splunk is able to collect and index data from many different sources, including logfiles written by web servers or business applications, syslog data streaming in from network devices, or the output of custom developed scripts. Even data that looks complex at first can be easily collected, indexed, transformed, and presented back to you in real time.

This chapter will walk you through the basic recipes that will act as the building blocks to get the data you want into Splunk. The chapter will further serve as an introduction to the sample datasets that we will use to build our own Operational Intelligence Splunk app. The datasets will be coming from a hypothetical, three-tier, e-commerce web application and will contain web server logs, application logs, and database logs.

Splunk Enterprise can index any type of data; however, it works best with time-series data (data with timestamps). When Splunk Enterprise indexes data, it breaks it into events, based on timestamps and/or event size, and puts them into indexes. Indexes are data stores that Splunk has engineered to be very fast, searchable, and scalable across a distributed server environment; they are commonly referred to as indexers. This is also why we refer to the data being put into Splunk as being indexed.

All data indexed into Splunk is assigned a source type. The source type helps identify the data format type of the event and where it has come from. Splunk has a number of preconfigured source types, but you can also specify your own. The example sourcetypes include `access_combined`, `cisco_syslog`, and `linux_secure`. The source type is added to the data when the indexer indexes it into Splunk. It is a key field that is used when performing field extractions and in many searches to filter the data being searched.

The Splunk community plays a big part in making it easy to get data into Splunk. The ability to extend Splunk has provided the opportunity for the development of inputs, commands, and applications that can be easily shared. If there is a particular system or application you are looking to index data from, there is most likely someone who has developed and published relevant configurations and tools that can be easily leveraged by your own Splunk Enterprise deployment.

Splunk Enterprise is designed to make the collection of data very easy, and it will not take long before you are being asked or you yourself try to get as much data into Splunk as possible—at least as much as your license will allow for!

Indexing files and directories

File- and directory-based inputs are the most commonly used ways of getting data into Splunk. The primary need for these types of inputs will be to index logfiles. Almost every application or system will produce a logfile, and it is generally full of data that you would want to be able to search and report on.

Splunk is able to continuously monitor for new data being written to existing files or new files added to a directory, and it is able to index this data in real time. Depending on the type of application that creates the logfiles, you would set up Splunk to either monitor an individual file based on its location or scan an entire directory and monitor all the files that exist within it. The later configuration is more commonly used when the logfiles being produced have unique filenames, for example, the name they have contains a timestamp.

This recipe will show you how to configure Splunk to continuously monitor and index the contents of a rolling logfile located on the Splunk server. The recipe specifically shows how to monitor and index the Linux system's `messages` logfile (`/var/log/messages`). However, the same principle can be applied to a logfile on a Windows system, and a sample file is provided. Do not attempt to index the Windows event logs this way, as Splunk has specific Windows event inputs for this.

Getting ready

To step through this recipe, you will need a running Splunk Enterprise server and access to read the `/var/log/messages` file on Linux. There are no other prerequisites. If you are not using Linux and/or do not have access to the `/var/log/messages` location on your Splunk server, please use the `cp01_messages.log` file that is provided and upload it to an accessible directory on your Splunk server.

Downloading the example code

You can download the example code files for all Packt books you have purchased from your account at `http://www.packtpub.com`. If you purchased this book elsewhere, you can visit `http://www.packtpub.com/support` and register to have the files e-mailed directly to you.

How to do it...

Follow the steps in the recipe to monitor and index the contents of a file:

1. Log in to your Splunk server.
2. From the home launcher in the top-right corner, click on the **Add Data** button.

3. In the **Choose a Data Type** list, click on **A file or directory of files**.

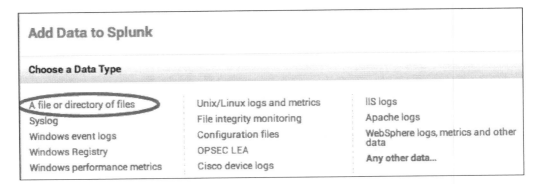

4. Click on **Next** in the **Consume any file on this Splunk server** option.

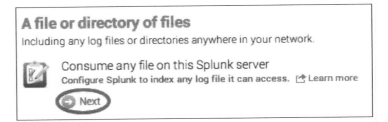

5. Select **Preview data before indexing** and enter the path to the logfile (`/var/log/messages` or the location of the `cp01_messages.log` file) and click on **Continue**.

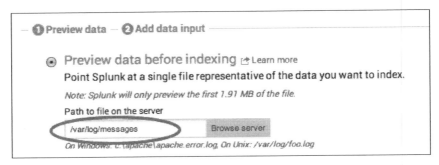

6. Select **Start a new source type** and click on **Continue**.

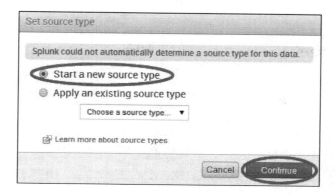

7. Assuming that you are using the provided file or the native `/var/log/messages` file, the data preview will show the correct line breaking of events and timestamp recognition. Click on the **Continue** button.

8. A **Review settings** box will pop up. Enter `linux_messages` as the source type and then, click on **Save source type**.

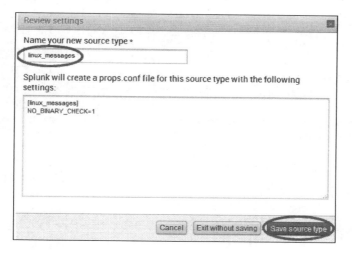

9. A **Sourcetype saved** box will appear. Select **Create input**.

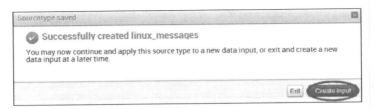

10. In the **Source** section, select **Continuously index data from a file or directory this Splunk instance can access** and fill in the path to your data.

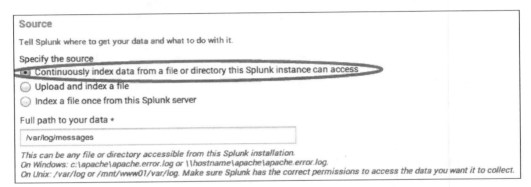

 If you are just looking to do a one-time upload of a file, you can select **Upload and Index** a file instead. This can be useful to index a set of data that you would like to put into Splunk, either to backfill some missing or incomplete data or just to take advantage of its searching and reporting tools.

11. Ignore the other settings for now and simply click on **Save**. Then, on the next screen, click on **Start searching**. In the search bar, enter the following search over a time range of **All time**:

```
sourcetype=linux_messages
```

 In this recipe, we could have simply used the common syslog source type; however, starting a new source type is often a better choice. The syslog format can look completely different depending on the data source. As knowledge objects, such as field extractions, are built on top of source types, using a single syslog source type for everything can make it challenging to search for the data you need.

How it works...

When you add a new file or directory data input, you are basically adding a new configuration stanza into an `inputs.conf` file behind the scenes. The Splunk server can contain one or more `inputs.conf` files, and these files are either located in `$SPLUNK_HOME/etc/system/local` or in the `local` directory of a Splunk app.

Splunk uses the **monitor** input type and is set to point to either a file or a directory. If you set the monitor to a directory, all files within that directory will be monitored. When Splunk monitors files, it initially starts by indexing all of the data that it can read from the beginning. Once complete, Splunk will maintain a record of where it last read data from, and if any new data comes into the file, it will read this data and advance the record. The process is nearly identical to using the tail command in Unix-based operating systems. If you are monitoring a directory, Splunk also provides many additional configuration options such as blacklisting files you don't want Splunk to index.

 For more information on Splunk's configuration files, visit `http://docs.splunk.com/Documentation/Splunk/latest/Admin/Aboutconfigurationfiles`.

There's more...

While adding inputs to monitor files and directories can be done through the web interface of Splunk as outlined in this recipe, there are other approaches to add multiple inputs quickly. These allow for customization of the many configuration options that Splunk provides.

Adding a file or directory data input via the CLI

Instead of going via the GUI, you could add a file or directory input via the Splunk **CLI** (**command-line interface**). Navigate to your `$SPLUNK_HOME/bin` directory and execute the following command (replacing the file or directory to be monitored with your own):

For Unix:

```
./splunk add monitor /var/log/messages -sourcetype linux_messages
```

For Windows:

```
splunk add monitor c:\filelocation\cp01_messages.log -sourcetype linux_messages
```

There are a number of different parameters that can be passed along with the file location to monitor. See the Splunk documentation for more on data inputs using the CLI (`http://docs.splunk.com/Documentation/Splunk/latest/Data/MonitorfilesanddirectoriesusingtheCLI`).

Adding a file or directory input via inputs.conf

Another common method of adding file and directory inputs is to manually add them to the `inputs.conf` configuration file directly. This approach is often used for large environments or when configuring Splunk forwarders to monitor for files or directories on endpoints.

Edit `$SPLUNK_HOME/etc/system/local/inputs.conf` and add your input. After your inputs are added, Splunk will need to be restarted to recognize these changes:

For Unix:

```
[monitor:///var/log/messages]
sourcetype = linux_messages
```

For Windows:

```
[monitor://c:\filelocation\cp01_messages.log]
sourcetype = linux_messages
```

Editing `inputs.conf` directly is often a much faster way of adding new files or directories to monitor when several inputs are needed. When editing `inputs.conf`, ensure that the correct syntax is used and remember that Splunk will need a restart for modifications to take effect. Additionally, specifying the source type in the `inputs.conf` file is the best practice to assign source types.

One-time indexing of data files via the Splunk CLI

Although you can select **Upload and Index a file** from the Splunk GUI to upload and index a file, there are a couple of CLI functions that can be used to perform one-time bulk loads of data.

Use the `oneshot` command to tell Splunk where the file is located and which parameters to use, such as the source type:

```
./splunk add oneshot XXXXXXX
```

Another way is to place the file you wish to index into the Splunk spool directory, `$SPLUNK_HOME/var/spool/splunk`, and then add the file using the `spool` command:

```
./splunk spool XXXXXXX
```

If using Windows, omit `./` that is in front of the Splunk commands, mentioned earlier.

Indexing the Windows event logs

Splunk comes with special `inputs.conf` configurations for some source types, including monitoring the Windows event logs. Typically, the Splunk **Universal Forwarder** (**UF**) would be installed on a Windows server and configured to forward the Windows events to the Splunk indexer(s). The configurations for `inputs.conf` to monitor Windows security, application, and system event logs in real time are as follows:

```
[WinEventLog://Application]
disabled = 0
[WinEventLog://Security]
disabled = 0
[WinEventLog://System]
disabled = 0
```

By default, the event data will go into the main index, unless another index is specified.

See also

- ▸ The *Getting data through network ports* recipe
- ▸ The *Using scripted inputs* recipe
- ▸ The *Using modular inputs* recipe

Getting data through network ports

Not every machine has the luxury of being able to write logfiles. Sending data over network ports and protocols is still very common. For instance, sending logs via syslog is still the primary method to capture network device data such as firewalls, routers, and switches.

Sending data to Splunk over network ports doesn't need to be limited to network devices. Applications and scripts can use socket communication to the network ports that Splunk is listening on. This can be a very useful tool in your back pocket, as there can be scenarios where you need to get data into Splunk but don't necessarily have the ability to write to a file.

This recipe will show you how to configure Splunk to receive syslog data on a UDP network port, but it is also applicable to the TCP port configuration.

Getting ready

To step through this recipe, you will need a running Splunk Enterprise server. There are no other prerequisites.

How to do it...

Follow the steps in the recipe to configure Splunk to receive network UDP data:

1. Log in to your Splunk server.

2. From the home launcher in the top-right corner, click on the **Add Data** button.

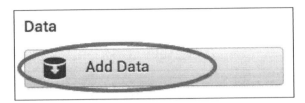

3. In the **Or Choose a Data Source** list, click on the **From a UDP port** link.

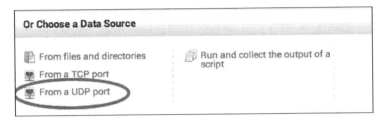

4. In the Source section, enter `514` in the **UDP port** field. On Unix/Linux, Splunk must be running as root to access privileged ports such as 514. An alternative would be to specify a higher port such as port 1514 or route data from 514 to another port using routing rules in `iptables`.

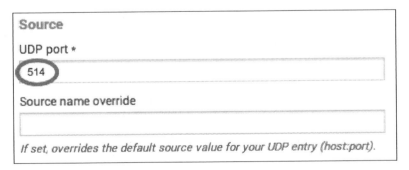

5. In the **Source type** section, select **From list** from the **Set sourcetype** drop-down list, and then, select **syslog** from the **Select source type from list** drop-down list.

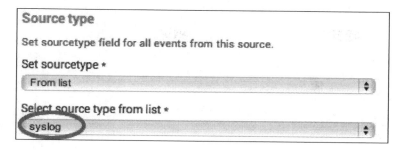

6. Click on **Save**, and on the next screen, click on **Start searching**. Splunk is now configured to listen on UDP port 514. Any data sent to this port now will be assigned the syslog source type. To search for the syslog source type, you can run the following search:

```
sourcetype=syslog
```

Understandably, you will not see any data unless you happen to be sending data to your Splunk server IP on UDP port 514.

How it works...

When you add a new network port input, you are basically adding a new configuration stanza into an `inputs.conf` file behind the scenes. The Splunk server can contain one or more `inputs.conf` files, and these files are either located in the `$SPLUNK_HOME/etc/system/local` or `local` directory of a Splunk app.

To collect data on a network port, Splunk will set up a socket to listen on the specified TCP or UDP port and will index any data it receives on that port. For example, in this recipe, you configured Splunk to listen on port 514 for UDP data. If data was received on that port, then Splunk would index it and assign a **syslog** source type to it.

Splunk also provides many configuration options that can be used with network inputs, such as how to resolve the host value to use on the collected data.

 For more information on Splunk's configuration files, visit `http://docs.splunk.com/Documentation/Splunk/latest/Admin/Aboutconfigurationfiles`.

There's more...

While adding inputs to receive data from network ports can be done through the web interface of Splunk as outlined in this recipe, there are other approaches to add multiple inputs quickly; these inputs allow for customization of the many configuration options that Splunk provides.

Adding a network input via the CLI

You can also add a file or directory input via the Splunk CLI. Navigate to your `$SPLUNK_HOME/bin` directory and execute the following command (just replace the protocol, port, and source type you wish to use):

For Unix:

```
./splunk add udp 514 -sourcetype syslog
```

For Windows:

```
splunk add udp 514 -sourcetype syslog
```

There are a number of different parameters that can be passed along with the port. See the Splunk documentation for more on data inputs using the CLI (`http://docs.splunk.com/Documentation/Splunk/latest/Data/MonitorfilesanddirectoriesusingtheCLI`).

Adding a network input via inputs.conf

Network inputs can be manually added to the `inputs.conf` configuration files. Edit `$SPLUNK_HOME/etc/system/local/inputs.conf` and add your input. You will need to restart Splunk after modifying the file.

```
[udp://514]
sourcetype = syslog
```

 It is best practice to not send syslog data directly to an indexer. Instead, always place a forwarder between the network device and the indexer. The Splunk forwarder would be set up to receive the incoming syslog data (`inputs.conf`) and will load balance the data across your Splunk indexers (`outputs.conf`). The forwarder can also be configured to cache the syslog data in the event that communication to the indexers is lost.

See also

- ► The *Indexing files and directories* recipe
- ► The *Using scripted inputs* recipe
- ► The *Using modular inputs* recipe

Using scripted inputs

Not all data that is useful for operational intelligence comes from logfiles or network ports. Splunk will happily take the output of a command or script and index it along with all of your other data.

Scripted inputs are a very helpful way to get that hard-to-reach data. For example, if you have third-party-supplied command-line programs that can output data you would like to collect, Splunk can run the command periodically and index the results. Typically scripted inputs are often used to *pull* data from a source, whereas network inputs await a *push* of data from a source.

This recipe will show you how to configure Splunk on an interval to execute your command and direct the output into Splunk.

Getting ready

To step through this recipe, you will need a running Splunk server and the provided scripted input script suited to the environment you are using. For example, if you are using Windows, use the `cp01_scripted_input.bat` file. This script should be placed in the `$SPLUNK_HOME/bin/scripts` directory. There are no other prerequisites.

How to do it...

Follow the steps in the recipe to configure a scripted input:

1. Log in to your Splunk server.
2. From the home launcher in the top-right corner, click on the **Add Data** button.

3. In the **Or Choose a Data Source** list, click on the **Run and collect the output of a script** link.

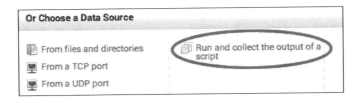

4. An **Add new** screen will be displayed, with a number of input fields. In the **Source** section, enter the full path for the command to be run, including any command-line arguments. All scripts must be located in a Splunk bin directory, either in $SPLUNK_ HOME/bin/scripts or an appropriate bin directory in a Splunk app.

5. Enter the value in the **Interval** field (in seconds) in which the script is to be run; the default value is 60.0 seconds.

6. In the **Source type** section, you have the option to select a predefined source type, or select **Manual** and enter your desired value. For the purposes of this recipe, select **Manual** as the sourcetype and enter cp01_scripted_input as the value for the sourcetype.

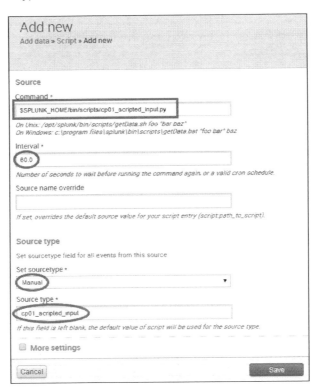

Data will be indexed into Splunk's default index, which is `main`. To change the destination index, you can check the box labeled **More Settings** and select the desired index from the drop-down list.

7. Click on **Save**, and on the next screen, click on **Start searching**. Splunk is now configured to execute the scripted input you provided every 60 seconds in accordance with the specified interval. You can search for the data returned by the scripted input using the following search over **All time**:

```
sourcetype=cp01_scripted_input
```

How it works...

When adding a new scripted input, you are directing Splunk to add a new configuration stanza into an `inputs.conf` file behind the scenes. The Splunk server can contain one or more `inputs.conf` files and these are located either in `$SPLUNK_HOME/etc/system/local` or the `local` directory of a Splunk app.

After creating a scripted input, Splunk sets up an internal timer and will execute the command that you have specified in accordance with the defined interval. It is important to note that Splunk will only run one instance of the script at a time, so if the script gets blocked for any reason, it will cause the script to not be executed again, until after it has been unblocked.

Since Splunk 4.2, any output of the scripted inputs that are directed to `stderr` (causing an error) will be captured in the `splunkd.log` file, which can be useful when attempting to debug the execution of a script. As Splunk indexes its own data by default, you can search for scripted input errors and alert on them if necessary.

For security reasons, Splunk will not execute scripts located outside of the `bin` directories mentioned earlier. In order to overcome this limitation, you can use a wrapper script (such as a shell script in Linux or batch file in Windows) to call any other script located on your machine.

See also

- ▶ The *Indexing files and directories* recipe
- ▶ The *Getting data through network ports* recipe
- ▶ The *Using modular inputs* recipe

Using modular inputs

Since Splunk 5.0, the ability to extend data input functionality has existed such that custom input types can be created and shared while still allowing minor customizations.

Modular inputs build further upon the scripted input model. Originally, any additional functionality required by the user had to be contained within a script. However, this presented a challenge, as no customization of this script could occur from within Splunk itself. For example, pulling data from a source for two different usernames might have needed two copies of a script or might have meant playing around with command-line arguments within your scripted input configuration.

By leveraging the modular input capabilities, developers are now able to encapsulate their code into a reusable app that exposes parameters in Splunk and allows for configuration through the processes familiar to Splunk administrators.

This recipe will walk you through how to install the Command Modular Input, which allows for periodic execution of commands and subsequent indexing of the command output. You will configure the input to collect the data outputted by the `vmstat` command in Linux and the `systeminfo` command in Windows.

Getting ready

To step through this recipe, you will need a running Splunk server with a connection to the Internet. There are no other prerequisites.

How to do it...

Follow the steps in this recipe to configure a modular input:

1. Log in to your Splunk server.
2. From the **Apps** menu in the upper left-hand corner of the home screen, click on **Find More Apps**.

3. In the search field, enter `command modular input` and click on the magnifying glass icon.

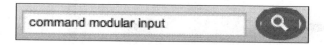

4. In the search results, click on the **Install free** button for **Command Modular Input**.

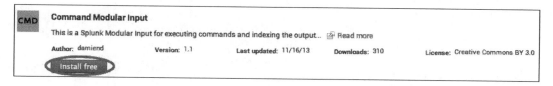

5. Enter your Splunk.com credentials and click on **Login**. Splunk should return with a message saying that the app was installed successfully.

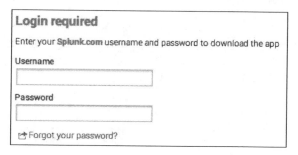

6. From the home launcher in the top-rightd corner, click on the **Settings** menu and then click on the **Data inputs** link.

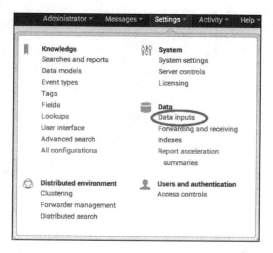

7. On the **Data inputs** page, click on the **Command** link under **Type**.

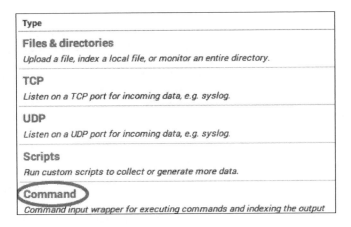

8. Then, click on **New**.

9. In the **Mod Input Name** field, enter SystemInfo.

   If you are using Linux, enter /usr/bin/vmstat in the **Command Name** field.

   If you are using Windows, enter C:\Windows\System32\systeminfo.exe in the **Command Name** field.

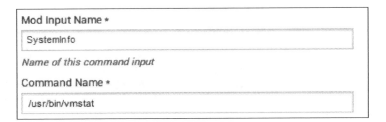

 Use a full path if the command to be executed cannot be found on the system PATH.

10. In the **Command Arguments** field, enter any argument that needs to be passed to the command listed in the **Command Name** field. In the **Command Execution Interval** field, enter a value in seconds for how often the command should be executed (in this case, we will use 60 seconds). If the output is streamed, then leave this field empty and check the **Streaming Output** field.

Command Arguments

Arguments string for the command. Environment variables in the format

☐ **Streaming Output ?**

Whether or not the command output is streaming(std out remains open) relevant.

Command Execution Interval

60

Interval time in seconds to execute the command, defaults to 60 seconds

11. In the **Source type** section, you have the option to select a predefined source type or select **Manual** and enter a value. For the purposes of this recipe, select **Manual** as the sourcetype and enter `cp01_modular_input` as the value for the sourcetype.

12. Click on **Save** to save the input. Splunk is now configured to execute the modular input you provided, every 60 seconds, in accordance with the specified interval. You can search for the data returned by the scripted input using the following search over **All time**:

```
sourcetype=cp01_modular_input
```

How it works...

Modular inputs are bundled as Splunk apps and, once installed, contain all the necessary configuration and code to display them in the **Data inputs** section of Splunk. In this recipe, you installed a modular input application that allows for periodic execution of commands. You configured the command to execute every minute and index the results of the command each time, giving the results a source type of `cp01_modular_input`.

Modular inputs can be written in a number of languages and need to follow only a set of interfaces that expose the configuration options and runtime behaviors. Depending on the design of the input, they will either run persistently or run on an interval and will send data to Splunk as they receive it.

 You can find several other modular inputs, including REST API, SNMP, and PowerShell, on the Splunk Apps site (`http://apps.splunk.com`).

There's more...

To learn how to create your own modular input, refer to the Modular Inputs section of the *Developing Views and Apps for Splunk Web* manual located at `http://docs.splunk.com/Documentation/Splunk/latest/AdvancedDev`.

See also

- ▸ The *Indexing files and directories* recipe
- ▸ The *Getting data through network ports* recipe
- ▸ The *Using scripted inputs* recipe

Using the Universal Forwarder to gather data

Most IT environments today range from multiple servers in the closet of your office to hundreds of endpoint servers located in multiple geographically distributed data centers.

When the data we want to collect is not located directly on the server where Splunk is installed, the Splunk Universal Forwarder (UF) can be installed on your remote endpoint servers and used to forward data back to Splunk to be indexed.

The Universal Forwarder is similar to the Splunk server in that it has many of the same features, but it does not contain Splunk web and doesn't come bundled with the Python executable and libraries. Additionally, the Universal Forwarder cannot process data in advance, such as performing line breaking and timestamp extraction.

This recipe will guide you through configuring the Splunk Universal Forwarder to forward data to a Splunk indexer and will show you how to set up the indexer to receive the data.

Getting ready

To step through this recipe, you will need a server with the Splunk Universal Forwarder installed but not configured. You will also need a running Splunk server. There are no other prerequisites.

> To obtain the Universal Forwarder software, you will need to go to `www.splunk.com/download` and register for an account if you do not already have one. Then, either download the software directly to your server or download it to your laptop or workstation and upload it to your server via a file-transfer process such as SFTP.

How to do it...

Follow the steps in the recipe to configure the Splunk Forwarder to forward data and the Splunk indexer to receive data:

1. On the server with the Universal Forwarder installed, open a command prompt if you are a Windows user or a terminal window if you are a Unix user.

2. Change to the $SPLUNK_HOME/bin directory, where $SPLUNK_HOME is the directory in which the Splunk forwarder was installed.

    For Unix, the default installation directory will be /opt/splunkforwarder/bin. For Windows, it will be C:\Program Files\SplunkUniversalForwarder\bin.

    > If using Windows, omit ./ in front of the Splunk command in the upcoming steps.

3. Start the Splunk forwarder if not already started, using the following command:

    `./splunk start`

4. Accept the license agreement.

5. Enable the Universal Forwarder to autostart, using the following command:

    `./splunk enable boot-start`

6. Set the indexer that this Universal Forwarder will send its data to. Replace the host value with the value of the indexer as well as the username and password for the Universal Forwarder.

    `./splunk add forward-server <host>:9997 -auth <username>:<password>`

    The username and password to log in to the forwarder (default is admin:changeme) is <username>:<password>.

> Additional receiving indexers can be added in the same way by repeating the command in the previous step with a different indexer host or IP. Splunk will automatically load balance the forwarded data if more than one receiving indexer is specified in this manner. Port 9997 is the default Splunk TCP port and should only be changed if it cannot be used for some reason.

On the receiving Splunk indexer server(s):

1. Log in to your receiving Splunk indexer server. From the home launcher, in the top-right corner click on the **Settings** menu item and then select the **Forwarding and receiving** link.

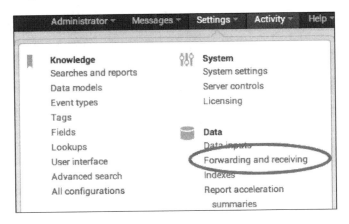

2. Click on the **Configure receiving** link.

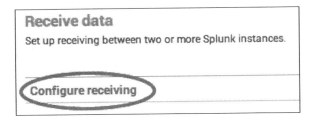

3. Click on **New**.

4. Enter 9997 in the **Listen on this port** field.

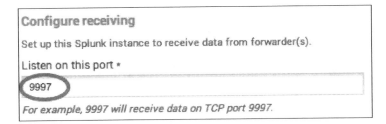

5. Click on **Save** and restart Splunk. The Universal Forwarder is installed and configured to send data to your Splunk server, and the Splunk server is configured to receive data on the default Splunk TCP port 9997.

How it works...

When you tell the forwarder which server to send data to, you are basically adding a new configuration stanza into an `outputs.conf` file behind the scenes. On the Splunk server, an `inputs.conf` file will contain a `[splunktcp]` stanza to enable receiving. The `outputs.conf` file on the Splunk forwarder will be located in `$SPLUNK_HOME/etc/system/local`, and the `inputs.conf` file on the Splunk server will be located in the local directory of the app you were in (the launcher app in this case) when configuring receiving.

Using forwarders to collect and forward data has many advantages. The forwarders communicate with the indexers on TCP port 9997 by default, which makes for a very simple set of firewall rules that need to be opened. Forwarders can also be configured to load balance their data across multiple indexers, increasing search speeds and availability. Additionally, forwarders can be configured to queue the data they collect if communication with the indexers is lost. This can be extremely important when collecting data that is not read from logfiles, such as performance counters or syslog streams, as the data cannot be re-read.

There's more...

While configuring the settings of the Universal Forwarder can be performed via the command-line interface of Splunk as outlined in this recipe, there are several other methods to update settings quickly and allow for customization of the many configuration options that Splunk provides.

Add the receiving indexer via outputs.conf

The receiving indexers can be directly added to the `outputs.conf` configuration file on the Universal Forwarder. Edit `$SPLUNK_HOME/etc/system/local/outputs.conf`, add your input, and then restart the UF. The following example configuration is provided, where two receiving indexers are specified. The `[tcpout-server]` stanza can be leveraged to add output configurations specific to an individual receiving indexer.

```
[tcpout]
defaultGroup = default-autolb-group

[tcpout:default-autolb-group]
disabled = false
server = mysplunkindexer1:9997,mysplunkindexer2:9997

[tcpout-server://mysplunkindexer1:9997]
[tcpout-server://mysplunkindexer2:9997]
```

If nothing has been configured in `inputs.conf` on the Universal Forwarder, but `outputs.conf` is configured with at least one valid receiving indexer, the Splunk forwarder will only send internal log data to the indexer. It is, therefore, possible to configure a forwarder correctly and be detected by the Splunk indexer(s), but not actually send any real data.

Loading the sample data for this book

While most of the data you will index with Splunk will be collected in real time, there might be instances where you have a set of data that you would like to put into Splunk, either to backfill some missing or incomplete data, or just to take advantage of its searching and reporting tools.

This recipe will show you how to perform one-time bulk loads of data from files located on the Splunk server. We will also use this recipe to load the data samples that will be used throughout subsequent chapters as we build our Operational Intelligence app in Splunk.

There are two files that make up our sample data. The first is `access_log`, which represents data from our web layer and is modeled on an Apache web server. The second file is `app_log`, which represents data from our application layer and is modeled on the `log4j` application log data.

Getting ready

To step through this recipe, you will need a running Splunk server and should have a copy of the sample data generation app (`OpsDataGen.spl`) for this book.

How to do it...

Follow the given steps to load the sample data generator on your system:

1. Log in to your Splunk server using your credentials.

2. From the home launcher, select the **Apps** menu in the top-left corner and click on **Manage Apps**.

3. Select **Install App from file**.

4. Select the location of the `OpsDataGen.spl` file on your computer, and then click on the **Upload** button to install the application.

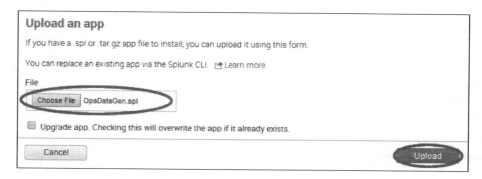

5. After installation, a message should appear in a blue bar at the top of the screen, letting you know that the app has installed successfully. You should also now see the OpsDataGen app in the list of apps.

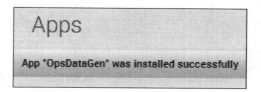

6. By default, the app installs with the data-generation scripts disabled. In order to generate data, you will need to enable either a Windows or Linux script, depending on your Splunk operating system. To enable the script, select the **Settings** menu from the top-right corner of the screen, and then select **Data inputs**.

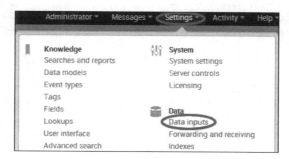

7. From the **Data inputs** screen that follows, select **Scripts**.

8. On the **Scripts** screen, locate the OpsDataGen script for your operating system and click on **Enable**.

   ❑ For Linux, it will be `$SPLUNK_HOME/etc/apps/OpsDataGen/bin/AppGen.path`

   ❑ For Windows, it will be `$SPLUNK_HOME\etc\apps\OpsDataGen\bin\AppGen-win.path`

The following screenshot displays both the Windows and Linux inputs that are available after installing the OpsDataGen app. It also displays where to click to enable the correct one based on the operating system Splunk is installed on.

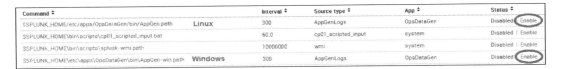

Command ⬍		Interval ⬍	Source type ⬍	App ⬍	Status ⬍
$SPLUNK_HOME/etc/apps/OpsDataGen/bin/AppGen.path	Linux	300	AppGenLogs	OpsDataGen	Disabled | Enable
$SPLUNK_HOME\bin\scripts\cp01_scripted_input.bat		60.0	cp01_scripted_input	system	Disabled | Enable
$SPLUNK_HOME\bin\scripts\splunk-wmi.path		10000000	wmi	system	Disabled | Enable
$SPLUNK_HOME\etc\apps\OpsDataGen\bin\AppGen-win.path	Windows	300	AppGenLogs	OpsDataGen	Disabled | Enable

9. Select the **Settings** menu from the top-right corner of the screen, select **Data inputs**, and then select **Files & directories**.

10. On the **Files & directories** screen, locate the two OpsDataGen inputs for your operating system and for each click on **Enable**.

    ❑ For Linux, it will be:

    `$SPLUNK_HOME/etc/apps/OpsDataGen/data/access_log`

    `$SPLUNK_HOME/etc/apps/OpsDataGen/data/app_log`

    ❑ For Windows, it will be:

    `$SPLUNK_HOME\etc\apps\OpsDataGen\data\access_log`

    `$SPLUNK_HOME\etc\apps\OpsDataGen\data\app_log`

The following screenshot displays both the Windows and Linux inputs that are available after installing the OpsDataGen app. It also displays where to click to enable the correct one based on the operating system Splunk is installed on.

Full path to your data ⬍	Set host ⬍	Source type ⬍	Set the destination index ⬍	Number of files ⬍	App ⬍		Status ⬍
$SPLUNK_HOME/etc/apps/OpsDataGen/data/access_log	Constant Value	access_combined	main		OpsDataGen	Linux	Disabled | Enable
$SPLUNK_HOME/etc/apps/OpsDataGen/data/app_log	Constant Value	log4j	main		OpsDataGen	Linux	Disabled | Enable
$SPLUNK_HOME\etc\apps\OpsDataGen\data\access_log	Constant Value	access_combined	main		OpsDataGen	Windows	Disabled | Enable
$SPLUNK_HOME\etc\apps\OpsDataGen\data\app_log	Constant Value	log4j	main		OpsDataGen	Windows	Disabled | Enable

11. The data will now be generated in real time. You can test this by navigating to the Splunk search screen and running the following search over an **All time (real-time)** time range:

    ```
    index=main sourcetype=log4j OR sourcetype=access_combined
    ```

After a short while, you should see data from both source types flowing into Splunk, and the data generation is now working as displayed in the following screenshot:

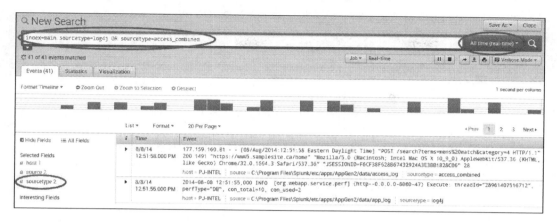

How it works...

In this case, you installed a Splunk application that leverages a scripted input. The script we wrote generates data for two source types. The `access_combined` source type contains sample web access logs, and the `log4j` source type contains application logs. These data sources will be used throughout the recipes in the book. Applications will also be discussed in more detail later on.

See also

▶ The *Indexing files and directories* recipe

▶ The *Getting data through network ports* recipe

▶ The *Using scripted inputs* recipe

Defining field extractions

Splunk has many built-in features, including knowledge on several common source types, which lets it automatically know what fields exist within your data. Splunk will, by default, also extract any key-value pairs present within the log data and all fields within JSON-formatted logs. However, often, fields within raw log data cannot be interpreted out of the box, and this knowledge must be provided to Splunk in order to make these fields easily searchable.

The sample data that we will be using in subsequent chapters contains data we wish to present as fields to Splunk. Much of the raw log data contains key-value fields that Splunk will extract automatically, but we need to tell Splunk how to extract one particular field that represents the page response time. To do this, we will be adding a custom field extraction, which will tell Splunk how to extract the field for us.

Getting ready

To step through this recipe, you will need a running Splunk server with the operational intelligence sample data loaded. There are no other prerequisites.

How to do it...

Follow the given steps to add a custom field extraction for response:

1. Log in to your Splunk server.

2. In the top-right corner, click on the **Settings** menu, and then click on the **Fields** link.

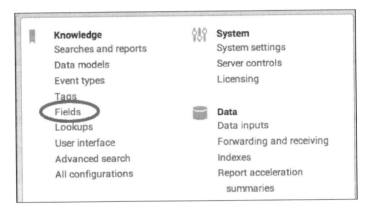

3. Click on the **Field extractions** link.

4. Click on **New**.

5. In the **Destination app** field, select the **search** app, and in the **Name** field, enter response. Set the **Apply to** dropdown to **sourcetype** and the **named** field to access_combined. Set the **Type** dropdown to **Inline**, and for the **Extraction/Transform** field, carefully enter the (?i)^(?:[^"]*"){8}\s+(?P<response>.+) regex.

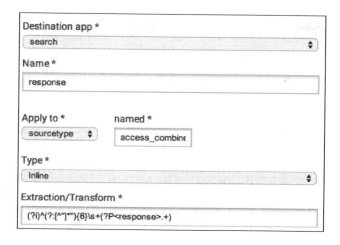

6. Click on **Save**.

7. On the **Field Extractions** listing page, find the recently added extraction, and in the **Sharing** column, click on the **Permissions** link.

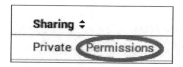

8. Update the **Object should appear in** setting to **All apps**. In the **Permissions** section, for the **Read** column, check **Everyone**, and in the **Write** column, check **admin**. Then, click on **Save**.

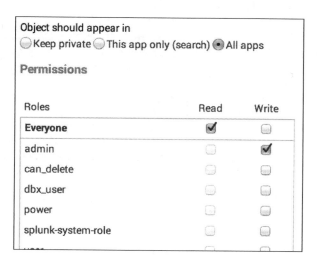

9. Navigate to the Splunk search screen and enter the following search over the **Last 60 minutes** time range:

```
index=main sourcetype=access_combined
```

You should now see a field called **response** extracted on the left-hand side of the search screen under the **Interesting Fields** section.

How it works...

All field extractions are maintained in the `props.conf` and `transforms.conf` configuration files. The stanzas in `props.conf` include an extraction class that leverages regular expressions to extract field names and/or values to be used at search time. The `transforms.conf` file goes further and can be leveraged for more advanced extractions such as reusing or sharing extractions over multiple sources, source types, or hosts.

See also

▶ The *Loading the sample data for this book* recipe

▶ The *Defining event types and tags* recipe

Defining event types and tags

Event types in Splunk are a way of categorizing common types of events in your data in order to make them easier to search and report on. One advantage of using event types is that they can assist in applying a common classification to similar events. Event types essentially turn chunks of search criteria into field/value pairs. Tags help you search groups of event data more efficiently and can be assigned to any field/value combination, including event types.

For example, Windows logon events could be given an event type of `windows_logon`, Unix logon events could be given an event type of `unix_logon`, and VPN logon events can be given an event type of `vpn_logon`. We could then tag these three event types with a tag of `logon_event`. A simple search for `tag="logon_event"` would then search across the Windows, Unix, and VPN source types and return all the logon events. Alternatively, if we want to search only for Windows logon events, we will search for `eventtype=windows_logon`.

This recipe will show how to define event types and tags for use with the sample data. Specifically, you will define an event type for successful web server events.

For more information on event types and tags in Splunk, please check out:

- ► `http://docs.splunk.com/Documentation/Splunk/latest/Knowledge/Abouteventtypes`
- ► `http://docs.splunk.com/Documentation/Splunk/latest/Knowledge/Abouttagsandaliases`

Getting ready

To step through this recipe, you will need a running Splunk server with the operational intelligence sample data loaded. There are no other prerequisites.

How to do it...

Follow the given steps to define an event type and associated tag:

1. Log in to your Splunk server.

2. From the home launcher in the top-right corner, click on the **Settings** menu item, and then click on the **Event types** link.

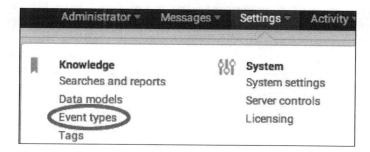

3. Click on the **New** button.

4. In the **Destination App** dropdown, select **search**. Enter `HttpRequest-Success` in the **Name** field. In the **Search string** text area, enter `sourcetype=access_combined status=2*`. In the **Tag(s)** field, enter `webserver`, and then click on **Save**.

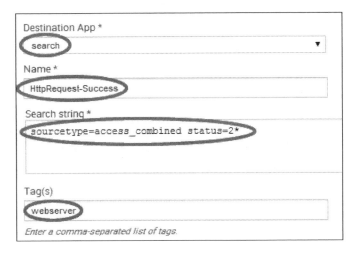

5. The event type is now created. To verify that this worked, you should now be able to search by both the event type and the tag that you created. Navigate to the Splunk search screen in the **Search & Reporting** app and enter the following search over the **Last 60 minutes** time range to verify that the eventtype is working:

    ```
    eventtype="HttpRequest-Success"
    ```

6. Enter the following search over the **Last 60 minutes** time range to verify that the tag is working:

    ```
    tag="webserver"
    ```

How it works...

Event types are applied to events at search time and introduce an **eventtype** field with user-defined values that can be used to quickly sift through large amounts of data. An event type is essentially a Splunk search string that is applied against each event to see if there is a match. If the event type search matches the event, the **eventtype** field is added with the value of the field being the user-defined name for that event type.

The common tag value allows for a grouping of event types. If multiple event types had the same tag, then your Splunk search could just search for that particular tag value, instead of needing to list out each individual event type value.

Event types can be added, modified, and deleted at any time without the need to change or reindex your data, as they are applied at search time.

Event types are stored in `eventtypes.conf` in either `$SPLUNK_HOME/etc/system/local/` or a custom app directory.

There's more...

While adding event types and tags can be done through the web interface of Splunk as outlined in this recipe, there are other approaches to add them in bulk quickly and allow for customization of the many configuration options that Splunk provides.

Adding event types and tags via eventtypes.conf and tags.conf

Event types in Splunk can be manually added to the `eventtypes.conf` configuration files. Edit (or create) `$SPLUNK_HOME/etc/system/local/eventtypes.conf` and add your event type. You will need to restart Splunk after this.

```
[HttpRequest-Success]
search = status=2*
```

Tags in Splunk can be manually added to the `tags.conf` configuration files. Edit (or create) `$SPLUNK_HOME/etc/system/local/tags.conf` and add your tag. You will need to restart Splunk after this.

```
[eventtype=HttpRequest-Success]
webserver = enabled
```

 In this recipe, you tagged an event type. However, tags do not always need to be associated with event types. You can tag any field/value combination found in an event. To create new tags independently, click on the **Settings** menu and select **Tags**.

See also

▸ The *Loading the sample data for this book* recipe

▸ The *Defining field extractions* recipe

Summary

The key takeaways from this chapter are:

- ▶ Splunk can easily monitor individual files or whole directories to collect the many logfiles you have access to
- ▶ Network ports can be used to collect data that is socket based, such as syslog
- ▶ The Splunk Universal Forwarder can be used to collect data that is not accessible from your Splunk server but is located remotely
- ▶ Leverage the Splunk community to get modular inputs for additional sources of data
- ▶ Use event types and field transforms to normalize your data to make searching easier

2
Diving into Data – Search and Report

In this chapter, we will cover the basic ways to search the data in Splunk. We will learn about:

- Making raw event data readable
- Finding the most accessed web pages
- Finding the most used web browsers
- Identifying the top-referring websites
- Charting web page response codes
- Displaying web page response time statistics
- Listing the top viewed products
- Charting the application's functional performance
- Charting the application's memory usage
- Counting the total number of database connections

Introduction

In the previous chapter, we learned about the various ways to get data into Splunk. In this chapter, we will dive right into the data and get our hands dirty.

The ability to search machine data is one of Splunk's core functions, and it should come as no surprise that many other features and functions of Splunk are heavily driven-off searches. Everything from basic reports and dashboards through to data models and fully featured Splunk applications are powered by Splunk searches behind the scenes.

The Search Processing Language (SPL)

Splunk has its own search language known as the **Search Processing Language** (**SPL**). This SPL contains hundreds of search commands, most of which also have several functions, arguments, and clauses. While a basic understanding of SPL is required in order to effectively search your data in Splunk, you are not expected to know all of the commands! Even the most seasoned ninjas do not know all the commands and regularly refer to the Splunk manuals, website, or Splunk Answers (`http://answers.splunk.com`).

> To get you on your way with SPL, be sure to check out the search command cheat sheet and download the handy quick reference guide available at `http://docs.splunk.com/Documentation/Splunk/latest/SearchReference/SearchCheatsheet`.

Searching

Searches in Splunk usually start with a base search, followed by a number of commands that are delimited by one or more pipe (|) characters. The result of a command or search to the left of the pipe is used as the input for the next command to the right of the pipe. Multiple pipes are often found in a Splunk search to continually refine data results as needed. As we go through this chapter, this concept will become very familiar to you.

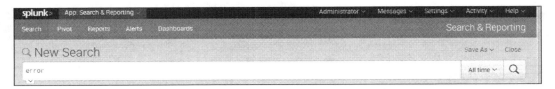

Splunk allows you to search for anything that might be found in your log data. For example, the most basic search in Splunk might be a search for a keyword such as `error` or an IP address such as `10.10.12.150`. However, searching for a single word or IP over the terabytes of data that might potentially be in Splunk is not very efficient. Therefore, we can use the SPL and a number of Splunk commands to really refine our searches. The more refined and granular the search, the faster the time to run and the quicker you get to the data you are looking for!

When searching in Splunk, try to filter as much as possible before the first pipe (|) character, as this will save CPU and disk I/O. Also, pick your time range wisely. Often, it helps to run the search over a small time range when testing it and then extend the range once the search is providing what you need.

Boolean operators

There are three different types of Boolean operators available in Splunk. These are AND, OR, and NOT. Case sensitivity is important here, and these operators must be in uppercase to be recognized by Splunk. The AND operator is implied by default and is not needed, but does no harm if used.

For example, searching for error OR success would return all events that contain either the word **error** or the word **success**. Searching for error success would return all events that contain the words **error** and **success**. Another way to write this would be error AND success. Searching web access logs for error OR success NOT mozilla would return all events that contain either the word **error** or **success**, but not those events that might also contain the word **mozilla**.

Common commands

There are many commands in Splunk that you will likely use on a daily basis when searching data within Splunk. These common commands are outlined in the following table:

Command	Description
chart / timechart	This command outputs results in a tabular and/or time-based output for use by Splunk charts.
dedup	This command de-duplicates results based upon specified fields, keeping the most recent match.
eval	This command evaluates new or existing fields and values. There are many different functions available for eval.
fields	This command specifies the fields to keep or remove in search results.
head	This command keeps the first X (as specified) rows of results.
lookup	This command looks up fields against an external source or list, to return additional field values.
rare	This command identifies the least common values of a field.
rename	This command renames fields.
replace	This command replaces the values of fields with another value.
search	This command permits subsequent searching and filtering of results.
sort	This command sorts results in either ascending or descending order.

Command	Description
stats	This command performs statistical operations on results. There are many different functions available for stats.
table	This command formats results into a tabular output.
tail	This command keeps only the last *X* (as specified) rows of results.
top	This command identifies the most common values of a field.
transaction	This command merges events into a single event based upon a common transaction identifier.

Time modifiers

The drop-down time range picker in the **graphical user interface** (**GUI**) to the right of the Splunk search bar allows users to select from a number of different preset and custom time ranges. However, in addition to using the GUI, you can also specify time ranges directly in your search string using the `earliest` and `latest` time modifiers. When a time modifier is used in this way, it will automatically override any time range that might be set in the GUI time range picker.

The `earliest` and `latest` time modifiers can accept a number of different time units: seconds (`s`), minutes (`m`), hours (`h`), days (`d`), weeks (`w`), months (`mon`), quarters (`q`), and years (`y`). Time modifiers can also make use of the `@` symbol to round down and snap to a specified time.

For example, searching for `sourcetype=access_combined earliest=-1d@d latest=-1h` will search all `access_combined` events from midnight, a day ago until an hour ago from now. Note that the snap (`@`) will round down such that if it were 12 p.m. now, we would be searching from midnight a day and a half ago until 11 a.m. today.

Working with fields

Fields in Splunk can be thought of as keywords that have one or more values. These fields are fully searchable by Splunk. At a minimum, every data source that comes into Splunk will have source, host, index, and sourcetype fields, but some sources might have hundreds of additional fields. If the raw log data contains key-value pairs or is in a structured format such as JSON or XML, then Splunk will automatically extract the fields and make them searchable. Splunk can also be told how to extract fields from the raw log data in the backend `props.conf` and `transforms.conf` configuration files.

Searching for specific field values is simple. For example, `sourcetype=access_combined status!=200` will search for events with a sourcetype field value of `access_combined` that has a status field with a value other than `200`.

Splunk has a number of built-in pretrained sourcetypes that ship with Splunk Enterprise that might work with out-of-the-box, common data sources. These are available at `http://docs.splunk.com/Documentation/Splunk/latest/Data/Listofpretrainedsourcetypes`.

In addition, **Technical Add-Ons** (**TAs**), which contain event types and field extractions for many other common data sources such as Windows events, are available from the Splunk app store at `http://apps.splunk.com`.

Saving searches

Once you have written a nice search in Splunk, you might wish to save the search such that you can use it again at a later date or use it for a dashboard. Saved searches in Splunk are known as **Reports**. To save a search in Splunk, you simply click on the **Save As** button on the top-right corner of the main search bar and select **Report**.

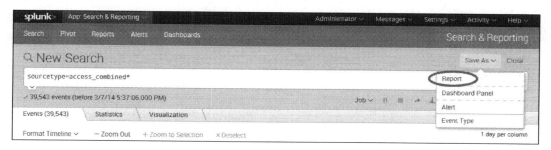

Making raw event data readable

When a basic search is executed in Splunk from the search bar, the search results are displayed in a raw event format by default. To many users, this raw event information is not particularly readable, and valuable information is often clouded by other less valuable data within the event. Additionally, if events span several lines, only a few events can be seen on screen at any one time.

In this recipe, we will write a Splunk search to demonstrate how we can leverage Splunk commands to make raw event data readable, tabulating events and displaying only the fields we are interested in.

Getting ready

To step through this recipe, you will need a running Splunk Enterprise server, with the sample data loaded from *Chapter 1, Play Time – Getting Data In*. You should be familiar with the Splunk search bar and search results area.

How to do it...

Follow the given steps to search and tabulate the selected event data:

1. Log in to your Splunk server.

2. Select the **Search & Reporting** application from the drop-down menu located in the top-left corner of the screen.

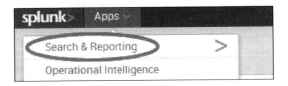

3. Set the time range picker to **Last 24 hours**, and type the following search into the Splunk search bar. Then, click on the magnifying glass icon or hit *Enter*.

   ```
   index=main sourcetype=access_combined
   ```

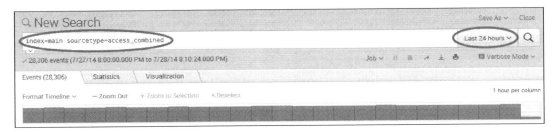

4. Splunk will return the results of the search and display the raw search events under the search bar.

5. Let's rerun the search, but this time, we will add the `table` command as follows:

   ```
   index=main sourcetype=access_combined | table _time,
   referer_domain, method, uri_path, status, JSESSIONID,
   useragent
   ```

6. Splunk will now return the same number of events, but instead of presenting the raw events to you, the data will be in a nicely formatted table, displaying only the fields we specified. This is much easier to read!

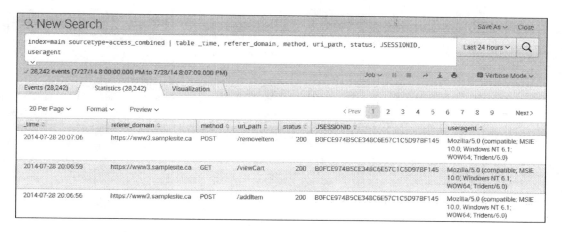

7. Save this search by clicking on **Save As** and then on **Report**. Give the report a name of `cp02_tabulated_webaccess_logs` and click on **Save**. On the next screen, click on **Continue Editing** to return to the search.

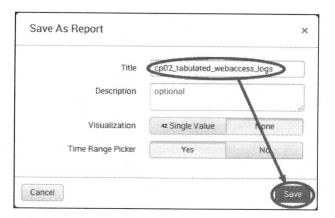

How it works...

Let's break down the search piece by piece.

Search fragment	Description
`index=main`	All data in Splunk is held in one or more indexes. While not strictly necessary, it is a good practice to specify the index (es) to search, as this will ensure a more precise search.
`sourcetype=access_combined`	This tells Splunk to search only the data associated with the `access_combined` sourcetype, which, in our case, is the web access logs.
`| table _time, referer_domain, method, uri_path, action, JSESSIONID, useragent`	Using the `table` command, we take the result of our search to the left of the pipe and tell Splunk to return the data in a tabular format. Splunk will only display the fields specified after the `table` command in the table of results.

In this recipe, you used the `table` command. The `table` command can have a noticeable performance impact on large searches. It should be used towards the end of a search, once all other processing on the data by other Splunk commands has been performed.

> The `stats` command is more efficient than the `table` command and should be used in place of `table` where possible. However, be aware that `stats` and `table` are two very different commands.

There's more...

The `table` command is very useful in situations where we wish to present data in a readable format. Additionally, tabulated data in Splunk can be downloaded as a CSV file, which many users find useful for offline processing in spreadsheet software or sending to others. There are some other ways we can leverage the `table` command to make our raw event data readable.

Tabulating every field

Often, there are situations where we might want to present every event within the data in a tabular format, without having to specify each field one by one. To do this, we simply use a wildcard (*) character as follows:

```
index=main sourcetype=access_combined | table *
```

Removing fields, then tabulating everything else

While tabulating every field using the wildcard (*) character is useful, you will notice that there are a number of Splunk internal fields, such as _raw, that appear in the table. We can use the `fields` command before the `table` command to remove fields as follows:

```
index=main sourcetype=access_combined | fields - sourcetype,
index, _raw, source date* linecount punct host time* eventtype |
table *
```

If we do not include the minus (-) character after the `fields` command, Splunk will keep the specified fields and remove all other fields.

> If you regularly need to remove a number of fields in your searches, you can write a macro to do this and then simply call the macro from your search. Macros are covered later in this book.

Finding the most accessed web pages

One of the data samples we loaded in *Chapter 1, Play Time – Getting Data In*, contained access logs from our web server. These have a Splunk sourcetype of access_combined and detail all pages accessed by users of our web application. We are particularly interested in knowing which pages are being accessed the most, as this information provides great insight into how our e-commerce web application is being used. It could also help influence changes to our web application such that rarely visited pages are removed, or our application is redesigned to be more efficient.

In this recipe, we will write a Splunk search to find the most accessed web pages over a given period of time.

Getting ready

To step through this recipe, you will need a running Splunk Enterprise server, with the sample data loaded from *Chapter 1, Play Time – Getting Data In*. You should be familiar with the Splunk search bar and the time range picker to the right of it.

How to do it...

Follow the given steps to search for the most accessed web pages:

1. Log in to your Splunk server.

2. Select the **Search & Reporting** application.

3. Set the range picker to **Last 24 hours** and type the following search into the Splunk search bar. Then, click on the magnifying glass icon or hit *Enter*.

   ```
   index=main sourcetype=access_combined | stats count by
   uri_path | sort - count
   ```

4. Splunk will return a list of pages, and a new field named **count** displays the total number of times the page has been accessed.

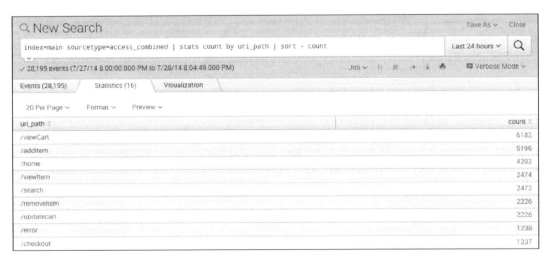

5. Save this search by clicking on **Save As** and then on **Report**. Give the report a name of cp02_most_accessed_webpages and click on **Save**. On the next screen, click on **Continue Editing** to return to the search.

How it works...

Let's break down the search piece by piece.

Search fragment	Description
`index=main`	All data in Splunk is held in one or more indexes. While not strictly necessary, it is a good practice to specify the index (es) to search, as this will ensure a more precise search.
`sourcetype=access_combined`	This tells Splunk to search only the data associated with the `access_combined` sourcetype, which, in our case, is the web access logs.
`| stats count by uri_path`	Using the `stats` command, we take the result of our search to the left-hand side of the pipe and tell Splunk to count the instances of each `uri_path`. The `uri_path` field is the name of the field associated with the website page.
`| sort - count`	Using the `sort` command, we take the `count` field generated by `stats` and tell Splunk to sort the results of the previous command in descending (-) order such that the most visited web page appears at the top of the results.

There's more...

We can further build upon the base search to provide different variations of the results.

Searching for the top 10 accessed web pages

We can modify the search from this recipe and replace the `stats` command with the `top` command. By default, this will display the top 10 web pages:

```
sourcetype=access_combined index=main | top uri_path
```

Here, we modified the search and replaced the `stats` command with the `top` command. By default, this will display the top 10 web pages. If we wanted to get the top 20 web pages, we can specify a limit value as follows:

```
sourcetype=access_combined index=main | top limit=20 uri_path
```

Searching for the most accessed pages by user

We can modify the search from this recipe and can use the distinct count (dc) function of the stats command to display a list of users and the unique pages they visited:

```
sourcetype=access_combined index=main | stats dc(uri_path) by user |
sort - user
```

The distinct count function ensures that if a user visits the same page multiple times, it is only counted as one visit. The user who visited the most number of unique pages will be at the top of the list, as we used a descending sort.

 For more information on the various functions that can be used with the stats command, please check out http://docs.splunk. com/Documentation/Splunk/latest/SearchReference/ CommonStatsFunctions.

See also

▸ The *Finding the most used web browsers* recipe

▸ The *Identifying the top-referring websites* recipe

▸ The *Charting web page response codes* recipe

Finding the most used web browsers

Users visiting our website use a variety of devices and web browsers. By analyzing the web access logs, we can understand which browsers are the most popular and, therefore, which browsers our site must support as a minimum. We can also use this same information to help identify the types of devices that people are using.

In this recipe, we will write a Splunk search to find the most used web browsers over a given period of time. We will then make use of both the eval and replace commands to clean up the data a bit.

Getting ready

To step through this recipe, you will need a running Splunk Enterprise server, with the sample data loaded from *Chapter 1, Play Time – Getting Data In*. You should be familiar with the Splunk search bar and the time range picker to the right of it.

How to do it...

Follow the given steps to search for the most used web browsers:

1. Log in to your Splunk server.

2. Select the **Search & Reporting** application.

3. Ensure that the time range picker is set to **Last 24 hours** and type the following search into the Splunk search bar. Then, click on the magnifying glass icon or hit *Enter*.

   ```
   index=main sourcetype=access_combined | eval
   browser=useragent | replace *Firefox* with Firefox,
   *Chrome* with Chrome, *MSIE* with "Internet Explorer",
   *Version*Safari* with Safari, *Opera* with Opera in browser
   | top limit=5 useother=t browser
   ```

4. Splunk will return a tabulated list of the top five most used web browsers on our site, by count and percent.

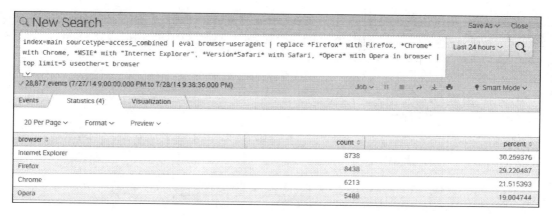

5. Save this search by clicking on **Save As** and then on **Report**. Give the report a name of cp02_most_used_webbrowsers and click on **Save**. On the next screen, click on **Continue Editing** to return to the search.

How it works...

Let's break down the search piece by piece.

Search fragment	Description
`index=main` `sourcetype=access_combined`	You should now be familiar with this search from the earlier recipes in this chapter.

Search fragment	Description
`| eval browser=useragent`	Using the `eval` command, we evaluate a new field called `browser` and populate it with the contents of the `useragent` field.
`| replace *Firefox* with Firefox, *Chrome* with Chrome, *MSIE* with "Internet Explorer", *Version*Safari* with Safari, *Opera* with Opera in browser`	Using the `replace` command, we use wildcards (`*`) within the content of the `browser` field to replace the values with shortened browser names. Note that values that contain spaces require quotes around them, for example, `"Internet Explorer"`.
`| top limit=5 useother=t browser`	Using the `top` command, we tell Splunk to find the top five web browsers and classify everything else under the value of `OTHER`.

In this recipe, we used both the `eval` and `replace` commands for illustrative purposes. This approach absolutely works, but a better approach might be to use Splunk's lookup functionality to lookup the `useragent` value and return the browser name and version. Lookups are covered later in this book.

There's more...

Often, the same field values can be used in different ways to provide additional insight. In this case, the `useragent` field can be used to inform the types of devices that access our site.

Searching the web browser data for the most used OS types

Let's modify the search to display the types of user operating systems (OSes) that access our website:

```
index=main sourcetype=access_combined | eval os=useragent |
replace *Windows* with Windows, *Macintosh* with Apple,
*Linux* with Linux in os | top limit=3 useother=t os
```

When the search is run you should see results similar to the following screenshot:

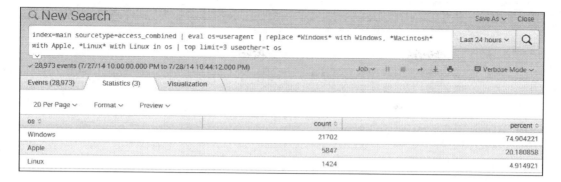

The search is similar, but this time we decided to pull the OS-related information from the useragent field and are using it to compare access between major OS types.

See also

▶ The *Finding the most accessed web pages* recipe

▶ The *Identifying the top-referring websites* recipe

▶ The *Charting web page response codes* recipe

Identifying the top-referring websites

Our web access logs continue to give us great information about our website and the users visiting the site. Understanding where our users are coming from provides insight into potential sales leads and/or which marketing activities might be working better than others. For this information, we look for the referer_domain field value within the log data.

In this recipe, we will write a Splunk search to find the top-referring websites.

Getting ready

To step through this recipe, you will need a running Splunk Enterprise server, with the sample data loaded from *Chapter 1, Play Time – Getting Data In*. You should be familiar with the Splunk search bar and the time range picker.

How to do it...

Follow the given steps to search for the top-referring websites:

1. Log in to your Splunk server.

2. Select the **Search & Reporting** application.

3. Ensure that the time range picker is set to **Last 24 hours** and type the following search into the Splunk search bar. Then, click on the magnifying glass icon or hit *Enter*.

   ```
   index=main sourcetype=access_combined | stats dc(clientip)
   AS Referals by referer_domain | sort - Referals
   ```

4. Splunk will return a tabulated list ordered by the amount of unique referrals each website has provided.

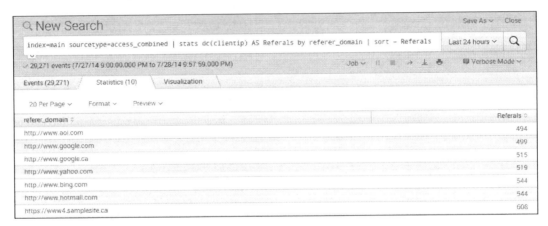

5. Save this search by clicking on **Save As** and then on **Report**. Give the report a name of `cp02_top_referring_websites` and click on **Save**. On the next screen, click on **Continue Editing** to return to the search.

How it works...

Let's break down the search piece by piece.

Search fragment	Description
`index=main sourcetype=access_combined`	You should now be familiar with this search from earlier recipes in this chapter.

Search fragment	Description
`| stats dc(clientip) AS Referals by referer_domain`	Using the `stats` command, we apply the distinct count (dc) function to `clientip` to count the unique IP addresses by `referer_domain` and rename the generated count field to `Referals`.
`| sort - Referals`	Using the `sort` command, we sort by the number of referrals in descending order.

There's more...

In this recipe, we did not use the `top` command, as this command only provides limited functionality. The `stats` command is far more powerful and has many available functions, including distinct count.

Searching for the top 10 referring websites using stats instead of top

Using the `stats` command in this recipe, we brought back all of the websites present in our web access logs and then sorted them by the number of unique referrals. Should we have wanted to only show the top 10, we can simply add the `head` command at the end of our search as follows:

```
index=main sourcetype=access_combined | stats dc(clientip) AS
Referals by referer_domain | sort -Referals | head 10
```

The `head` command keeps the first specified number of rows. In this case, as we have a descending sort, by keeping the first 10 rows, we are essentially keeping the top 10.

 There is a great guide in the Splunk documentation to understanding all of the different functions for `stats`, `chart` and `timechart`, which are available at `http://docs.splunk.com/Documentation/Splunk/latest/SearchReference/CommonStatsFunctions`.

See also

▶ The *Finding the most used web browsers* recipe

▶ The *Charting web page response codes* recipe

▶ The *Displaying web page response time statistics* recipe

Charting web page response codes

Log data often contains seemingly cryptic codes that have all sorts of meanings. This is true of our web access logs, where there is a status code that represents a web page response. This code is very useful, as it can tell us whether certain events were successful or not. For example, error codes found in purchase events are less than ideal, and if our website was at fault, then we might have lost a sale.

In this recipe, we will write a Splunk search to chart web page responses against the various web pages on the site.

Getting ready

To step through this recipe, you will need a running Splunk Enterprise server, with the sample data loaded from *Chapter 1, Play Time – Getting Data In*. You should be familiar with the Splunk search bar and the time range picker.

How to do it...

Follow the given steps to chart web page response codes over time:

1. Log in to your Splunk server.
2. Select the **Search & Reporting** application.
3. Ensure that the time range picker is set to **Last 24 hours** and type the following search into the Splunk search bar. Then, click on the magnifying glass icon or hit *Enter*.

   ```
   index=main sourcetype=access_combined | chart
   count(eval(like(status,"2%"))) AS Success,
   count(eval(like(status,"4%") OR like(status,"5%"))) AS
   Error by uri_path
   ```

4. Splunk will return a tabulated list of web pages, detailing for each page how many events were successful and how many generated errors.

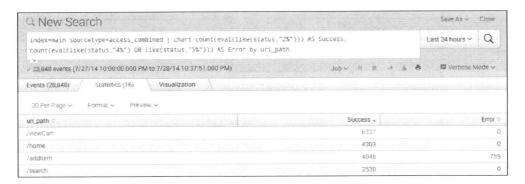

5. Click on the **Visualization** tab, and you will see this data represented in a column chart (by default).

6. Save this search by clicking on **Save As** and then on **Report**. Give the report a name of `cp02_webpage_response_codes` and click on **Save**. On the next screen, click on **Continue Editing** to return to the search.

How it works...

In this recipe, we selected to search by the `uri_path` field. This field represents the various web pages on the site. Let's break down the search piece by piece.

Search fragment	Description
`index=main` `sourcetype=access_combined`	You should now be familiar with this search from earlier recipes in this chapter.

`  chart count(eval`
`(like(status,"2%"))) AS Success,`
`count(eval(like(status,"4%")`
`OR like(status,"5%"))) AS`
`Error by uri_path`
	Stripping away the complexity for a moment, this is very similar to performing a `stats count by uri_path`. However, in this case, we are using the `chart` command and only counting success and error status codes.

	As the `status` field is essentially just a code, we are evaluating whether the code represents success or error. We do this using an inline `eval` command with `like` function. The `like` function allows us to specify the start of the status field value and then wildcard it with a `%` sign. Any status codes beginning with 2 represent success events, and any status codes beginning with either a 4 or a 5 represent an error.

There's more...

Hopefully, you can start to see the power of the **Search Processing Language** (**SPL**), as we start to ramp up the complexity a bit. We can now take this search a little further to provide a bit more insight.

Totaling success and error web page response codes

We can further amend the search to show only the `addItem` and `checkout` web pages events, which seem a little more relevant to sales intelligence. Additionally, using the `addcoltotals` command, we can add up the total success and error events.

```
index=main sourcetype=access_combined uri_path="/addItem" OR
uri_path="/checkout" | chart count(eval(like(status,"2%"))) AS
Success, count(eval(like(status,"4%") OR like(status,"5%"))) AS
Error by uri_path | addcoltotals label=Total labelfield=uri_path
```

When this updated search is run you should see results similar to the following screenshot:

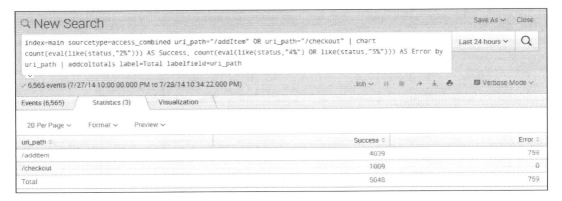

We use `labelfield=uri_path` and `label=Total` to tell Splunk to place a value of `Total` in the `uri_path` field column.

See also

- ▸ The *Identifying the top-referring websites* recipe
- ▸ The *Displaying web page response time statistics* recipe
- ▸ The *Listing the top viewed products* recipe

Displaying web page response time statistics

No one likes to wait for a web page to load, and we certainly do not want users of our web application waiting either! Within our web access logs, there is a field named `response` that tracks the total time the page has taken to load in milliseconds.

In this recipe, we will track the average page load time over the past week at different times of the day.

Getting ready

To step through this recipe, you will need a running Splunk Enterprise server, with the sample data loaded from *Chapter 1, Play Time – Getting Data In*. You should be familiar with the Splunk search bar and the time range picker.

How to do it...

Follow the given steps to search and calculate web page response time statistics over the past week:

1. Log in to your Splunk server.

2. Select the **Search & Reporting** application.

3. Ensure that the time range picker is set to **Last 7 Days** and type the following search into the Splunk search bar. Then, click on the magnifying glass icon or hit *Enter*.

   ```
   sourcetype=access_combined | timechart span=6h
   avg(response) AS avg_response | eval
   avg_response=round(avg_response/1000,2)
   ```

4. Splunk will return a tabulated list, detailing the average response times for every 6-hour period, going back a week.

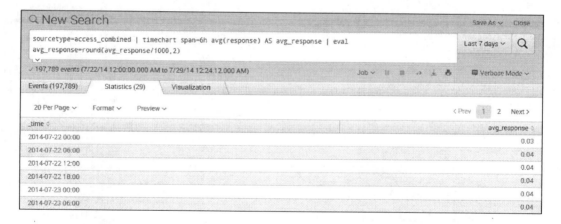

5. This is great, but hard to visualize in tabular form. Click on the **Visualization** tab, and you will see this data represented in a column chart (by default).

6. Click on the **Column** link above the chart and select **Line**. Splunk now presents this data in a nice line chart, and we can now see the average response times at different times of the day much more clearly.

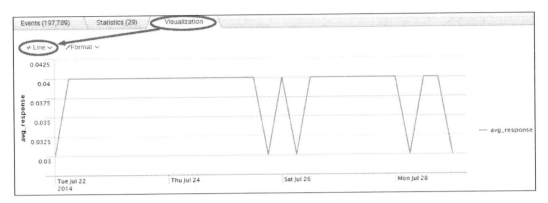

7. Save this search by clicking on **Save As** and then on **Report**. Give the report a name of cp02_webpage_response_times and click on **Save**. On the next screen, click on **Continue Editing** to return to the search.

How it works...

Let's break down the search piece by piece.

Search fragment	Description
index=main sourcetype=access_combined	You should now be familiar with this search from earlier recipes in this chapter.
| timechart span=6h avg(response) AS avg_response	Using the timechart command, we specify a span of 6 hours. We then use the avg function on the response field. Splunk will add up all the response times in the 6-hour period and then calculate the average response time during that period.
| eval avg_response=round(avg_resp onse/1000,2)	Using the eval command, we calculate the average response time in seconds by dividing the average time (which is in milliseconds) by 1000, to give us the time in seconds. The number 2 at the end is part of the round function and tells Splunk to round to 2 decimal places.

There's more...

The `timechart` command offers some great functionality. Searches like this can be extended further to graphically compare several weeks against one another to spot anomalies and other issues.

Displaying web page response time by action

We can further amend the search to offer granular information on average response times by the type of action being performed. This might pinpoint some actions that are less responsive than others. For example, we might want to ensure that the checkout page remains at an optimal load time. For the following search to work, you must complete the *Defining field extractions* recipe in *Chapter 1*, *Play Time – Getting Data In*, to extract the response field:

```
sourcetype=access_combined uri_path=* | timechart span=6h
avg(response) by uri_path | foreach *
[eval <<FIELD>>=round(<<FIELD>>/1000,2)]
```

We are now searching for web page events and then we will calculate the average time by page (`uri_field`). This results in a table of multiple columns, where each column represents a different web page. When we visualize this on a line graph, we now see many different lines on the same chart—pretty cool! You will notice that we used a pretty advanced Splunk search command earlier named `foreach`. This is essentially a `for` type loop that cycles through each of the column fields in the table and applies a calculation to convert the average time by page from milliseconds to seconds while rounding the value to two decimal places.

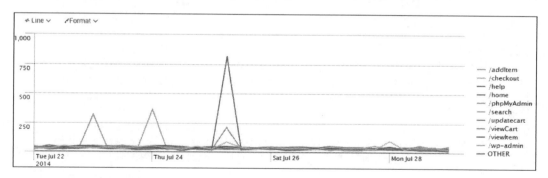

See also

- ▶ The *Charting web page response codes* recipe
- ▶ The *Listing the top viewed products* recipe
- ▶ The *Identifying the top-referring websites* recipe

Listing the top viewed products

Our web access logs capture the product IDs (the item field in the logs) that users are viewing and adding to their shopping carts. Understanding the top products that people view can help influence our sales and marketing strategy and even product direction. Additionally, products viewed on an e-commerce website might not always necessarily translate into sales of that product.

In this next recipe, we will write a Splunk search to **chart** the top 10 products that users successfully view and compare against the number of successful shopping cart additions for each product. For example, if a product has a high number of views, but the product is not being added to carts, this could indicate that something is not right—perhaps, the pricing of the product is too high.

Getting ready

To step through this recipe, you will need a running Splunk Enterprise server, with the sample data loaded from *Chapter 1, Play Time – Getting Data In*. You should be familiar with the Splunk search bar and the time range picker.

How to do it...

Follow the given steps to search for the top products being searched over the past week:

1. Log in to your Splunk server.
2. Select the **Search & Reporting** application.
3. Ensure that the time range picker is set to **Last 7 days** and type the following search into the Splunk search bar. Then, click on the magnifying glass icon or hit *Enter*.

   ```
   index=main sourcetype=access_combined uri_path="/viewItem"
   OR uri_path="/addItem" status=200  | dedup JSESSIONID
   uri_path item | chart count(eval(uri_path="/viewItem")) AS
   view, count(eval(uri_path="/addItem")) AS add by item |
   sort - view | head 10
   ```

4. Splunk will return a tabulated list of items (products), detailing the number of times a product was successfully viewed versus the number of times a product was actually added to the shopping cart.

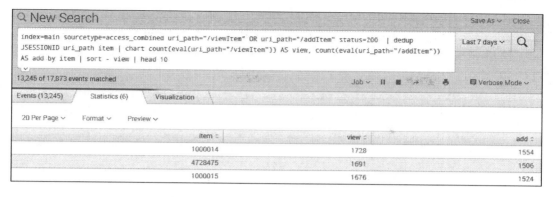

5. Save this search by clicking on **Save As** and then on **Report**. Give the report a name of cp02_top_products_viewed and click on **Save**. On the next screen, click on **Continue Editing** to return to the search.

How it works...

In this recipe, our search returned a count by item of how many items were viewed versus how many were added to the cart. In this case, the item field represents a unique item ID that pertains to a specific product. Let's break down the search piece by piece.

Search fragment	Description
index=main sourcetype=access_combined	You should now be familiar with this search from earlier recipes in this chapter.
uri_path="/viewItem" OR uri_path="/addItem" status=200	Following the best practice of making our search as granular as possible, we are only searching for events that contain uri_paths related to viewing items and adding items and have a successful status code of 200. This type of granularity will greatly limit the amount of records we search, making our search a lot faster.
| dedup JSESSIONID uri_path item	Using the dedup command, we are de-duplicating our data by the JSESSIONID, the uri_path, and the item values. Why? Well, because a user in a given session could view a product many times in that session before adding it, so we want to ensure that we only count one view and one addition per user session of a product.

Search fragment	Description
`| chart count (eval(uri_path="/viewItem")) AS view, count (eval(uri_path="/addItem")) AS add by item`	Using the `chart` and `eval` commands, we count the number of views and adds by item.
`| sort - view | head 10.`	Using the `sort` command, we sort in descending order on the view field such that the items with the most views are at the top. We then leverage the `head` command to keep only the first 10 rows of data, leaving us with the top 10 searched products.

There's more...

This recipe provides us with some insight into product views and subsequent shopping cart additions that might then lead on to a sale. However, we can keep adding to the search to make it even easier to understand the relationship between the two.

Searching for the percentage of cart additions from product views

We can further amend the search from this recipe to evaluate a new column that calculates the percentage of product views being added to the cart. We do this using the `eval` command and some basic math as follows:

```
index=main sourcetype=access_combined uri_path="/viewItem" OR
uri_path="/addItem" status=200  | dedup JSESSIONID uri_path item |
chart count(eval(uri_path="/viewItem")) AS view,
count(eval(uri_path="/addItem")) AS add by item | sort - view |
head 10 | eval  cart_conversion=round(add/view*100)."%"
```

We firstly evaluate a new field called `cart_conversion` and then calculate the percentage, dividing purchase by view and multiplying by 100. We use the round function of `eval` to eliminate decimal places, and then we tack on the % character at the end. Now, we can easily see what percentage of views lead to cart additions.

See also

▶ The *Displaying web page response time statistics* recipe

▶ The *Identifying the top-referring websites* recipe

▶ The *Finding the most used web browsers* recipe

Charting the application's functional performance

Another of the data samples we loaded in *Chapter 1, Play Time – Getting Data In,* contained application logs from our application server. These have a Splunk sourcetype of `log4j` and detail the various calls that our application makes to the backend database in response to user web requests, in addition to providing insight into memory utilization and other health-related information. We are particularly interested in tracking how our application is performing in relation to the time taken to process user-driven requests for information.

In this recipe, we will write a Splunk search to find out how our application is performing. To do this, we will analyze database call transactions and chart the maximum, mean, and minimum transaction durations over the past week.

Getting ready

To step through this recipe, you will need a running Splunk Enterprise server, with the sample data loaded from *Chapter 1, Play Time – Getting Data In.* You should be familiar with the Splunk search bar and the time range picker.

How to do it...

Follow the given steps to chart the application's functional performance over the past week:

1. Log in to your Splunk server.

2. Select the **Search & Reporting** application.

3. Ensure that the time range picker is set to **Last 24 hours** and type the following search into the Splunk search bar. Then, click on the magnifying glass icon or hit *Enter*.

   ```
   index=main sourcetype=log4j | transaction maxspan=4h
   threadId | timechart span=6h max(duration) AS max,
   mean(duration) AS mean, min(duration) AS min
   ```

4. Splunk will return a tabulated list, detailing the maximum, mean, and minimum database transaction durations for every 6-hour period, going back over the last 24 hours.

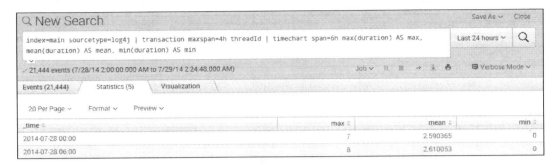

5. This is great, but hard to visualize in tabular form. Click on the **Visualization** tab, and you will see this data represented in a column chart (by default).

6. Click on the chart type link in the upper-left of the chart (next to the **Format** link) and select **Line** if not already selected. Splunk now presents this data in a nice line chart, and we can now see the maximum, mean, and minimum levels much more clearly.

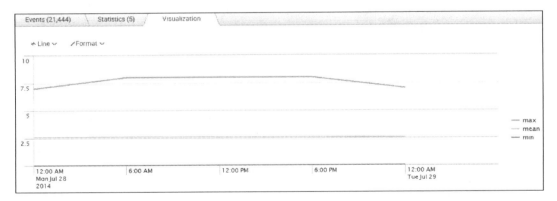

7. Save this search by clicking on **Save As** and then on **Report**. Give the report a name of cp02_application_performance and click on **Save**. On the next screen, click on **Continue Editing** to return to the search.

How it works...

Let's break down the search piece by piece.

Search fragment	Description
`index=main` `sourcetype=log4j`	In this example, we are searching for our application logs, which have the `log4j` sourcetype.
`| transaction maxspan=4h` `threadId`	Using the `transaction` command, we essentially consolidate multiple events with a common `threadId` into single event, multiline transactions. The `maxspan` function tells Splunk to only look at events with the same `threadId` that are within 4 hours of each other. The `transaction` command also calculates a new field called `duration`. This is the duration in seconds from the first event in the transaction to the last event in the transaction.

`| timechart span=6h`
`max(duration) AS max,`
`mean(duration) AS mean,`
`min(duration) AS min`
	Using the `timechart` command, we specify a span of 6 hours. We then use the `max`, `mean`, and `min` functions on the `duration` field. Splunk will analyze the durations in the 6-hour period and then calculate the `max`, `mean`, and `min` durations during this period.

> The `transaction` command is an extremely thirsty search command. When using this command, be sure to use the `maxspan` function where possible, as this helps focus on transactions grouped only within the specified `maxspan` timeframe.

There's more...

In this recipe, we leveraged the `transaction` command. This is a very useful and powerful function, and we will revisit it in more depth and complexity later in the book.

See also

- ▶ The *Charting the application's memory usage* recipe
- ▶ The *Counting the total number of database connections* recipe

Charting the application's memory usage

In addition to measuring functional performance of database transactions, we are also interested in understanding how our application is performing from a memory usage perspective. Analyzing this type of information can help identify memory leaks in our application or high-memory utilization that might be affecting the user experience and causing our application to slow down.

In this next recipe, we will analyze the memory usage of our application over time.

Getting ready

To step through this recipe, you will need a running Splunk Enterprise server, with the sample data loaded from *Chapter 1, Play Time – Getting Data In*. You should be familiar with the Splunk search bar and the time range picker.

How to do it...

Follow the given steps to chart the application memory usage over the past day:

1. Log in to your Splunk server.

2. Select the **Search & Reporting** application.

3. Ensure that the time range picker is set to **Last 24 hours** and type the following search into the Splunk search bar. Then, click on the magnifying glass icon or hit *Enter*.

   ```
   index=main sourcetype=log4j perfType="MEMORY" | eval
   mem_used_pc=round((mem_used/mem_total)*100) | eval
   mem_remain_pc=(100-mem_used_pc) | timechart span=15m
   avg(mem_remain_pc) avg(mem_used_pc)
   ```

4. Splunk will return a tabulated list, detailing all the events that meet our search criteria.

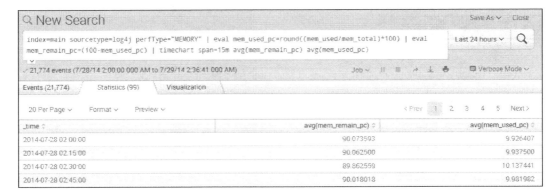

5. This is great, but hard to visualize in tabular form. Click on the **Visualization** tab, and you will see this data represented in a column chart (by default).

6. Click on the column link above the chart and select **Area**. Then, click on the **Format** link and change the **Stack Mode** to stacked and click on **Apply**. Splunk now presents this data in an area chart, allowing us to easily see if there are times during the day when our application might be getting low on memory. In this case, our sample data looks to be using very little memory.

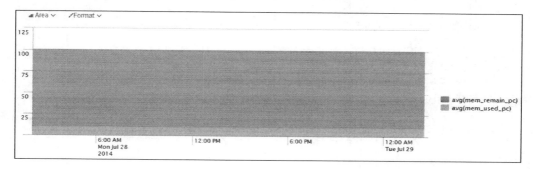

7. Save this search by clicking on **Save As** and then on **Report**. Give the report a name of cp02_application_memory and click on **Save**. On the next screen, click on **Continue Editing** to return to the search.

How it works...

Let's break down the search piece by piece.

Search fragment	Description
index=main sourcetype=log4j perfType="MEMORY"	In this example, we are searching for our application logs, which have the log4j sourcetype. We also select to view only the memory-related events.
| eval mem_used_pc=round ((mem_used/mem_total)*1 00)	Using the eval command, we calculate the percentage of memory used from the mem_used and mem_total fields in our application log.
| eval mem_remain_pc=(100- mem_used_pc)	Using the eval command again, we calculate the remaining percentage of memory from the used percentage of memory that we just calculated in the previous step.
| timechart span=15m avg(mem_remain_pc) avg(mem_used_pc)	Using the timechart command, we calculate the average remaining percentage of memory and used percentage of memory for every 15-minute interval over the past day.

See also

▶ The *Charting the application's functional performance* recipe

▶ The *Counting the total number of database connections* recipe

Counting the total number of database connections

Our application currently only allows for a limited amount of concurrent database connections. As our application user base grows, we need to proactively monitor these connections to ensure that we do not hit our concurrency limit or to know when we need to further scale out the database infrastructure.

In the last recipe of this chapter, we will monitor database transactions over the past week to identify if there are certain times or days when we might be close to our concurrency limit.

Getting ready

To step through this recipe, you will need a running Splunk Enterprise server, with the sample data loaded from *Chapter 1, Play Time – Getting Data In*. You should be familiar with the Splunk search bar and the time range picker.

How to do it...

Follow the given steps to search for the total number of database connections over the past 30 days:

1. Log in to your Splunk server.

2. Select the **Search & Reporting** application.

3. Ensure that the time range picker is set to **Last 7 days** and type the following search into the Splunk search bar. Then, click on the magnifying glass icon or hit *Enter*.

   ```
   index=main sourcetype=log4j perfType="DB" | eval
   threshold=con_total/100*70 | where con_used>=threshold |
   timechart span=4h count(con_used) AS CountOverThreshold
   ```

4. Splunk will return a tabulated list, detailing all the events that meet our search criteria.

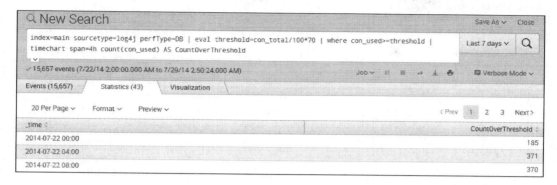

5. This is great, but hard to visualize in a tabular form. Click on the **Visualization** tab, and you will see this data represented by a chart.

6. Click on the chart type link in the upper-left of the chart (next to the **Format** link) and select **Line** if not already selected. Splunk now presents this data in a line chart, allowing us to easily see any spikes during certain times of the week.

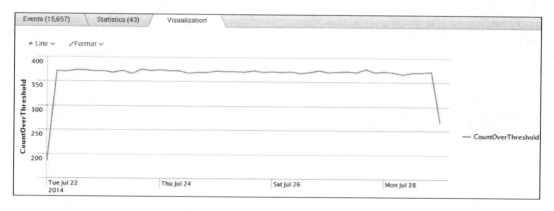

7. Save this search by clicking on **Save As** and then on **Report**. Give the report a name of cp02_application_db_connections and click on **Save**. On the next screen, click on **Continue Editing** to return to the search.

How it works...

Let's break down the search piece by piece:

Search fragment	Description
```index=main sourcetype=log4j perfType="DB"```	In this example, we are searching for our application logs, which have the log4j sourcetype. We also select to view only the events related to database (DB).
```| eval threshold=con_total/100 *70```	Using the eval command, we calculate a new field called threshold, which is 70 percent of the total connections permitted.
```| where con_used>=threshold```	Using the where command, we search for only events that are greater than or equal to the 70 percent threshold we just defined.
```| timechart span=4h count(con_used) AS CountOverThreshold```	Finally, we count the number of times over a 4-hour period in which the connection limit is greater than or equal to our threshold.

See also

▸ The *Charting the application's functional performance* recipe

▸ The *Charting the application's memory usage* recipe

Summary

The key takeaways from this chapter are as follows:

▸ Splunk has a very powerful **Search Processing Language** (**SPL**)

▸ The SPL contains many commands and functions to transform raw data into meaningful insight

▸ The same data can be manipulated to produce operational intelligence and business insights by just varying the SPL commands used

3
Dashboards and Visualizations – Make Data Shine

In this chapter, we will learn how to build dashboards and create visualizations of your data. We will learn about:

- Creating an Operational Intelligence dashboard
- Using a pie chart to show the most accessed web pages
- Displaying the unique number of visitors
- Using a gauge to display the number of errors
- Charting the number of method requests by type and host
- Creating a timechart of method requests, views, and response times
- Using a scatter chart to identify discrete requests by size and response time
- Creating an area chart of the application's functional statistics
- Using a bar chart to show the average amount spent by category
- Creating a line chart of item views and purchases over time

Introduction

In the previous chapter, we learned all about Splunk's **Search Processing Language** (**SPL**) and how it can be leveraged to search and report your data. In this chapter, we're going to build on this knowledge and use some of Splunk's visualization capabilities to make our data shine! You will learn how to create a dashboard through the Splunk UI and proceed to add the reports that were built in the previous chapter to it. Two more dashboards will then be created as a result of the remaining recipes.

Visualizations are a cornerstone for proper data presentation. By visualizing data in a manner that we as humans are accustomed to, you enable the user to better relate to what is being presented and have a proper understanding of how to react. When using Splunk for operational intelligence, you will be hard pressed to find a report that is not being visually represented in some fashion. Everyone from the front-line staff to C-level executives looks to Splunk's visualizations to make better sense of the data that their systems and applications are producing. Through the creation and use of dashboards, these visualizations can then be arranged and centralized to meet the needs of your organization.

About Splunk dashboards

A dashboard represents the most common type of view within Splunk and provides the means to bring together one or more reports and display them on a single page. Each report is placed on a dashboard as a panel and powered by the search you created. Typically, the panels will be populated with data once the dashboard is loaded. A report within a panel can display tabular data or one of the number of visualizations we will cover in this chapter.

Using dashboards for operational intelligence

In the world of operational intelligence, dashboards are one of the key tools to unlock pivotal information and provide a holistic view of systems and applications through a single pane. Dashboards are built to collectively display information to key audiences such as operators, administrators, or executives. They act as a window to how your environment is performing and allow you to obtain the right information at the right time in one place, in order to make timely and actionable decisions.

Enriching data with visualizations

Data on its own can be hard for us, as humans, to make sense of easily and can be extremely tedious to analyze. Visualizations provide a powerful way to bring data to life. Presenting data in a visual context enables those viewing it to better understand the relationship one value has to another, identify patterns, build correlations between datasets, and plot out trends. Colors that we easily relate to can be applied to visualizations in order to direct attention and highlight specific data points. For example, a value being within an acceptable range might be colored green, but when this value increases, it might change to yellow and eventually to red when it's within an unacceptable range. Humans associate red with bad and green with good; therefore, a red value nicely conveys the need to draw attention to itself.

Let's now apply this to an Operational Intelligence example. Imagine that you have a distributed environment of web servers that are generating large amounts of erratic data. Inside each of these events is a field that represents the response time of when that event occurred. If you were left having to analyze these events row by row in a table, it could take a very long time to find the events with values outside of the norm. Using visualizations such as a scatter chart, you could plot your event data and easily be able to identify these discrete events that lie outside of the primary cluster of events.

Available visualizations

One of the great benefits of Splunk is that there are numerous out-of-the-box visualizations that can be easily overlaid on your data. The type of visualization and common usage is outlined in the following table:

Visualization	Common usage
Line chart	This is commonly used to display data over time. If more than one data series is specified, each line on the chart will have a different color. Line charts can be stacked to help understand the relation of a given series of data to the rest of the plotted series.
Area chart	This works in the same way as a line chart, but the area below the line is shaded in color to emphasize quantities.
Column chart	This displays data values as vertical columns and is most commonly used when the frequency of values needs to be compared. Column charts can also be stacked to highlight the importance of different data types within the chart.
Bar chart	This displays data values as horizontal bars and works in the same way as column charts, but with its axis reversed.
Pie chart	This is one-dimensional and displays data values as segments of a pie. It is most commonly used to highlight or compare the proportion of numerical values.
Scatter chart	This displays data values as a series of plotted squares. It is commonly used when trying to identify discrete values in data that fall within the confines of regular events.
Single value	This displays data as a single value and is mostly used to display a sum or total, for example, the total number of errors in the last hour.
Radial gauge	This resembles a speedometer with a needle to signify the current value across an arced range. It is most commonly used on real-time dashboards to draw attention to the current state of a given metric. Thresholds can be defined to signify what values are acceptable (green), escalating (yellow), and severe (red).
Filler gauge	This resembles a thermometer with a liquid-like indicator. As the value changes, the volume of liquid rises and falls as well as changes color. As with the radial gauge, it is most commonly found on real-time dashboards and can have custom thresholds defined.

Visualization	Common usage
Marker gauge	Similar to the filler gauge, a marker gauge is already filled with values as defined by the thresholds, and it has a sliding marker to signify what the current value is. It is found most commonly on real-time dashboards.
Map	This is commonly used to illustrate geographic distributions of data. Data points on the map can be charted to highlight distinct counts of values within the same geographic region.
Heat map	Tabular values can have a heat map overlay applied to them so that the highest values are shaded red, while the lowest values are shaded blue. It is most commonly used when trying to draw attention visually to the variation of values in a table.
Sparkline	Sparkline visualizations are like mini line charts and are applied within a table to each row. They provide insight into the identification of patterns that might not have otherwise been properly represented by the resulting data in the table.

 For more information on the available visualizations, visit `http://docs.splunk.com/Documentation/Splunk/latest/Viz/Visualizationreference`.

Best practices for visualizations

Here are some best practices to consider when adding visualizations to your dashboards:

- Use visualizations to provide insight in a way that cannot be easily represented by tabular data.

- It can sometimes be useful to have a chart supported with a table, as a table can make finding absolute numbers easier.

- Provide enough information, but not too much. Do not overload charts with data that is not pertinent to achieving the goal of the visualization.

- Do not overload dashboards with visualizations. Spread visualizations out among a few dashboards rather than overloading one specific dashboard.

- Stacked charts are your friend, especially with area charts. If not stacked, area charts can have instances where large values dominate the chart, obscuring other values.

- Scale visualizations properly. Know when it is best to use linear versus log.

- Label your visualizations clearly so that the audience can understand what they are looking at and do not have to assume.

- ▶ Use appropriate visualizations for the task at hand. Here is some guidance:
  - ❏ **Comparisons over time**: Use line and column charts
  - ❏ **Comparisons among items**: Use bar and column charts
  - ❏ **Relationships**: Use scatter charts
  - ❏ **Distribution**: Use column or bar charts sorted or a scatter chart
  - ❏ **Static composition**: Use column charts stacked at 100 percent or a pie chart
  - ❏ **Changing composition**: Use column or area charts stacked, or column or area charts stacked at 100 percent
- ▶ Make proper use of colors and thresholds when leveraging single value visualizations and gauge charts.
- ▶ You can change the orientation of most visualizations; make use of your best judgment as required.

Creating an Operational Intelligence dashboard

Before this chapter gets into everything that is great about visualizations, it is best to first cover the process of creating a dashboard. In this recipe, you will create a dashboard from scratch using the Splunk Web UI that we will then use for other recipes in this chapter.

Getting ready

To step through this recipe, you will need a running Splunk Enterprise server, with the sample data loaded from *Chapter 1, Play Time – Getting Data In,* and the completed recipes from *Chapter 2, Diving into Data – Search and Report.* You should be familiar with navigating the Splunk user interface.

How to do it...

Follow the given steps to create an Operational Intelligence dashboard:

1. Log in to your Splunk server.
2. Select the default **Search & Reporting** application.

3. From the menu bar, click on the **Dashboards** link.

4. On the **Dashboards** screen, click on the **Create New Dashboard** button.

5. The **Create New Dashboard** screen will pop up. Enter `Website Monitoring` in the **Title** field. The **ID** field will be automatically populated; leave it as it is. The **Description** field can be left blank for now, but ensure that the **Shared in App** permission is selected. Finally, click on **Create Dashboard**.

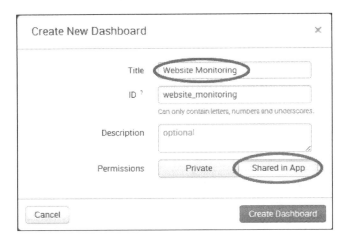

6. The newly created **Website Monitoring** dashboard will appear in the edit mode. We will add panels to the dashboard in the next few recipes. For now, just click on the **Done** button.

You have now created a blank dashboard ready to be populated with reports and visualizations.

How it works...

When creating a dashboard through the user interface, Splunk builds the underlying dashboard object code in simple XML for you behind the scenes. Following this, the dashboard object will then be used as a container for the reports you add to it. You can always view the source code of the dashboard by clicking on the **Edit** button and then, from the drop-down menu, you can click on **Edit Source**. The simple XML source code for the dashboard will be displayed in the editor. Dashboards and simple XML will be covered in more detail in the next chapter.

There are several ways in which dashboards can be created in the Splunk user interface. In this recipe, we essentially created an empty dashboard, which is ready to be filled with visualized reports. Splunk also allows dashboards to be created at the time of adding reports as you will see later in this chapter.

There's more...

When creating a dashboard, the default permission is for it to be private (only accessible by the user who created it). You might wish to share this or other dashboards with other users or groups who have an interest in these reports.

Changing dashboard permissions

To change the permissions on a dashboard you must first return to the **Dashboards** screen. This can be accomplished by clicking on the **Dashboards** menu, as outlined in step 3 of this recipe. Within the **Dashboards** screen, you will see the **Website Monitoring** dashboard that you created during the course of this recipe. Under the **Actions** column, you will see a clickable link labeled **Edit**; click on this link. A drop-down panel will appear; click on the item labeled **Edit Permissions**. The resulting pop-up window that appears will allow you to define permissions on a role-by-role basis and limit these permissions to be restrictive within the working application or globally for all applications.

 When creating dashboards through the GUI in Splunk, the default permission level should be private. However, in this recipe, you selected the **Shared in App** permissions button when creating the dashboard. This ensures that the new dashboard is automatically shared with everyone who has permissions to the application and saves you from having to edit permissions after creating it. On the backend, dashboards with application permissions are stored in the respective application directory structure. Dashboards with private permissions are stored in the respective user directory.

Using a pie chart to show the most accessed web pages

The sample data loaded in *Chapter 1, Play Time – Getting Data In*, provides a wealth of information on how customers are interacting with our online shopping website. In the *Finding the most accessed web pages* recipe in *Chapter 2, Diving into Data – Search and Report*, we saw how to find the most accessed web pages. The output of that recipe was displayed in a tabular format that could be hard for the viewer to grasp the proportional differences between web page access amounts. We will now take a look at how to use pie charts. By taking the same data and visually presenting it using a pie chart, we will enable the viewer to more easily identify the proportion of requests between different web pages. Visual representation of data, even if the data is very simple, can lead to better decision making in times of need.

In this recipe, you will use the report named `cp02_most_accessed_webpages`, which you created in *Chapter 2, Diving into Data – Search and Report*. You will graphically display the output of the report using a pie chart and add it to the **Website Monitoring** dashboard that we just created.

Getting ready

To step through this recipe, you will need a running Splunk Enterprise server, with the sample data loaded from *Chapter 1, Play Time – Getting Data In*. You should be familiar with the Splunk search bar, the time range picker, and the search tabs (**Events**, **Statistics**, and **Visualization**).

How to do it...

Follow the given steps to use a pie chart to show the most accessed web pages:

1. Log in to your Splunk server.
2. Select the default **Search & Reporting** application.
3. From the menu bar, click on the **Reports** link. This will display a list of all the reports we created and saved in *Chapter 2, Diving into Data – Search and Report*.

4. Locate the report line item named cp02_most_accessed_webpages and click on **Open in Search**.

5. Splunk will run the saved report with the search outlined in the following code. This will return a list of pages together with a count field that totals the number of times each page has been accessed.

    ```
    index=main sourcetype=access_combined | stats count by
    uri_path | sort - count
    ```

6. On completion of the search, the results will be displayed within the **Statistics** tab. As we will be creating a pie chart, click on the **Visualization** tab.

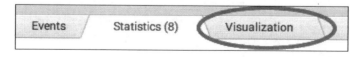

7. As there are a number of visualizations within Splunk, the **Pie** visualization may not be displayed by default within the **Visualization** tab. Click on the dropdown to list the visualization types and then select **Pie**.

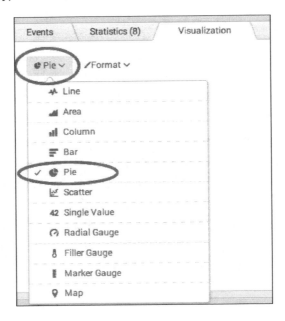

8. Now, the data will be visualized as a pie chart, as shown in the following screenshot:

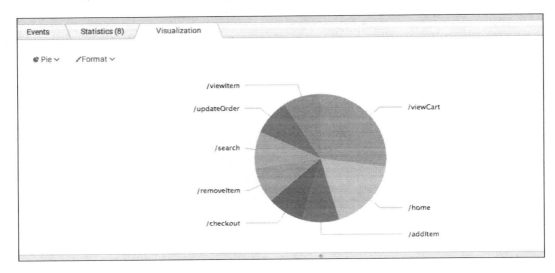

9. Let's add it to the **Website Monitoring** dashboard you created in the first recipe. Click on **Save As**, and then, from the drop-down menu, click on **Dashboard Panel**.

10. The **Save As Dashboard Panel** screen will pop up. Select **Existing** to use an existing dashboard, and select the **Website Monitoring** dashboard from the list. For **Panel Title**, enter **Most Accessed Webpages** and select for the panel to be powered by a report. Then, click on **Save**, as shown in the following screenshot:

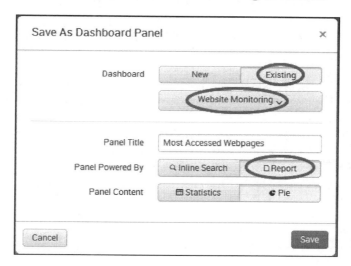

11. The next screen will confirm that the dashboard has been created and the panel has been added. Click on **View Dashboard** to see for yourself.

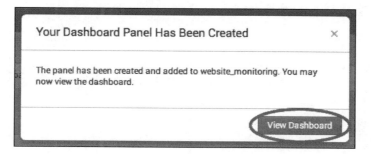

How it works...

To review how the search works in detail, refer to the *Finding the most accessed web pages* recipe in *Chapter 2, Diving into Data – Search and Report*.

The **Visualization** tab simply takes the tabular output, which is essentially a value split by another value, and overlays the given visualization. In this case, it was a total count of events split by the web page name, which you overlaid with the pie chart visualization.

There's more...

We can further build on the base search to provide different variations of the results and make use of other visualizations.

Searching for the top 10 accessed web pages

If we modify the report search and replace the `stats` command with the `top` command, by default it will display the top 10 web pages:

```
index=main sourcetype=access_combined | top uri_path
```

Here, we modified the report search and replaced the `stats` command with the `top` command. By default, this will display the top 10 web pages. You can then select the **Visualization** tab, and choose **Column** to see the results displayed as a column chart. Then, by clicking on **Format**, you can access a menu that allows you to extend the control over the chart by applying specific values such as customizing the *x* and *y* axes, placement or removal of the legend, and more.

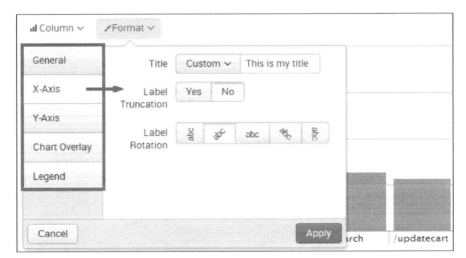

See also

▶ The *Creating an Operational Intelligence dashboard* recipe
▶ The *Displaying the unique number of visitors* recipe
▶ The *Using a gauge to display the number of errors* recipe

Displaying the unique number of visitors

It is always good to understand the number of page views and those that are accessed most, but sometimes, it is even better to understand how many of these page views are from unique visitors. Through the web access logs, we can get an understanding of how many unique visitors we have had to our website. For example, it could be helpful to understand whether times of high load are due to the true number of sessions on the website.

In this recipe, you will write a Splunk search to find the unique number of visitors to the website over a given period of time. You will then graphically display this value on a dashboard using the single value visualization.

Getting ready

To step through this recipe, you will need a running Splunk Enterprise server, with the sample data loaded from *Chapter 1, Play Time – Getting Data In*. You should be familiar with the Splunk search bar, the time range picker, and the **Visualization** tab. It is not required but is advisable that you complete all the recipes up until this point.

How to do it...

Follow the given steps to display the unique number of website visitors:

1. Log in to your Splunk server.
2. Select the default **Search & Reporting** application.
3. Ensure that the time range picker is set to **Last 24 hours**, and type the following search into the Splunk search bar. Then, click on the magnifying glass icon or hit *Enter*.

   ```
   index=main sourcetype=access_combined | stats
   dc(JSESSIONID)
   ```

4. Splunk will return a single value that represents the distinct count (unique) of values in the field named **JSESSIONID**.
5. Click on the **Visualization** tab.

6. As there are a number of visualizations within Splunk, the **Single Value** visualization might not be displayed by default within the **Visualization** tab. Click on the dropdown that lists the visualization types, and select **Single Value**.

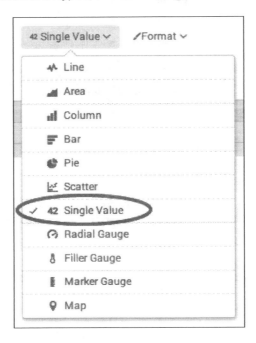

7. Your data should now be visualized as a single value.

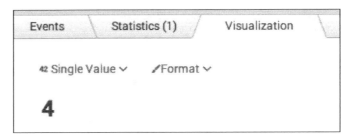

8. Save this search by clicking on **Save As** and then on **Report**. Name the report `cp03_unique_visitors` and click on **Save**. On the next screen, click on **Add to Dashboard**.

9. You will now add this to the **Website Monitoring** dashboard. Select the button labeled **Existing**, and from the drop-down menu that appears, select the **Website Monitoring** dashboard. For the **Panel Title** field value, enter Unique Visitors and select for the panel to be powered by **Report**. Then, click on **Save**.

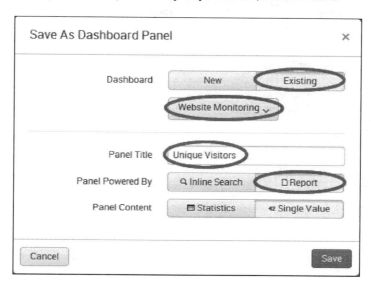

10. The next screen will confirm that the dashboard has been created and the panel has been added. Click on **View Dashboard** to see for yourself. The single value visualization should be placed below the pie chart you created in the previous recipe.

11. You will now arrange the dashboard such that the pie chart panel and single value panel are side by side. Click on the **Edit** button, and from the drop-down menu, select **Edit Panels**.

12. A gray bar will now appear at the top of your panel. Using this bar, click-and-drag the panel to now be aligned on the same row as the pie chart panel, as shown in the following screenshot:

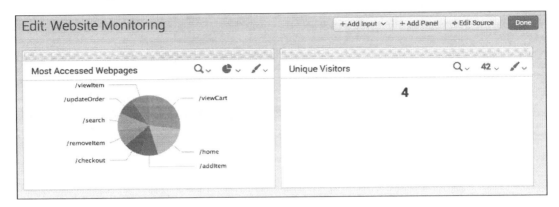

13. Finally, click on **Done** to save the changes to your dashboard.

 You will learn more about the functions and features of the Dashboard Editor in the next chapter. For the purposes of this chapter, you will be simply moving panels around on a dashboard.

How it works...

Let's break down the search piece by piece.

Search fragment	Description
`index=main` `sourcetype=access_combined`	You should now be familiar with this search from the earlier recipes in this book.
`| stats dc(JSESSIONID)`	Using the `stats` command, you call the distinct count (`dc`) function to count the total number of unique values for the field named `JSESSIONID`. The `JSESSIONID` field is chosen as each visitor to the website will be given a random session identifier whose value is stored in this field. The `clientip` field, for example, was not chosen here, as you can have multiple users coming to a website from the same IP address through the use of **NAT** (short for **Network Address Translation**).

The **Visualization** tab simply takes the numeric output of the stats command and overlays the given visualization. In this case, you overlaid single value visualization on a distinct count of visitor sessions.

There's more...

A single value on the dashboard is very useful, but providing some visual colors and context to the value can prove even more useful.

Adding labels to a single value panel

Run the same search from this recipe, and when the search completes, click on the **Visualization** tab and choose the **Single Value** visualization type. Next, click on the **Format** button, and in the drop-down menu that appears, you have the option to enter text values for **Before Label**, **After Label**, and **Under Label**.

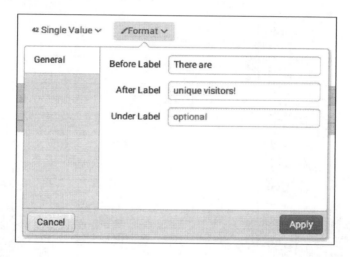

After entering your desired values, click on **Apply**. The changes will appear immediately, as shown in the following screenshot:

You can now save this single value report as a panel on a dashboard, as you did before, but can leave the **Panel Title** field empty as the description of the value is now part of the data itself.

Coloring the value based on ranges

After adding labels, it can be useful to provide some visual color to the numeric value displayed, based on a given range within which the number might be. Modify the search as follows:

```
index=main sourcetype=access_combined | stats dc(JSESSIONID) AS
count | rangemap field=count low=0-1 elevated=2-5 default=severe
```

This search renames the `dc(JSESSIONID)` field to `count`. The `rangemap` command is then used to assign a range value (`low`, `elevated`, or `severe`) based on the value of the count field. The single value visualization uses the given range value to apply a color to the visualization. If it is within the low range, the color will be green; if it is elevated, the color will be yellow; and if severe, it will be red.

> For more information on the `rangemap` command, visit `http://docs.splunk.com/Documentation/Splunk/latest/SearchReference/Rangemap`.

See also

▶ The *Using a pie chart to show the most accessed web pages* recipe

▶ The *Using a gauge to display the number of errors* recipe

▶ The *Charting the number of method requests by type and host* recipe

Using a gauge to display the number of errors

Not every user interaction with a website will go smoothly. There are times when accessed pages will report an unsuccessful status code. Understanding this number and being able to apply acceptable low, medium, and high thresholds enables a better understanding of the current user experience when there are a higher number of errors than acceptable.

In this recipe, you will write a Splunk search to find the total number of errors over a given period of time. You will then graphically represent this value on the dashboard using a radial gauge.

Getting ready

To step through this recipe, you will need a running Splunk Enterprise server, with the sample data loaded from *Chapter 1, Play Time – Getting Data In*. You should be familiar with the Splunk search bar, the time range picker, and the **Visualization** tab. It is not required but is advisable that you complete all the recipes up until this point.

How to do it...

Follow the given steps to use a gauge visualization to display the number of web access errors:

1. Log in to your Splunk server.
2. Select the default **Search & Reporting** application.
3. Ensure that the time range picker is set to **Last 24 hours**, and type the following search into the Splunk search bar. Then, click on the magnifying glass icon or hit *Enter*.

   ```
   index=main sourcetype=access_combined NOT status="200" |
   stats count
   ```

4. Splunk will return the total count of events where the status was anything but successful.
5. Click on the **Visualization** tab.
6. As there are a number of visualizations within Splunk, the single value visualization might not be displayed by default within the **Visualization** tab. Click on the dropdown that lists the visualization types, and select **Radial Gauge**.
7. Your data should now be visualized as a gauge, and the needle on the gauge is likely all the way into the red—this is because the thresholds need to be adjusted.

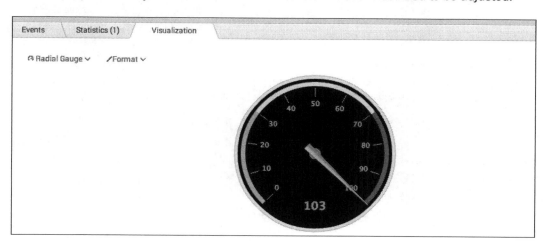

8. To adjust the thresholds on the radial gauge, click on the **Format** button. Then, from the drop-down menu, click on the **Color Ranges** tab, and finally, click on the **Manual** button.

9. From within the **Manual Color Ranges** screen, you can now adjust the values to acceptable amounts such that the needle sits in the middle of the yellow range; then, click on **Apply**.

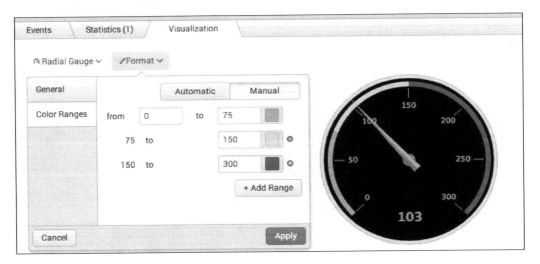

10. Save this report by clicking on **Save As** and then on **Report**. Name the report `cp03_webaccess_errors` and click on **Save**. On the next screen, click on **Add to Dashboard**.

11. You will now add this report to the **Website Monitoring** dashboard. Select the button labeled **Existing**, and from the drop-down menu that appears, select the **Website Monitoring** dashboard. For the **Panel Title** field value, enter `Total Number of Errors` and select for the panel to be powered by a **Report**; then, click on **Save**.

12. The next screen will confirm that the dashboard has been created and the panel has been added. Click on **View Dashboard** to see for yourself. The radial gauge visualization should be now positioned on the dashboard below the previous two panels.

13. Arrange the dashboard so that the radial gauge panel is to the right of the single value panel. Click on the **Edit** button, and from the drop-down menu, select **Edit Panels**. Move the radial gauge panel accordingly.

14. Finally, click on **Done** to save the changes to your dashboard. The dashboard should now look like the following screenshot:

How it works...

Let's break down the search piece by piece.

Search fragment	Description

`index=main`
`sourcetype=access_combined`
`NOT status="200"`
	You should be familiar with this search from the earlier recipes in this chapter. However, we added the search criteria to *not* return any event where the `status` field is equal to `200` (success).

`| stats count`	Using the `stats` command, we count the total number of events that are returned.

The **Visualization** tab simply takes the numeric output of the `stats` command and overlays the given visualization. In this case, you overlaid a radial gauge visualization on the total count of events that was not successful.

There's more...

In this recipe, we did not use the other two types of gauges: the filler gauge and marker gauge. It is advisable to try out the other gauges, as they might be the preferred single value visualization for your intended audience.

> For more information on the available single value visualizations, visit `http://docs.splunk.com/Documentation/Splunk/latest/Viz/Visualizationreference#Single-value_visualizations`.

See also

▶ The *Displaying the unique number of visitors* recipe

▶ The *Charting the number of method requests by type and host* recipe

▶ The *Creating a timechart of method requests, views, and response times* recipe

Charting the number of method requests by type and host

In our environment where multiple hosts are responding to web requests for customers who browse the website, it is good to get an idea of the current number of each method request split by the host. Methods relate to request/response actions between a customer's web client and our web hosts. Having this type of information can enable you to understand if these requests are being balanced properly across the hosts or if one host is receiving the majority of the load.

In this recipe, you will write a Splunk search to chart the number of method requests split by type and host. You will then graphically represent these values on a dashboard using a column chart.

Getting ready

To step through this recipe, you will need a running Splunk Enterprise server, with the sample data loaded from *Chapter 1, Play Time – Getting Data In*. You should be familiar with the Splunk search bar, the time range picker, and the **Visualization** tab. It is not required but is advisable that you also complete all the recipes up until this point.

How to do it...

Follow the given steps to chart the number of method requests by type and host:

1. Log in to your Splunk server.

2. Select the default **Search & Reporting** application.

3. Ensure that the time range picker is set to **Last 24 hours**, and type the following search into the Splunk search bar. Then, click on the magnifying glass icon or hit *Enter*.

   ```
   index=main sourcetype=access_combined | chart count by
   host,method
   ```

4. Splunk will return a tabulated list of total counts for each method request split by host.

5. Click on the **Visualization** tab.

6. Click on the dropdown that lists the visualization types, and select **Column**.

7. Your data should now be visualized as shown in the following screenshot:

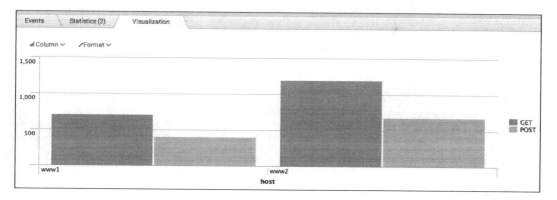

8. Save this report by clicking on **Save As** and then on **Report**. Name the report cp03_
methods_by_host, and click on **Save**. On the next screen, click on **Add to Dashboard**.

9. You will now add this to the **Website Monitoring** dashboard. Select the button labeled
Existing, and from the drop-down menu that appears, select the **Website Monitoring**
dashboard. For the **Panel Title** field value, enter Method Requests by Type and
Host, and select for the panel to be powered by a **Report**; then, click on **Save**.

10. The next screen will confirm that the dashboard has been created and the panel has
been added. Click on **View Dashboard** to see for yourself.

11. Edit the dashboard to position the column chart visualization below the previously
added panels.

How it works...

Let's break down the search piece by piece.

Search fragment	Description
index=main sourcetype=access_combined	You should now be familiar with this search from the earlier recipes.
| chart count by host,method	The chart command is simply performing a count of events split by host and method. This produces the total count of each method for a given host.

The **Visualization** tab simply takes the tabulated output of the stats command and overlays
the given visualization. In this case, you overlaid a column chart visualization on the total
count for each method split by host.

See also

▶ The *Using a gauge to display the number of errors* recipe

▶ The *Creating a timechart of method requests, views, and response times* recipe

▶ The *Using a scatter chart to identify discrete requests by size and response time* recipe

Creating a timechart of method requests, views, and response times

Having the right single values displayed on a dashboard can be beneficial to understanding key metrics, but can also be limiting in providing true operational intelligence on how different metrics of our website affect one another. By plotting values such as the number of method requests, number of total views, and average response times over a given time range, you can begin to understand if there is any correlation between these numbers. This can be very beneficial in understanding things such as if the average response time of pages is growing due to the number of active POST requests to the website or if one type of request is making up for the majority of the total number of requests at that given time.

In this recipe, you will create a Splunk search using the timechart command to plot values over a given time period. You will then graphically represent these values using a line chart.

Getting ready

To step through this recipe, you will need a running Splunk Enterprise server, with the sample data loaded from *Chapter 1, Play Time – Getting Data In*. You should be familiar with the Splunk search bar, the time range picker, and the **Visualization** tab. It is not required but is advisable that you also complete all the recipes up until this point.

How to do it...

Follow the given steps to create a timechart of method requests, views, and response times:

1. Log in to your Splunk server.

2. Select the default **Search & Reporting** application.

3. Ensure that the time range picker is set to **Last 7 days**, and type the following search into the Splunk search bar. Then, click on the magnifying glass icon or hit *Enter*.

```
index=main sourcetype=access_combined | eval
GET_response=if(method=="GET",response,0) | eval
POST_response=if(method=="POST",response,0) | timechart
span=5m avg(GET_response) AS Avg_GET_Response,
avg(POST_response) AS Avg_POST_Response,
count(eval(method=="GET")) AS GET_Total,
count(eval(method=="POST")) AS POST_Total, count AS
Total_Visits
```

4. Splunk will return a time series chart of values for the average response time of GET and POST requests, the count of GET and POST requests, and the total count of web page visits.

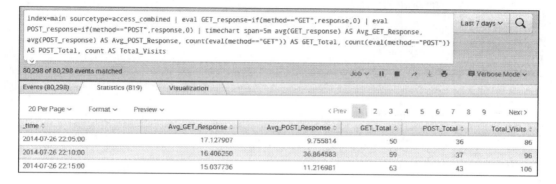

5. Click on the **Visualization** tab, and select **Line** from the drop-down listing of visualization types to visualize the data represented as a line chart.

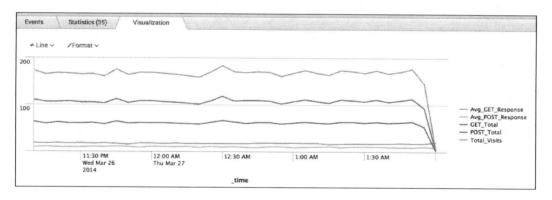

6. Save this report by clicking on **Save As** and then on **Report**. Name the report cp03_method_view_reponse, and click on **Save**. On the next screen, click on **Add to Dashboard**.

7. You will now add this report to the **Website Monitoring** dashboard. Select the button labeled **Existing**, and from the drop-down menu that appears, select the **Website Monitoring** dashboard. For the **Panel Title** field value, enter `Website Response Performance` and select for the panel to be powered by **Report**; then, click **Save**.

8. The next screen will confirm that the dashboard has been created and the panel has been added. Click on **View Dashboard** to see for yourself. The line chart visualization should be now positioned on the dashboard below the previously added panels.

9. Arrange the dashboard so that the line chart panel is on the right-hand side of the column chart panel created in the previous recipe. Click on the **Edit** button, and from the drop-down menu, select **Edit Panels**. Move the line chart panel accordingly.

10. Finally, click on **Done** to save the changes to your dashboard.

How it works...

Let's break down the search piece by piece.

Search fragment	Description
`index=main sourcetype=access_ combined`	You should now be familiar with this search from the earlier recipes in this book.
`| eval GET_response=if(method =="GET",response,0)`	Using the `eval` command, we create a new field called `GET_response`, whose value is based on the return value of the `if` function. In this case, if the method is `GET`, then the value returned is the value of the `response` field; otherwise, the value returned is `0`.
`| eval POST_response=if (method=="POST", response,0)`	Using the `eval` command, we create a new field called `POST_response`, whose value is based on the return value of the `if` function. In this case, if the method is `POST`, then the value returned is the value of the `response` field; otherwise, the value returned is `0`.
`timechart span=5m avg(GET_response) AS Avg_GET_Response, avg(POST_response) AS Avg_POST_Response, count(eval(method==" GET")) AS GET_Total, count(eval(method==" POST")) AS POST_Total, count AS Total_Visits`	Using the `timechart` command, we first specify a span of 5 minutes. Next, we calculate the average value for the given span of `GET_response` and `POST_response`. Next, we count the total number of `GET` and `POST` events. Finally, the total number of events, both `GET` and `POST`, are counted. Note that we make use of the `AS` operator to rename the fields so that they are meaningful and easy to understand when displayed on our chart.

The **Visualization** tab takes the time series output of the timechart command and overlays the given visualization. In this case, you are overlaying the line chart visualization.

There's more...

In this recipe, we looked at the values represented as a whole across our web server environment. However, in instances like ours where web traffic is balanced across multiple servers, it is a good idea to split the values based on their respective hosts.

Method requests, views, and response times by host

It is very easy to obtain a more granular view of events split by the host where the events are occurring. All we need to do is add the by clause to the end of our previous Splunk search as follows:

```
index=main sourcetype=access_combined | eval
GET_response=if(method=="GET",response,0) | eval
POST_response=if(method=="POST",response,0) | timechart span=5m
avg(GET_response) AS Avg_GET_Response, avg(POST_response) AS
Avg_POST_Response, count(eval(method=="GET")) AS GET_Total,
count(eval(method=="POST")) AS POST_Total, count AS Total_Visits
by host
```

As simple as this is, we can now visualize values broken down by the host on which these values originated. In a distributed environment, this can be most crucial to understanding where latency or irregular volumes exist.

See also

▶ The *Charting the number of method requests by type and host* recipe

▶ The *Using a scatter chart to identify discrete requests by size and response time* recipe

▶ The *Creating an area chart of the application's functional statistics* recipe

Using a scatter chart to identify discrete requests by size and response time

As shown by the recipes up until this point, there is vast intelligence that can be attained by building visualizations that summarize the current application state, analyze performance data over time, or compare values to one another. However, what about those discrete events that appear off in the distance at odd or random times? These events might not be correctly reflected when looking at a column chart, single value gauge, or pie chart, as to most calculations, they are just a blip in the radar somewhere off in the distance. However, there could be times where these discrete events are indicative of an issue or simply the start of one.

In this recipe, you will write a very simple Splunk search to plot a few elements of web request data in the tabular format. The real power comes next where you will graphically represent these values using a scatter chart.

Getting ready

To step through this recipe, you will need a running Splunk Enterprise server, with the sample data loaded from *Chapter 1, Play Time – Getting Data In*. You should be familiar with the Splunk search bar, the time range picker, and the **Visualization** tab. It is not required but is advisable that you complete the recipes up until this point.

How to do it...

Follow the given steps to use a scatter chart to identify discrete requests by size and response time:

1. Log in to your Splunk server.

2. Select the default **Search & Reporting** application.

3. Ensure that the time range picker is set to **Last 24 hours**, and type the following search into the Splunk search bar. Then, click on the magnifying glass icon or hit *Enter*.

   ```
   index=main sourcetype=access_combined | eval kb=bytes/1024
   | table method kb response
   ```

4. Splunk will return a tabulated list of the `method`, `kb`, and `response` fields for each event.

5. Click on the **Visualization** tab and select **Scatter** from the drop-down list of visualization types to see the data represented as a scatter plot chart. You should see the cluster of normal activity and then some discrete values that are off on their own.

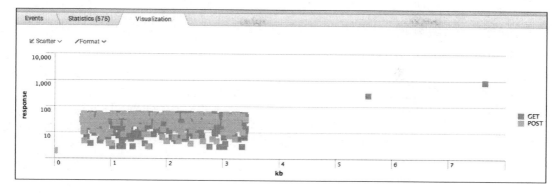

6. Save this report by clicking on **Save As** and then on **Report**. Name the report cp03_discrete_requests_size_response, and click on **Save**. On the next screen, click on **Add to Dashboard**.

7. You will now add this to the **Website Monitoring** dashboard. Select the button labeled **Existing**, and from the drop-down menu that appears, select the **Website Monitoring** dashboard. For the **Panel Title** field value, enter Discrete Requests by Size and Response and select for the panel to be powered by a **Report**; then, click on **Save**.

8. The next screen will confirm that the dashboard has been created and the panel has been added. Click on **View Dashboard** to see for yourself. The scatter chart visualization should be now positioned on the dashboard below the previously added panels.

How it works...

Let's break down the search piece by piece.

Search fragment	Description
`index=main` `sourcetype=access_combined`	You should now be familiar with this search from the earlier recipes in this book.
`| eval kb=bytes/1024`	Using the `eval` command, we convert the size of the request from bytes to kilobytes. For presentation purposes, this makes it easier to read and relate.
`| table method kb response`	Using the `table` command, we plot our data points that will be represented on the scatter chart. The first field, `method`, will present the data that appears in the legend. The second field, `kb`, represents the *x*-axis value. Finally, the third field, `response`, represents the *y*-axis value.

There's more...

Aside from simply plotting data points for a scatter chart in the tabular form, you can leverage the `timechart` command and its available functions to better identify and provide more context to these discrete values.

Using time series data points with a scatter chart

The Splunk search you ran in this recipe can be modified to make use of the `timechart` command and all of the functions it has to offer. Using the **Visualization** tab and scatter chart, run the following Splunk search over **Last 24 hours**:

```
index=main sourcetype=access_combined | eval kb=bytes/1024 |
timechart span=5m mean(kb) min(kb) max(kb)
```

As you can see, with the `timechart` command, you are first bucketing the events into 5-minute intervals as specified by the `span` parameter. Next, the `mean`, `min`, and `max` values of the `kb` field for that given time span are calculated. This way, if there is an identified discrete value, you can see more clearly what drove that span of events to be discrete. An example of this can be found in the following screenshot. In this scatter chart, we have highlighted one discrete value that is far outside the normal cluster of events. You can see why this might have stood out using the `min` and `max` values from this event series.

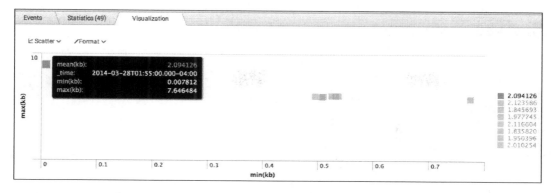

See also

▶ The *Creating a timechart of method requests, views, and response times* recipe

▶ The *Creating an area chart of the application's functional statistics* recipe

▶ The *Using a bar chart to show the average amount spent by category* recipe

Creating an area chart of the application's functional statistics

Understanding not only how your web page is performing and responding to requests but also underlying applications that you rely on is critical to the success of any website. You need to have a constant pulse on how the application is behaving and if any trends are emerging or correlations are being observed between interdependent pieces of data. The experience a customer has with your website is reliant on the constant high performance of all of its components.

In this recipe, you will write a Splunk search using the `timechart` command to plot web application memory and response time statistics over a given time period. You will then graphically present these values using an area chart.

Getting ready

To step through this recipe, you will need a running Splunk Enterprise server, with the sample data loaded from *Chapter 1, Play Time – Getting Data In*. You should be familiar with the Splunk search bar, the time range picker, and the **Visualization** tab. It is not required but is advisable that you complete all the recipes up until this point.

How to do it...

Follow the given steps to create an area chart of the application's functional statistics:

1. Log in to your Splunk server.

2. Select the default **Search & Reporting** application.

3. Ensure that the time range picker is set to **Last 24 hours**, and type the following search into the Splunk search bar. Then, click on the magnifying glass icon or hit *Enter*.

    ```
    index=main sourcetype=log4j | eval
    mem_used_MB=(mem_used/1024)/1024 | eval
    mem_total_MB=(mem_total/1024)/1024 | timechart span=1m
    values(mem_total_MB) AS Total_Mem_Avail_MB, count AS
    Total_Calls, avg(mem_used_MB) AS Avg_Mem_Used_MB,
    avg(response_time) AS Avg_Response_Time
    ```

4. Splunk will return a time series chart of values for the average response time of GET and POST requests, the count of GET and POST requests, and the total count of web page visits.

5. Click on the **Visualization** tab and select **Area** from the drop-down list of visualization types to see the data represented as an area chart. Note how the data is stacked for better visual representation of the given data.

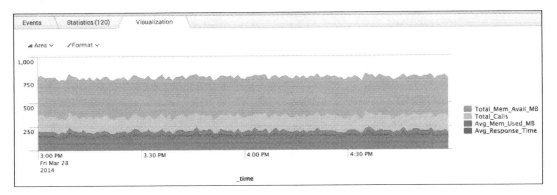

6. Save this report by clicking on **Save As** and then on **Report**. Name the report cp03_ webapp_functional_stats, and click on **Save**. On the next screen, click on **Add to Dashboard**.

7. You will now add this to the **Website Monitoring** dashboard. Select the button labeled **Existing**, and from the dropdown menu that appears, select the **Website Monitoring** dashboard. For the **Panel Title** field value, enter Web Application Functional Statistics and select for the panel to be powered by a **Report**; then, click on **Save**.

8. The next screen will confirm that the dashboard has been created and the panel has been added. Click on **View Dashboard** to see for yourself.

How it works...

Let's break down the search piece by piece.

Search fragment	Description
`index=main` `sourcetype=log4j`	In this example, we are searching for our application's logs that have the `log4j` sourcetype.
`| eval mem_used_MB=` `(mem_used/1024)/1024`	Using the `eval` command, we calculate the amount of memory currently being used, in megabytes.

`| eval mem_total_MB=`
`(mem_total/1024)/102`
`4`
	Using the `eval` command again, we calculate the total amount of memory that is available for use, in megabytes.

`| timechart span=1m`
`values(mem_total_MB)`
`AS`
`Total_Mem_Avail_MB,`
`count AS`
`Total_Calls,`
`avg(mem_used_MB) AS`
`Avg_Mem_Used_MB,`
`avg(response_time)`
`AS Avg_Response_Time`
	Using the `timechart` command, we first specify a span of 1 minute for our events. Next, we use the values function to retrieve the value stored in the `mem_total_MB` field. The `count` function is then used to calculate the total amount of function calls during the given time span. The `average` function is then called twice to calculate the average amount of memory used and average response time for the function call during the given time span. Note that we make use of the `AS` operator to rename the fields so that they are meaningful and easy to understand when displayed on our chart.

The **Visualization** tab takes the time series output of the `timechart` command and overlays the given visualization. In this case, you overlaid an area chart.

See also

▶ The *Using a scatter chart to identify discrete requests by size and response time* recipe

▶ The *Using a bar chart to show the average amount spent by category* recipe

▶ The *Creating a line chart of item views and purchases over time* recipe

Using a bar chart to show the average amount spent by category

Throughout this chapter, you have been building visualizations to provide insight into the operational performance of our e-commerce website. It can also be useful to understand the customer's view and the factors that might drive them to the website. This type of information is traditionally most useful for product or marketing folks. However, it can also be useful to gain an understanding around whether an item is increasing in popularity and/or if this could ultimately lead to additional customers and heavier load on the site.

In this recipe, you will write a Splunk search to calculate the average amount of money spent split out by product category. You will then graphically present this data using a bar chart on a new **Product Monitoring** dashboard.

Getting ready

To step through this recipe, you will need a running Splunk Enterprise server, with the sample data loaded from *Chapter 1, Play Time – Getting Data In*. You should be familiar with the Splunk search bar, the time range picker, and the **Visualization** tab. It is not required but is advisable that you complete all the recipes up until this point.

How to do it...

Follow the given steps to use a bar chart to show average amount spent by category:

1. Log in to your Splunk server.

2. Select the default **Search & Reporting** application.

3. Ensure that the time range picker is set to **Last 24 hours**, and type the following search into the Splunk search bar. Then, click on the magnifying glass icon or hit *Enter*.

   ```
   index=main sourcetype=log4j | transaction sessionId
   maxspan=30m | search requestType="checkout" | stats
   avg(total) AS Avg_Spent by category
   ```

4. Splunk will return a tabulated list, detailing the category and the associated average amount spent.

5. Click on the **Visualization** tab and select **Bar** from the drop-down list of visualization types to see the data represented as a bar chart.

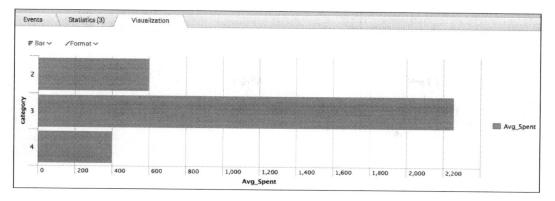

6. Save this report by clicking on **Save As** and then on **Report**. Name the report `cp03_ average_spent_category`, and click on **Save**. On the next screen, click on **Add to Dashboard**.

7. You will now add this to a new **Product Monitoring** dashboard. Select the button labeled **New** and enter a dashboard title of `Product Monitoring`. For the **Panel Title** field value, enter `Average Spent by Category`, and select for the panel to be powered by a **Report**; then, click on **Save**.

8. The next screen will confirm that the dashboard has been created and the panel has been added. Click on **View Dashboard** to see for yourself.

How it works...

Let's break down the search piece by piece.

Search fragment	Description
`index=main sourcetype=log4j`	In this example, we are searching for our application's logs that have the `log4j` sourcetype.
`| transaction sessionId maxspan=30m`	Using the `transaction` command, we group together all events that share the same `sessionId` in a 30-minute span.
`| search requestType="checkout" paymentReceived="Y"`	Using the `search` command, we limit the grouped results to those that have only a `checkout` event and where the payment was received. In this visualization, a purchase does not qualify for consideration if it did not successfully process.
`| stats avg(total) AS Avg_Spent by category`	Using the `stats` command, we calculate the average total amount spent by category. Note that we make use of the `AS` operator to rename the field so that it is meaningful and easy to understand when displayed on our chart.

The **Visualization** tab simply takes the time series output of the `stats` command and overlays the given visualization. In this case, you overlaid a bar chart visualization.

See also

▶ The *Creating an area chart of the application's functional statistics* recipe

▶ The *Creating a line chart of item views and purchases over time* recipe

▶ The *Using a scatter chart to identify discrete requests by size and response time* recipe

Creating a line chart of item views and purchases over time

Continuing on from the last recipe, you will look to further improve your understanding of customer activities by now looking at a chart of item views and actual purchases over a given time period. This will allow you to understand if customers who are viewing an item actually follow through with purchasing the given item.

In the last recipe of this chapter, you will write a Splunk search to chart item views and purchases over a given time period. You will then graphically present this data using a line chart.

Getting ready

To step through this recipe, you will need a running Splunk Enterprise server, with the sample data loaded from *Chapter 1, Play Time – Getting Data In*. You should be familiar with the Splunk search bar, the time range picker, and the **Visualization** tab. It is not required but is advisable that you complete all the recipes up until this point.

How to do it...

Follow the given steps to create a line chart of item views and purchases over time:

1. Log in to your Splunk server.

2. Select the default **Search & Reporting** application.

3. Ensure that the time range picker is set to **Last 24 hours**, and type the following search into the Splunk search bar. Then, click on the magnifying glass icon or hit *Enter*.

   ```
   index=main sourcetype=access_combined | timechart span=5m
   count(eval(uri_path="/viewItem")) AS Item_Views,
   count(eval(uri_path="/checkout")) AS Purchases
   ```

4. Splunk will return a time series-based chart, listing the count of item views and count of purchases over the given time period.

5. Click on the **Visualization** tab and select **Line** from the drop-down list of visualization types to represent the data as a line chart.

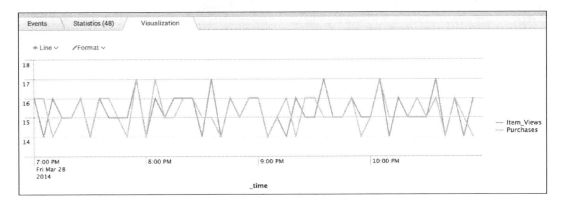

6. Save this report by clicking on **Save As** and then on **Report**. Name the report `cp03_item_views_purchases`, and click on **Save**. On the next screen, click on **Add to Dashboard**.

7. You will now add this to the **Product Monitoring** dashboard. Select the button labeled **Existing**, and from the drop-down menu that appears, select the **Product Monitoring** dashboard. For the **Panel Title** field value, enter `Item Views vs. Purchases`, and select for the panel to be powered by a `Report`; then, click on **Save**.

8. The next screen will confirm that the dashboard has been created and the panel has been added. Click on **View Dashboard** to see for yourself.

9. Arrange the dashboard so that the line chart panel is to the right of the bar chart panel created in the previous recipe. Click on the **Edit** button, and from the drop-down menu, select **Edit Panels**. Move the line chart panel accordingly.

10. Finally, click on **Done** to save the changes to your dashboard.

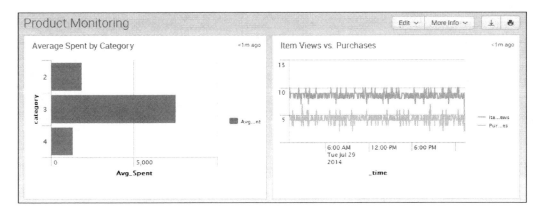

How it works...

Let's break down the search piece by piece.

Search fragment	Description
`index=main` `sourcetype=access_combined`	In this example, we are searching for our application's logs that have the `log4j` sourcetype.

`| timechart span=5m`
`count(eval(uri_path="/viewItem"))`
`AS Item_Views,`
`count(eval(uri_path="/checkout"))`
`AS Purchases`
	Using the `timechart` command, we count the total number of times an item is viewed and the total number of purchases that occurred.

See also

- ▸ The *Creating an area chart of the application's functional statistics* recipe
- ▸ The *Using a bar chart to show the average amount spent by category* recipe

Summary

The key takeaways from this chapter are as follows:

- ▸ Dashboards provide a means to bring together multiple visualizations into a central view
- ▸ Visualizations bring data to life by placing it in a visual context, making it easy for the viewer to distinguish patterns, trends, and relationships within their data
- ▸ Review and make use of the best practices of visualization
- ▸ Splunk comes loaded with meaningful and powerful visualizations that can be overlaid on common search commands

4

Building an Operational Intelligence Application

In this chapter, we will learn how to build and modify a Splunk application. You will learn about:

- ▶ Creating an Operational Intelligence application
- ▶ Adding dashboards and reports
- ▶ Organizing the dashboards more efficiently
- ▶ Dynamically drilling down on activity reports
- ▶ Creating a form to search web activities
- ▶ Linking web page activity reports to the form
- ▶ Displaying a geographical map of visitors
- ▶ Scheduling the PDF delivery of a dashboard

Introduction

In the previous chapter, we were introduced to Splunk's awesome dashboarding and visualization capabilities. We created several basic dashboards and populated them with various operational intelligence-driven visualizations. In this chapter, we will continue to build on what we have learned in the previous chapters and further advance our Splunk dashboarding knowledge. You will learn how to create a Splunk application and populate it with several dashboards. You will also learn to use some of Splunk's more advanced dashboarding capabilities such as forms, drill downs, and maps.

Splunk applications (or **apps**) are best thought of as workspaces designed specifically around certain use cases. In this chapter, we will be building a new application that focuses specifically on operational intelligence. Splunk apps can vary in complexity from a series of saved reports and dashboards, through to complex, fully-featured standalone solutions. After logging in to Splunk for the first time, you are actually interfacing with Splunk through the **launcher** application, which displays a dashboard that lists other applications installed on the system. The **Search & Reporting** application that we have been using throughout this book so far is an example of another bundled Splunk application.

 Several vendors, developers, and customers have developed applications that can be used to get you started with your datasets. Most of these applications are available for free download from the Splunk App store at http://apps.splunk.com.

In this chapter, you will also start to get to grips with the dashboard forms functionality. The best way to think about forms in Splunk is that they are essentially dashboards with an interface, allowing users to easily supply values to the underlying dashboard searches. For example, a basic form in Splunk would be a dashboard with a user-selectable time range at the top. The user might then select to run the dashboard over the last 24 hours, and all the searches that power the dashboard visualizations will run over this selected time range.

Forms, by their very nature, require inputs. Luckily, for us, Splunk has a number of common form inputs out of the box that can be readily used using the dashboard editor or SimpleXML. The available form inputs and an explanation of their common usage are detailed in the following table:

Input	Common usage
Dropdown	This is used to display lists of user selectable values. Dropdowns can be populated dynamically using Splunk searches and even filtered based on the user selection of another dropdown. Users can also select single values or multiple values.
Radio	This is used for simple yes/no or single selection type values. You can only select one value at a time with radio buttons, unlike dropdowns.
Text	This is a simple textbox, allowing the user to type whatever value they want to search for. The textbox is great for searching for wildcard type values, such as field values of abc*.
Time	This is a time range picker. This is exactly the same as the time range picker found on the main Splunk search dashboard. You can add a time range for the entire dashboard or for individual dashboard panels.

Dashboards in Splunk are coded behind the scenes in something known as SimpleXML. This SimpleXML code can be edited directly or by use of Splunk's interactive, **GUI**-based dashboard editor. For the most part, this chapter will focus on using the GUI-based dashboard editor, which allows for dashboards to be edited without touching a line of code—nice! However, you will be introduced to direct SimpleXML editing in order to take advantage of more advanced capabilities and options.

Ok, enough of discussion; let's get started!

Creating an Operational Intelligence application

This recipe will show you how to create an empty Splunk app that we will use as the starting point in building our Operational Intelligence application.

Getting ready

To step through this recipe, you will need a running Splunk Enterprise server, with the sample data loaded from *Chapter 1, Play Time – Getting Data In*. You should have also completed the recipes from the earlier chapters. You should be familiar with navigating the Splunk user interface.

How to do it...

Follow the given steps to create the Operational Intelligence application:

1. Log in to your Splunk server.

2. From the top menu, select **Apps** and then select **Manage Apps**.

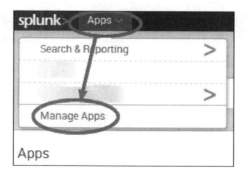

3. Click on the **Create app** button.

4. Complete the fields in the box that follows. Name the app `Operational Intelligence` and give it a folder name of `operational_intelligence`. Add in a version number and provide an author name. Ensure that **Visible** is set to **Yes**, and the **barebones** template is selected.

5. When the form is completed, click on **Save**. This should be followed by a blue bar with the message, **Successfully saved operational_intelligence**.

Congratulations, you just created a Splunk application!

How it works...

When an app is created through the Splunk GUI, as in this recipe, Splunk essentially creates a new folder (or directory) named `operational_intelligence` within the `$SPLUNK_HOME/etc/apps` directory. Within the `$SPLUNK_HOME/etc/apps/operational_intelligence` directory, you will find four new subdirectories that contain all the configuration files needed for our barebones Operational Intelligence app that we just created.

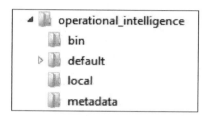

The eagle-eyed among you would have noticed that there were two templates, `barebones` and `sample_app`, out of which any one could have been selected when creating the app. The `barebones` template creates an application with nothing much inside of it, and the `sample_app` template creates an application populated with sample dashboards, searches, views, menus, and reports. If you wish to, you can also develop your own custom template if you create lots of apps, which might enforce certain color schemes for example.

There's more...

As Splunk apps are just a collection of directories and files, there are other methods to add apps to your Splunk Enterprise deployment.

Creating an application from another application

It is relatively simple to create a new app from an existing app without going through the Splunk GUI, should you wish to do so. This approach can be very useful when we are creating multiple apps with different `inputs.conf` files for deployment to Splunk Universal Forwarders.

Taking the app we just created as an example, copy the entire directory structure of the `operational_intelligence` app and name it `copied_app`.

```
cp -r $SPLUNK_HOME$/etc/apps/operational_intelligence/*
$SPLUNK_HOME$/etc/apps/copied_app
```

Within the directory structure of `copied_app`, we must now edit the `app.conf` file in the default directory.

Open `$SPLUNK_HOME$/etc/apps/copied_app/default/app.conf` and change the label field to `My Copied App`, provide a new description, and then save the `conf` file.

```
#
# Splunk app configuration file
#
[install]
is_configured = 0

[ui]
is_visible = 1
label = My Copied App

[launcher]
author = John Smith
description = My Copied application
version = 1.0
```

 If you are working on Windows and receive an "access denied" error, go see your administrator.

Now, restart Splunk, and the new **My Copied App** application should now be seen in the application menu.

```
$SPLUNK_HOME$/bin/splunk restart
```

Downloading and installing a Splunk app

Splunk has an entire application website with hundreds of applications, created by Splunk, other vendors, and even users of Splunk. These are great ways to get started with a base application, which you can then modify to meet your needs.

If the Splunk server that you are logged in to has access to the Internet, you can click on the **Apps** menu as you did earlier and then select the **Find More Apps** button. From here, you can search for apps and install them directly.

An alternative way to install a Splunk app is to visit `http://apps.splunk.com` and search for the app. You will then need to download the application locally. From your Splunk server, click on the **Apps** menu and then on the **Manage Apps** button. After that, click on the **Install App from File** button and upload the app you just downloaded, in order to install it.

Once the app has been installed, go and look at the directory structure that the installed application just created. Familiarize yourself with some of the key files and where they are located.

When downloading applications from the Splunk apps site, it is best practice to test and verify them in a nonproduction environment first. The Splunk apps site is community driven and, as a result, quality checks and/or technical support for some of the apps might be limited.

See also

- ▸ The *Adding dashboards and reports* recipe
- ▸ The *Organizing the dashboards more efficiently* recipe
- ▸ The *Dynamically drilling down on activity reports* recipe

Adding dashboards and reports

As we saw in the previous chapter, dashboards are a great way to present many different pieces of information. Rather than having lots of disparate dashboards across your Splunk environment, it makes a lot of sense to group related dashboards into a common Splunk application, for example, putting operational intelligence dashboards into a common Operational Intelligence application.

In this recipe, you will learn how to move the dashboards and associated reports you created in the last couple of chapters into our new Operational Intelligence application.

Getting ready

To step through this recipe, you will need a running Splunk Enterprise server, with the sample data loaded from *Chapter 1, Play Time – Getting Data In*. You should have also completed the recipes from the earlier chapters. You should be familiar with navigating the Splunk user interface.

How to do it...

Follow these steps to move your dashboards into the new application:

1. Log in to your Splunk server.
2. Select the newly created **Operational Intelligence** application.

3. From the top menu, select **Settings** and then select the **User interface** menu item.

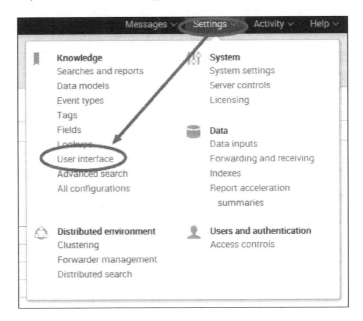

4. Click on the **Views** section.

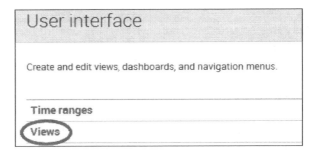

5. In the **App Context** dropdown, select **Searching & Reporting (search)** or whatever application you were in when creating the dashboards in the previous chapter:

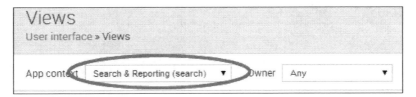

6. Locate the **website_monitoring** dashboard row in the list of views and click on the **Move** link to the right of the row.

7. In the **Move Object** pop up, select the **Operational Intelligence (operational_ intelligence)** application that was created earlier and then click on the **Move** button.

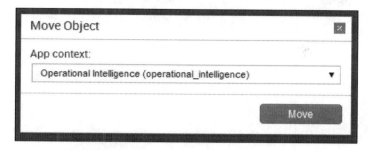

8. A message bar will then be displayed at the top of the screen to confirm that the dashboard was moved successfully.

9. Repeat from step 5 to move the **product_monitoring** dashboard as well.

10. After the **Website Monitoring** and **Product Monitoring** dashboards have been moved, we now want to move all the reports you created in the previous recipes, as these power the dashboards and provide operational intelligence insight. From the top menu, select **Settings** and this time select **Searches, reports, and alerts**.

11. Select the **Search & Reporting (search)** context and filter by *cp0** to view the searches (reports) created in *Chapter 2, Diving into Data – Search and Report*, and *Chapter 3, Dashboards and Visualizations – Make Data Shine*. Click on the **Move** link of the first *cp0** search in the list.

12. Select to move the object to the **Operational Intelligence (operational_intelligence)** application and click on the **Move** button.

13. A message bar will then be displayed at the top of the screen to confirm that the dashboard was moved successfully.

14. Select the **Search & Reporting (search)** context and repeat from step 11 to move all the other searches over to the new Operational Intelligence application—this seems like a lot but will not take you long!

All of the dashboards and reports are now moved over to your new Operational Intelligence application.

How it works...

In the previous recipe, we revealed how Splunk apps are essentially just collections of directories and files. Dashboards are XML files found within the $SPLUNK_HOME/etc/apps directory structure. When moving a dashboard from one app to another, Splunk is essentially just moving the underlying file from a directory inside one app to a directory in the other app. In this recipe, you moved the dashboards from the **Search & Reporting** app to the **Operational Intelligence** app, as represented in the following screenshot:

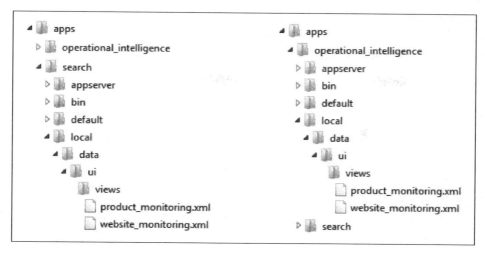

As visualizations on the dashboards leverage the underlying saved searches (or reports), you also moved these reports to the new app so that the dashboards maintain permissions to access them. Rather than moving the saved searches, you could have changed the permissions of each search to **Global** such that they could be seen from all the other apps in Splunk. However, the other reason you moved the reports was to keep everything contained within a single Operational Intelligence application, which you will continue to build on going forward.

It is best practice to avoid setting permissions to **Global** for reports and dashboards, as this makes them available to all the other applications when they most likely do not need to be. Additionally, setting global permissions can make things a little messy from a housekeeping perspective and crowd the lists of reports and views that belong to specific applications. The exception to this rule might be for knowledge objects such as tags, event types, macros, and lookups, which often have advantages to being available across all applications.

There's more...

As you went through this recipe, you likely noticed that the dashboards had application-level permissions, but the reports had private-level permissions. The reports are private as this is the default setting in Splunk when they are created. This private-level permission restricts access to only your user account and admin users. In order to make the reports available to other users of your application, you will need to change the permissions of the reports to **Shared in App** as we did when adjusting the permissions of reports.

Changing the permissions of saved reports

Changing the sharing permission levels of your reports from the default **Private** to **App** is relatively straightforward:

1. Ensure that you are in your newly created **Operational Intelligence** application.

2. Select the **Reports** menu item to see the list of reports.

3. Click on **Edit** next to the report you wish to change the permissions for. Then, click on **Edit Permissions** from the drop-down list.

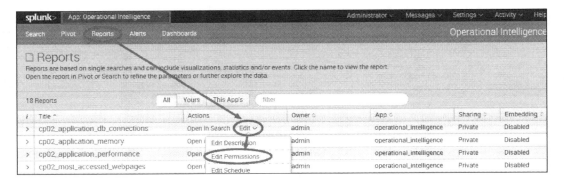

4. An **Edit Permissions** pop-up box will appear. In the **Display for** section, change from **Owner** to **App**, and then, click on **Save**.

5. The box will close, and you will see that the **Sharing** permissions in the table will now display **App** for the specific report. This report will now be available to all the users of your application.

See also

▶ The *Creating an Operational Intelligence application* recipe

▶ The *Organizing the dashboards more efficiently* recipe

▶ The *Dynamically drilling down on activity reports* recipe

Organizing the dashboards more efficiently

In this recipe, you will learn how to use Splunk's dashboard editor to use more efficient visualizations and organize the dashboards more efficiently. This feature was introduced in Splunk 6 and enhanced even further in Splunk 6.1.

Getting ready

To step through this recipe, you will need a running Splunk Enterprise server, with the sample data loaded from *Chapter 1, Play Time – Getting Data In*, and should have completed the earlier recipes in this chapter. You should also be familiar with navigating the Splunk user interface.

How to do it...

Follow these steps to organize the dashboards more efficiently:

1. Log in to your Splunk server.
2. Select the **Operational Intelligence** application.
3. Click on the **Dashboards** menu item.

4. You should see the **Product Monitoring** and **Website Monitoring** dashboards that we moved into the Operational Intelligence app in the previous recipe. Select the **Website Monitoring** dashboard, and it will be displayed.

5. You will notice that there are several visualizations on the dashboard; in Splunk, they are known as panels. Select **Edit Panels** from the **Edit** menu.

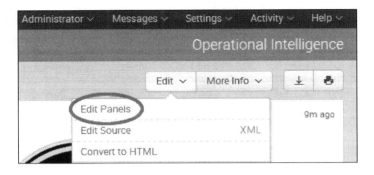

6. In the **Total Number of Errors** panel, change **Radial Gauge** to **Single Value** visualization, by clicking on the radial gauge icon and selecting **Single Value**.

7. Move the other panels around until your dashboard resembles the layout in the following screenshot. Notice how we have our single value panels at the top, our various charts in the middle, and then, our time series-based charts at the bottom.

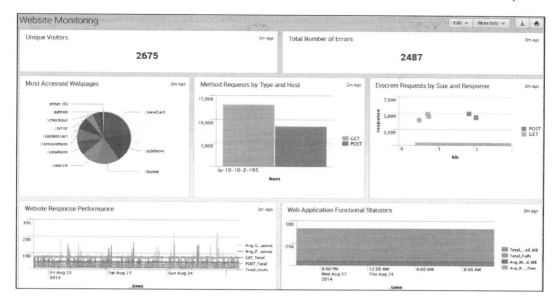

8. Click on the **Done** button when complete. I think you will agree that this dashboard looks a lot better than the earlier one! Everything fits on the screen for the most part, and it is much easier on the eye.

How it works...

In this recipe, we started to experience the power of Splunk's amazing dashboard editor. The dashboard editor provides a nice usable interface that essentially shields the user from what is happening underneath the covers. When we edit dashboard panels and visualizations in this manner, Splunk is actually writing the required SimpleXML code into the respective view's XML file on your behalf. When you click on **Done**, the file is essentially saved with the newly written XML under the covers. If you are hungry for more, don't worry; we are just getting started with the editor. There is plenty more to come later in this chapter!

Dashboards in Splunk are also called views. In the management interface and in the backend, they are commonly known as views, but in the application menu, they are called dashboards. We may use the terms interchangeably in this book.

There's more...

Instead of using the dashboard editor, you can edit the SimpleXML directly.

Modifying the SimpleXML directly

Let's take a look at the SimpleXML that is behind the **Website Monitoring** dashboard. Ensure that the dashboard is displayed on screen. Then, click on the **Edit** button as you did earlier, but instead of clicking on **Edit Panels**, click on **Edit Source**. The underlying SimpleXML source code will now be displayed.

Dashboards in SimpleXML consist of rows, panels, and visualization elements. Dashboards can have many rows (`<row></row>`), but around three rows is advisable. Within each row, you can have multiple panels (`<panel></panel>`), and within each panel, you can have multiple visualization elements (for example, `<chart></chart>` for a chart). On the **Website Monitoring** dashboard, you should see three row elements and multiple panels with a single dashboard element on each panel.

We can edit the SimpleXML directly to swap the single elements around on the top row of the dashboard. Simply select the first panel group as shown in the following screenshot:

```
<dashboard>
  <label>Website Monitoring</label>
  <description/>
  <row>
    <panel>
      <single>
        <title>Unique Visitors</title>
        <searchName>cp03_unique_visitors</searchName>
      </single>
    </panel>
    <panel>
      <single>
        <title>Total Number of Errors</title>
        <searchName>cp03_webaccess_errors</searchName>
      </single>
    </panel>
  </row>
```

Move this panel group below the second panel group as shown in the following screenshot:

```
<dashboard>
  <label>Website Monitoring</label>
  <description/>
  <row>
    <panel>
      <single>
        <title>Total Number of Errors</title>
        <searchName>cp03_webaccess_errors</searchName>
      </single>
    </panel>
    <panel>
      <single>
        <title>Unique Visitors</title>
        <searchName>cp03_unique_visitors</searchName>
      </single>
    </panel>
  </row>
```

Then, once done, click on the **Save** button. This is an extremely simple example, but you should start to see how we can edit the code directly rather than use the dashboard editor.

Note that there might be some `<option>` data within the panel groups that we have removed in the screenshots to simplify things. However, ensure that you move everything within the panel group.

Familiarizing yourself with SimpleXML and how to tweak it manually will provide more functionality and likely make the process of creating a dashboard a lot more efficient.

> A great way to learn SimpleXML can be to modify something using the Splunk dashboard editor and then select to view the code to see what has happened in the underlying SimpleXML code. Splunk also has a great SimpleXML reference that allows for quick access to many of the key SimpleXML elements. Visit `http://docs.splunk.com/Documentation/Splunk/latest/Viz/PanelreferenceforSimplifiedXML` for more information.

See also

- The *Adding dashboards and reports* recipe
- The *Dynamically drilling down on activity reports* recipe
- The *Creating a form to search web activities* recipe

Dynamically drilling down on activity reports

When viewing a dashboard in Splunk, there is usually a very high probability that you will look at a chart or report and want to know more details about the information that you are looking at.

Splunk dashboards can be configured to let the user drill down into more details. By linking results or data points to an underlying dashboard or report, information about what the user clicked on can provide them with the next level of detail or the next step in the process they are following.

This recipe will show you how you can configure reports to drill down into subsequent searches and other dashboards so that you can link them together into a workflow that gets the user to the data they are interested in seeing within your Operational Intelligence application.

Getting ready

To step through this recipe, you will need a running Splunk Enterprise server, with the sample data loaded from *Chapter 1, Play Time – Getting Data In,* and should have completed the earlier recipes in this chapter. You should also be familiar with navigating the Splunk user interface.

How to do it...

Follow these steps to configure a dashboard report with row drilldown capabilities:

1. Log in to your Splunk server.
2. Select the **Operational Intelligence** application.
3. Click on the **Dashboards** menu.

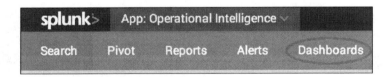

4. Click on the **Create New Dashboard** button.

5. Name the dashboard `Visitor Monitoring` and set the **Permissions** field to **Shared in App**.

6. Click on **Create Dashboard**.

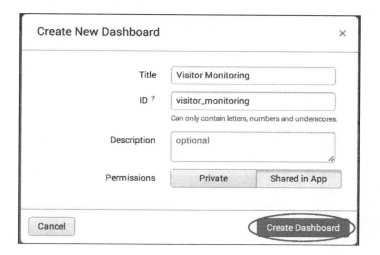

7. When the empty dashboard is displayed, click on the **Add Panel** button.

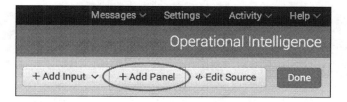

8. Set the **Content Title** panel to `Session Listing`.

9. Set the **Search String** field to the following search:

```
index=main sourcetype=access_combined | iplocation clientip |
fillnull value="Unknown" City, Country, Region| replace "" with
"Unknown" in City, Country, Region | stats count by JSESSIONID,
clientip, City, Country, Region | fields clientip, City, Region,
Country
```

10. Set the time range to **Last 24 hours**:

11. Click on the **Add Panel** button.

12. Click on the panel graph icon and ensure that the graph is a **Statistics Table**:

13. Click on the panel edit icon, select the **Row** option for the **Drilldown** setting, and click on the **Apply** button.

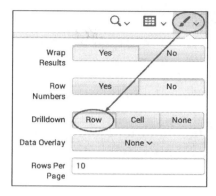

14. Click on the **Done** button to finish editing the dashboard.

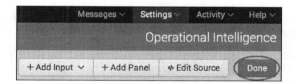

15. Click on a row in the dashboard table, and Splunk will now drill down to the search screen and execute a search that is filtered by the `clientip` value in the row you selected to drill down on.

How it works...

The drilldown feature of dashboards can be utilized to get your users to the next set of data they need. When they click on a table entry or a part of a chart, they set off a search that can drill down into more details of the item they clicked. The behavior of the drilldown is controlled by the configuration of the panel in the SimpleXML but also has a few options displayed by the dashboard editor.

When displaying a table of results, there are three options that can be chosen from.

Option	Description
Row	When a row is clicked, the search that is launched by the drilldown is based on the *x*-axis value, which is the first column in the row.
Cell	When a particular cell is clicked, the search that is launched by the drilldown is based on both the *x*-axis and *y*-axis values represented by that cell.
None	The drilldown functionality is disabled. When a user clicks on the table, the page will not change.

When displaying a chart, there are two options for the drilldown behavior that can be chosen from.

Option	Description
On	When a row is clicked, the search that is launched by the drilldown is based on the values of the portion of that chart.
Off	The drilldown functionality is disabled. When a user clicks on the table, the page will not change.

When the drilldown search is started after the table or chart is clicked on, it is generally derived by taking the original search, backing off the final transforming commands, and then adding the values that were selected depending on the drilldown setting.

 When a new panel item is added, such as a chart, table, or map, the default drilldown is always turned on by default.

There's more...

The drilldown options can be customized and provide many different options to control the behavior when dashboards are clicked on.

Disabling the drilldown feature in tables and charts

To disable the drilldown feature, you can specify the **None** option in the **Drilldown** setting of the edit panel form or add/modify the following SimpleXML option to the panel source:

```
<option name="drilldown">none</option>
```

 A full reference of drilldown options can be found in the Splunk documentation at http://docs.splunk.com/Documentation/ Splunk/latest/Viz/PanelreferenceforSimplifiedXML#Pa nel_visualization_elements.

See also

▸ The *Organizing the dashboards more efficiently* recipe

▸ The *Creating a form to search web activities* recipe

▸ The *Linking web page activity reports to the form* recipe

Creating a form to search web activities

Presenting users with dashboards is a great way to visualize data, as we have seen. However, often, people like to "slice n dice" data in many different ways, and to do this, we need to make our dashboards more interactive. We can do this using the dashboard forms functionality of Splunk, which allows users to filter dashboard visualizations and data based upon the criteria that are important to them.

This recipe will build on the tabular **Visitor Monitoring** dashboard you created in the previous recipe to allow for granular filtering of the tabulated results.

Getting ready

To step through this recipe, you will need a running Splunk Enterprise server, with the sample data loaded from *Chapter 1, Play Time – Getting Data In*, and should have completed the earlier recipes in this chapter. You should also be familiar with navigating the Splunk user interface.

How to do it...

Follow these steps to create a form to filter data on a dashboard:

1. Log in to your Splunk server.
2. Select the **Operational Intelligence** application.
3. Click on the **Dashboards** menu item.
4. Select to view the **Visitor Monitoring** dashboard we created in the previous recipe.
5. Once loaded, click on the **Edit** dropdown and then on **Edit Panels**.
6. Click on **Add Input** and then select **Time**.

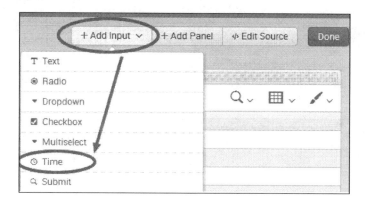

7. Click on **Add Input** again, and this time, select **Text**.

8. A new text input named **field2** will appear. Above the text input, you will see a little pencil icon. Click on the pencil icon to edit the input. A pop up will be displayed.

9. Complete the box with the values in the following table:

Field	Value
Label	IP
Search on Change	Should be checked
Token	ip
Default	*
Token Suffix	*

Then, click on **Apply**.

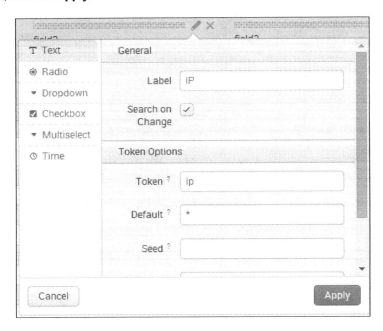

10. The box will disappear, and you will see that the input is now titled IP.

11. Repeat from step 7 to add and edit the three other textbox fields (one at a time) using the following values for each:

Textbox field	Field	Value
field3	Label	City
	Search on Change	Should be checked
	Token	city
	Default	*
	Token Suffix	*
field4	Label	Region
	Search on Change	Should be checked
	Token	region
	Default	*
	Token Suffix	*
field5	Label	Country
	Search on Change	Should be checked
	Token	country
	Default	*
	Token Suffix	*

12. Once complete, you should have a total of five fields. Let's now do a bit of rearrangement. Move the **Time input** field on the far right-hand side so that it is the last input field at the top. Additionally, check the **Autorun dashboard** checkbox on the far right-hand side.

13. Click on the pencil icon above the time input and change the default time range from **All Time** to **Last 24 Hours**. Then, click on **Apply**.

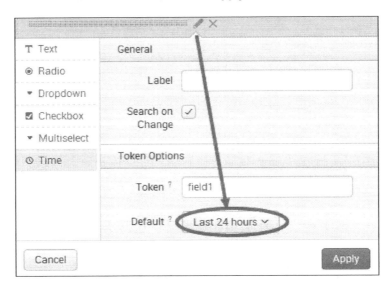

14. Next, click on **Done** in the top-right corner of the screen to finish editing the form. You should see all your fields nicely labeled across the top with wildcard asterisks (*****) in each textbox.

15. Next, we need to link the new fields we just created with the table. Click on **Edit** and then on **Edit Panels**.

16. Select **Edit Search String** in the panel with the table. A pop-up box will appear with the current search string.

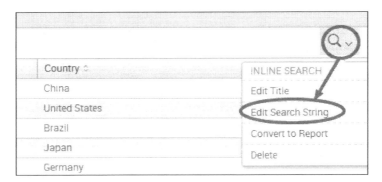

17. Replace the existing search string with the following search string. The modifications to the search have been highlighted.

```
index=main sourcetype=access_combined clientip="$ip$" |
iplocation clientip  | fillnull value="Unknown" City,
Country, Region| replace "" with "Unknown" in City,
Country, Region | stats count by JSESSIONID, clientip,
City, Country, Region | fields clientip, City, Region,
Country | search City="$city$" Region="$region$"
Country="$country$"
```

18. Change **Time Range Scope** to **Shared Time Picker (field1)**.

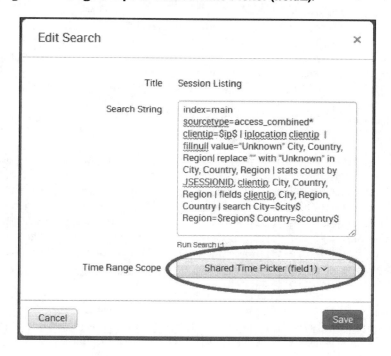

19. Click on **Save** and then on **Done**.

20. Refresh/reload the dashboard in your browser.

21. That's it! You now have a nice form-driven table. Try testing it out. For example, if you want to filter by all IP addresses that begin with 134, simply enter 134 into the IP textbox and press *Enter*.

How it works...

In this recipe, we only used the GUI editor, which means that Splunk was changing the underlying SimpleXML for us. As soon as we added the first input field, Splunk changed the opening SimpleXML `<dashboard>` element to a form `<form>` element behind the scenes. Each of the five inputs we added are contained within a `<fieldset>` element. For each of the inputs, Splunk creates an `<input>` element, and each input type can have a number of fields: some optional some required. One of the key fields for each type is the **Token** field, the values of which are then used by searches on the dashboard. We assigned a token name to each input, such as `ip`, `city`, and `country`. Other fields that we populated for the text inputs were the **Default** and **Suffix** field values of *. This tells Splunk to search for everything (*) by default if nothing is entered into the textbox and to add a wildcard (*) suffix to everything entered into the textbox. This means that if we were to search for a city using a value of `Tor`, Splunk will search for all the cities that begin with Tor (`Tor*`), such as Toronto. We also checked the **Search on Change** box, which forces a rerun of any searches in the dashboard should we change a value of the input. After completing the editing of the inputs, we selected to autorun the dashboard, which adds `autoRun="true"` in the `<fieldset>` element of the SimpleXML and ensures that the dashboard runs as soon as it is loaded with the default values rather than waiting for something to be submitted in the form.

Once we built the form inputs and configured them appropriately, we needed to tell the searches that power the dashboard visualizations to use the tokens from each of the form inputs. The **Token** field for each input will contain the value for that input. We edited the search for the table on the dashboard and added additional search criteria to force Splunk to search, based upon these tokens. Token names must be encapsulated by $ signs, so our `ip` token is entered into the search as `$ip$`, and our country token is entered as `$country$`. We also told our search to use the `Shared Time Picker` input rather than its own time range. This allows us to then search using the time picker input we added to the form.

The end result is that anything entered into the form inputs is encapsulated into the respective tokens, and the values of these tokens are then passed to the search that powers the table in the dashboard. If we change the value of an input, then the value of the input's token in the search changes, the search immediately reruns, and the search results in the table change accordingly.

There's more...

In this recipe, we began to scratch the surface of form building, using only textbox inputs and the time picker. Later in this book, we will leverage the drop-down input, and you will learn how to prepopulate drop-down values as a result of a search and learn how to filter drop-down values as a result of other drop-down selections.

Adding a Submit button to your form

In this recipe, you probably will have noticed that there was no **Submit** button. The reason for this was primarily because no **Submit** button was needed. We selected to autorun the dashboard and selected **Search on Change** for each input. However, there are times when you might not want the form to run as soon as something is changed; perhaps, you want to modify multiple inputs and then search. Additionally, many users like the reassurance of a **Submit** button, as it is commonly used on forms across websites and applications.

Adding a **Submit** button is extremely simple. When the dashboard is in the editing mode, simply click on the **Add Input** dropdown and select **Submit**. You will notice that a green **Submit** button now appears on the form. If you now edit the text inputs and uncheck the **Search on Change** checkbox for each of them, the form will only be submitted when someone clicks on the **Submit** button.

See also

- ▶ The *Dynamically drilling down on activity reports* recipe
- ▶ The *Linking web page activity reports to the form* recipe
- ▶ The *Displaying a geographical map of visitors* recipe

Linking web page activity reports to the form

Form searches in Splunk do not need to be limited to displaying events and table-driven data. Rich visualizations can also be linked to forms and be updated when the forms are submitted.

This recipe will show you how you can extend a form to include charts and other visualizations that can be driven by the form created to show visitor traffic and location data.

Getting ready

To step through this recipe, you will need a running Splunk Enterprise server, with the sample data loaded from *Chapter 1, Play Time – Getting Data In*, and should have completed the earlier recipes in this chapter. You should also be familiar with navigating the Splunk user interface.

How to do it...

Follow these steps to add a web page activity chart and link it to a form:

1. Log in to your Splunk server.

2. Select the default **Operational Intelligence** application.

3. Select the **Dashboards** menu item.

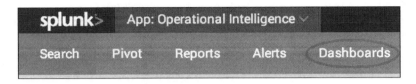

4. Select the **Visitor Monitoring** dashboard.

5. Click on the **Edit** button and then on **Edit Panels**.

6. Click on the **Add Panel** button.

7. In the **Add Panel** window, set the **Content Title** field to Sessions Over Time.

8. Set the **Search String** field to the following search:

```
index=main sourcetype=access_combined clientip="$ip$" |
iplocation clientip | fillnull value="Unknown" City,
Country, Region| replace "" with "Unknown" in City,
Country, Region | search City="$city$" Region="$region$"
Country="$country$" | timechart dc(JSESSIONID)
```

9. Set the **Time Range Scope** field to **Shared Time Picker (field1)**.

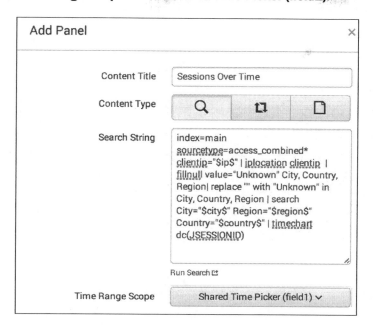

10. Click on the **Add Panel button**.

11. After the panel is added to the bottom of the dashboard, click on the chart-type panel icon located at the top-right corner of the panel you just added.

12. Click on the **Line** chart type.

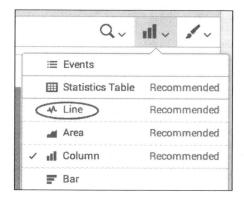

13. Click on the edit panel icon.

14. Update the **X-Axis** label with **Custom Title** set to `Time`.

15. Update the **Y-Axis** label with **Custom Title** set to `Unique Sessions`.

16. Set the **Legend** option to **None**.

17. Click on **Apply**, and the pop-up box will disappear with the changes reflected on the panel.

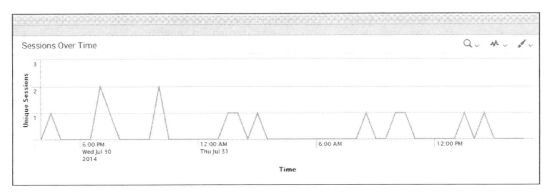

18. Next, click on **Done** to finish editing the dashboard.

19. Filter by an IP of 134 or similar again, and you should see that the chart panel also changes along with the table panel.

How it works...

Adding a chart to the dashboard works in a manner very similar to the way in which the original form was created. You can utilize the field variables defined in the form in the inline search that is used for the chart. Splunk will set them when the form is submitted. The panel can also utilize the time range that was used in the form or contain a separate time range dropdown.

By building a form and several different charts and tables, you can build a very useful form-driven dashboard. One of the great uses of a form-driven dashboard is for investigative purposes. In this example, you can take any of the fields and, for instance, see what all sessions are coming from a particular country and then see the level of activity over the time period you are interested in.

There's more...

Additional customizations can be added to the charts in order to give them more meaning.

Adding an overlay to the Sessions Over Time chart

You can have Splunk overlay a field value on top of your existing chart to provide trendlines and so on. Add the following line to the end of the inline search used for the Sessions Over Time search:

```
| eventstats avg(dc(JSESSIONID)) as average | eval
average=round(average,0)
```

Then, add the following line to the SimpleXML of the panel:

```
<option name="charting.chart.overlayFields">average</option>
```

```
<row>
  <panel>
    <chart>
      <title>Sessions Over Time</title>
      <searchString>index=main sourcetype=access_combined clientip="$ip$" | iplocation client
      <earliestTime>$field1.earliest$</earliestTime>
      <latestTime>$field1.latest$</latestTime>
      <option name="charting.chart.overlayFields">average</option>
      <option name="charting.axisLabelsX.majorLabelStyle.overflowMode">ellipsisNone</option>
      <option name="charting.axisLabelsX.majorLabelStyle.rotation">0</option>
```

It will then add a line that charts the average of the session count over top of the actual values.

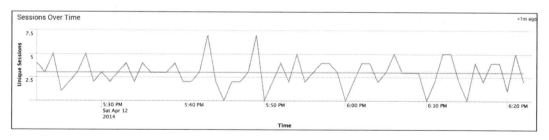

See also

 ▸ The *Creating a form to search web activities* recipe

 ▸ The *Displaying a geographical map of visitors* recipe

 ▸ The *Scheduling the PDF delivery of a dashboard* recipe

Displaying a geographical map of visitors

Operational intelligence doesn't always need to come in the form of pie charts, bar charts, and data tables. With a wide range of operational data being collected from IT systems, there is the opportunity to display this data in ways that can be more meaningful to users or help present it in ways that can be easier to identify trends or anomalies.

One way that always provides great visibility is by representing your data using a geographical map. With geolocation data available for many different data types, it becomes very easy to plot them. Using IP addresses from web server logs is a very common use case for this type of visualization. Splunk allows for the easy addition of a map to a dashboard with all the capabilities to zoom and update the portion of the map that the user is viewing.

This recipe will show you how you can configure a map panel within a dashboard and link it to a search that contains IP addresses in order to visualize where in the world the IP traffic is originating from.

Getting ready

To step through this recipe, you will need a running Splunk Enterprise server, with the sample data loaded from *Chapter 1, Play Time – Getting Data In*, and should have completed the earlier recipes in this chapter. You should also be familiar with navigating the Splunk user interface.

How to do it...

Follow these steps to add a map to your form-driven dashboard:

1. Log in to your Splunk server.
2. Select the **Operational Intelligence** application.
3. Click on the **Dashboards** menu item.

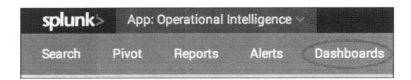

4. Select the **Visitor Monitoring** dashboard.

5. Click on the **Edit** button and then click on the **Edit Panels** option.

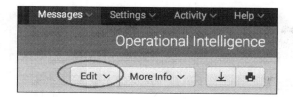

6. Click on the **Add Panel** button.

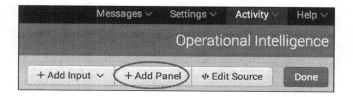

7. In the **Add Panel** window, set the **Content Title** field to `Sessions By Location`.

8. Set the **Search String** field to the following search:

```
index=main sourcetype=access_combined clientip="$ip$" | iplocation
clientip | fillnull value="Unknown" City, Country, Region|
replace "" with "Unknown" in City, Country, Region | search
City="$city$" Region="$region$" Country="$country$" | geostats
count
```

9. Set the **Time Range Scope** field to **Shared Time Picker (field1)**.

10. Click on the **Add Panel** button.

11. After the panel is added to the bottom of the dashboard, click on the chart-type panel icon on the top-left corner of the newly added panel.

12. Click on the **Map** chart type.

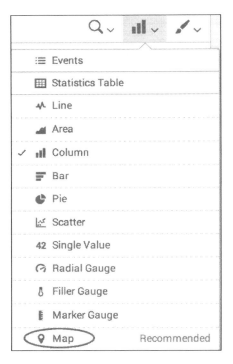

13. Click on **Done** to finish editing the dashboard.

14. Filter by an IP of 134 or similar again, and you should now see that the map panel also changes along with the table and chart panels you added earlier.

How it works...

Mapping support has been available in Splunk 4 using a third-party developed application. Since Spunk 6, native map support has been available and can be used easily within your dashboards.

The rendering of the map is done in the same way in which most browser-based maps are generated using many small images known as tiles that are put together in a grid layout and swapped in and out depending on the zoom level and the visible area being requested. As a result of this, the browser and services do not need to load an entire world's worth of image data into memory.

Splunk supports both a native tile server that can be used to serve the actual map images or can be configured to use the external OpenStreetMap service (openstreetmap.org). The native tiles do not have a very granular level of mapping detail but will work in situations where there is no external connectivity or security reasons for not calling the external service.

The map panel depends on the result of the geostats command which looks for the necessary latitude and longitude fields in the search results and adds its own fields that the map can use to render the data properly. The geostats command is commonly paired with the iplocation command to map the network traffic-originating locations.

The built-in IP location data within Splunk is provided by Splunk as part of Splunk Enterprise but is not always the most up-to-date data available from the Internet. It's often best practice to purchase a third-party service to get the most accurate and real-time data available, especially when it is used on critical security-monitoring dashboards and searches.

The map panel has many different configuration options that can be used to specify the initial latitude, longitude, and zoom level that should be applied when the map is initially loaded as well as the minimum and maximum zoom levels. Drilldown in the maps is also supported.

> A full reference of map drilldown options can be found in the Splunk documentation at http://docs.splunk.com/Documentation/Splunk/latest/Viz/PanelreferenceforSimplifiedXML#Panel_visualization_elements.

There's more...

The map panel option can also be configured in several different ways in Splunk.

Adding a map panel using SimpleXML

A map panel can be added directly to a dashboard by adding the following SimpleXML when editing the dashboard source:

```
<map>
        <title>Count by location</title>
        <searchString>index=main sourcetype=access_combined
        clientip="$ip$" | iplocation clientip | fillnull
        value="Unknown" City, Country, Region| replace "" with
        "Unknown" in City, Country, Region | search City="$city$"
        Region="$region$" Country="$country$" | geostats
        count</searchString>
        <earliestTime>-24h@m</earliestTime>
        <latestTime>now</latestTime>
        <option name="mapping.data.maxClusters">100</option>
        <option name="mapping.drilldown">all</option>
        <option name="mapping.map.center">(0,0)</option>
</map>
```

Mapping different distributions by area

The `geostats` command takes an aggregation term as its main argument. This term is what is used to render the pie charts that are located on the map. In this recipe, we simply ran `|` `geostats count`, which is the most commonly used command and simply does a single count. However, you can break out the data by product, and then the pie charts will provide segmented visual information and can be moused over to see the breakdown.

```
MySearch | geostats count by product
```

See also

▶ The *Linking web page activity reports to the form* recipe

▶ The *Scheduling the PDF delivery of a dashboard* recipe

Scheduling the PDF delivery of a dashboard

Getting operational intelligence to users who need it the most can be challenging. They can be users who are not IT savvy, don't have the correct access to the right systems, or are executives about to walk into a client meeting to go over the latest result data.

Sometimes, all a user needs is to have data e-mailed to their inbox every morning so that they can review it on their commute to the office or have an assistant prepare for a morning briefing. Splunk allows the user to schedule a dashboard so that it can be delivered as a PDF document via e-mail to a customizable list of recipients.

This recipe will show you how to schedule the delivery of a dashboard within the Operational Intelligence application as a PDF document to an internal e-mail distribution list.

Getting ready

To step through this recipe, you will need a running Splunk Enterprise server, with the sample data loaded from *Chapter 1, Play Time – Getting Data In,* and should have completed the earlier recipes in this chapter. You should also be familiar with navigating the Splunk user interface. You should also have configured your e-mail server to work with Splunk such that Splunk can actually send e-mails to specified addresses.

How to do it...

Follow these steps to schedule a PDF delivery of your dashboard:

1. Log in to your Splunk server.
2. Select the **Operational Intelligence** application.
3. Click on the **Dashboards** menu item.

4. From the dashboard listing, select the dashboard you would like to deliver as a PDF document. Only the **Website Monitoring** and **Product Monitoring** dashboards can leverage PDF delivery, as the PDF delivery function is not (currently) compatible with the dashboards driven by form inputs.
5. Once the selected dashboard loads, click on the **Edit** drop-down menu in the top-right corner of the screen.
6. Click on the **Schedule PDF Delivery** option.

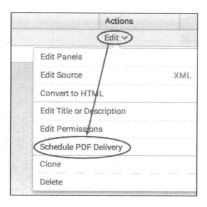

7. On the **Edit PDF Schedule** form, check the **Schedule PDF** box.

8. Modify the **Schedule** field to suit your needs. Update the dropdown and select the appropriate schedule type.

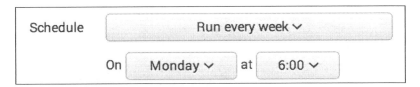

9. Enter the list of e-mail addresses you wish to send the PDF to in **the Email To** field using commas to separate multiple e-mail addresses.

10. Select the priority of the e-mail.

11. Customize the **Subject** field with the content of the message subject you would like the recipients to see.

12. Customize the **Message** field with the content of the message you would like the recipients to see.

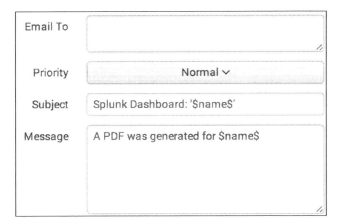

13. Update the layout options of the generated PDF by updating the **Paper Size** and **Paper Layout** options.

14. You can test your PDF and e-mail formatting using the preview options. Click on the **Send Test Email** link to send to the recipients the dashboard as it looks when the link is clicked. Then, click on the **Preview PDF** link to view a version of the PDF as it looks when the link is clicked. Sending a test e-mail will require that your Splunk administrator has configured the appropriate SMTP settings in Splunk.

15. Click on the **Save** button, and the PDF delivery of the dashboard is now scheduled.

How it works...

Since Splunk 5 was released, Splunk Enterprise has been natively able to produce PDFs of dashboards and reports. Prior to Version 5, it required a separate add-on app that only worked on Linux servers and required other operating system dependencies. The new integrated PDF features allow quicker and easier access to generate PDFs either via a schedule and e-mailed or directly from the Web.

There are still some situations that will not be able to produce PDFs such as form-driven dashboard, dashboards created using advanced XML, and SimpleXML dashboards that still contain Flash components. There are also some features such as heat map overlays that will not render properly.

PDFs are generated when requested by native libraries built into Splunk that render what would normally be output as HTML and encode this into the PDF. It's not an easy feat, as you have to take the page layout and orientation into consideration as the PDF is much more constrained than the browser window.

When delivering a scheduled PDF of a dashboard, you are using the same mechanism that scheduled reports and alerts are using. The `sendemail` command is the backbone of the process and allows many different configuration options for the format of the message, including a full range of tokens that can be inserted into the subject and body of the messages that are replaced with job- and schedule-specific details.

For more information on the configuration options to schedule reports and dashboards, check out `http://docs.splunk.com/Documentation/Splunk/latest/Report/Schedulereports`.

See also

▶ The *Displaying a geographical map of visitors* recipe

Summary

The key takeaways from this chapter are as follows:

▶ Organize your dashboards and knowledge into a custom Splunk app

▶ Modify the layout of dashboards so that information can be displayed effectively

▶ Layer your operational data and utilize drilldown options to dive deeper when needed

▶ Use new visualizations, such as maps, to convey more meaningful data

▶ Deliver data to key stakeholders without needing to log in to Splunk

5

Extending Intelligence – Data Models and Pivoting

In this chapter, we will introduce the Splunk data model and pivoting functionality. We will learn about:

- ▶ Creating a data model for web access logs
- ▶ Creating a data model for application logs
- ▶ Accelerating data models
- ▶ Pivoting total sales transactions
- ▶ Pivoting purchases by geographical location
- ▶ Pivoting slowest responding web pages
- ▶ Pivot charting top error codes

Introduction

In many of the previous chapters, we leveraged Splunk's **Search Processing Language (SPL)** quite a bit in order to build searches, reports, and dashboards. In this chapter, we will learn how to leverage Splunk's data model and Pivot functionality and demonstrate how these can be leveraged by less technical users to easily build reports, charts, and dashboards.

The first set of recipes in this chapter involves building Splunk data models. Data models allow Splunk datasets to be mapped, together with associated knowledge, into a hierarchical structure that encapsulates a number of Splunk searches behind the scenes. These models power Splunk's Pivot tool and allow users to create dynamic reports and dashboards, without the need to write any searches. Data models are somewhat analogous to relational database schemas; in that, they present data to Pivot as rows and columns.

Data models are typically built by individuals who are familiar with Splunk's SPL using the Data Model Editor. Data models have a hierarchical structure made up of objects, object types, object constraints, and object attributes. A data model consists of one or more objects and each object will be a certain object type. Each object will have one or more object constraints and contain one or more object attributes.

There are four different object types and these are outlined in the following table:

Object type	Description
Event objects	These represent a type of event, such as application log events or web access log events. They are likely to be the most commonly used type.
Search objects	These represent a Splunk search that includes commands that transform the data into the data you wish to represent, such as a search that aggregates data over time.
Transaction objects	These represent transaction type searches that group related events over time.
Child objects	These inherit constraints and attributes from their parent objects but allow for further filtering of events and have additional constraints and attributes of their own.

All data model objects are defined by one or more object constraints, which help filter out irrelevant events and these are outlined in the following table:

Object constraint	Description
Event object constraints	This is limited to a simple constraint, essentially the first part of a search before the pipe (for example, `sourcetype=x field=y`)
Search object constraints	The constraint is the object's full search string that may include a number of transforming commands and pipes
Transaction object constraints	The constraint is the transaction definition, which must identify group objects and group by fields
Child object constraints	This is limited to a simple constraint, essentially the first part of a search before the pipe (for example, `sourcetype=x field=y`)

All data model objects have one or more object attributes. These are basically fields within the dataset being modeled and the available attribute types are outlined in the following table:

Object attributes	Description
Auto-Extracted	These are fields that Splunk automatically extracts based upon extractions already defined for the sourcetypes in the dataset being modeled.
Eval-Expression	This is a field generated as a result of an `eval` expression.
Lookup	This is a field where one or more fields are added to the events as a result of a lookup.
Regular Expression	This is a field that is extracted from the event data using the entered regular expression.
Geo IP	This a lookup that takes IPs and adds geographical fields such as `lon`, `lat`, `city`, `country`, and so on.

The Common Information Model add-on app contains a number of predefined data models that comply with Splunk's **Common Information Model** (**CIM**). The CIM add-on can be used when modeling data to ensure compatibility or to take advantage of the prebuilt data models to Pivot and report. The add-on is available for download at `http://apps.splunk.com/app/1621/`.

Once we have built our data models in this chapter, you will learn how to accelerate them. An accelerated data model leverages Splunk's underlying **High Performance Analytics Store** (**HPAS**), building summaries alongside the buckets of data in the associated indexes and allows for significant performance increases in Pivot-based reporting across extremely large datasets.

For more information on data models, please review the Knowledge Manager documentation at `http://docs.splunk.com/Documentation/Splunk/latest/Knowledge/Aboutdatamodels`.

The second half of this chapter is dedicated to using Splunk's Pivot tool in order to search and report on the data we have modeled. Pivot enables users to report on data within Splunk, without having to use the SPL. The Pivot interface provides drag-and-drop functionality, allowing for easy reporting and visualization of Splunk datasets. As Pivot leverages data models and their associated objects for reporting, a data model must be created before Pivot can be used.

The fundamentals of data models and Pivot can be quite challenging to get to grips with initially and there is no better way to learn than to get our hands dirty and start modeling and pivoting in Splunk; so, let's do that!

Creating a data model for web access logs

In this first recipe, you will create a data model for our web access logs. You will be using Splunk's Data Model Editor to do this and define a number of object types, and add constraints and attributes.

Getting ready

To step through this recipe, you will need a running Splunk Enterprise server, with the sample data loaded from *Chapter 1, Play Time – Getting Data In*, and the completed recipes from earlier chapters. You should be familiar with navigating the Splunk user interface.

How to do it...

Follow the steps in this recipe to create the **Web Access** data model:

1. Log in to your Splunk server.

2. Select the **Operational Intelligence** application.

3. Select the **Settings** menu item at the top-right corner of the screen, and then select **Data models**:

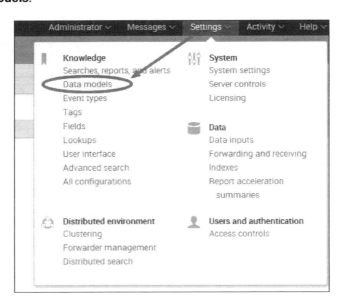

4. An empty list of data models to manage will load. Click on the **New Data Model** button located at the top-right corner of the screen:

5. A pop-up box will be displayed. Enter Web Access in the **Title** field and as you type, the ID will automatically populate. Ensure the selected app is **Operational Intelligence**, and then click on the **Create** button:

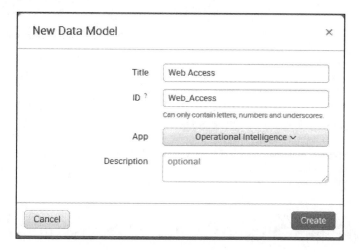

6. This will create an empty data model and the Data Model Editor will be displayed. Next, create an object type. Select the **Add Object** dropdown and select **Root Event**:

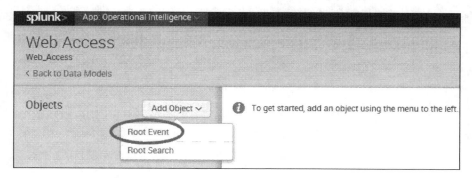

7. The **Add Event Object** page will be displayed. Enter `All Web Access` in the **Object Name** field and in the **Constraints** box, enter the search syntax `index=main sourcetype=access_combined`. Once these have been entered, click on the **Preview** button and a few web access log events will be displayed in the preview area. Following this, click on **Save**, to save the event object type:

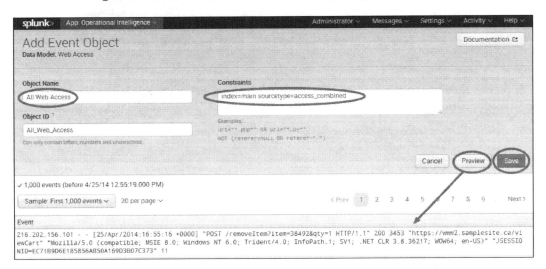

8. After saving the object type, the Data Model Editor will be displayed with the newly created **All Web Access** object displayed. Some inherited attributes will be seen on the right-hand side. You will now add a few more. Click on the **Add Attribute** dropdown and select **Auto-Extracted**.

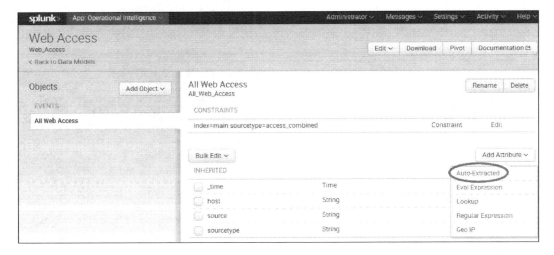

9. A pop-up box will be displayed with all the fields that Splunk has already extracted for the web access logs. You can select specific fields for the model, but to keep things simple, let's select them all by checking the checkbox next to the **Field** column heading at the top of the field list. Notice that all fields will then get checked. Once complete, click on **Save** and all these fields will now become attributes for the data model object.

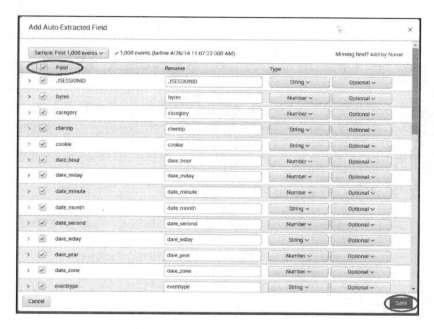

10. You will now add an evaluated attribute to add a status category. Click on the **Add Attribute** dropdown again, but this time select **Eval Expression**:

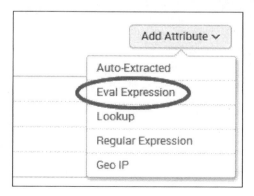

11. The **Add Attributes with an Eval Expression** screen will be displayed. In the **Eval Expression** box, enter the following search syntax to match the status code in the events to a descriptive category:

```
case(like(status,"1%"),"Informational",
like(status,"2%"),"Success", like(status,"3%"),"Redirect",
like(status,"4%"),"Client Error", like(status,"5%"),"Server
Error")
```

12. Enter `status_category` in the **Field Name** field and leave all other fields with the defaults. Then click on the **Preview** button. You should see the new **status_category** field populated in the preview results. Click on **Save** to save this newly evaluated attribute:

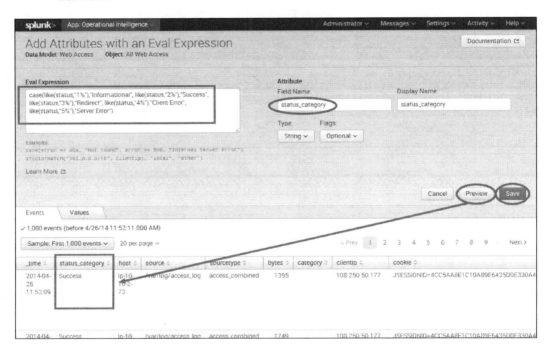

13. You will now use this newly created **status_category** object attribute to create a couple of child object types for error and success events. From the Data Model Editor, select the **Add Object** dropdown again, but this time select **Child**:

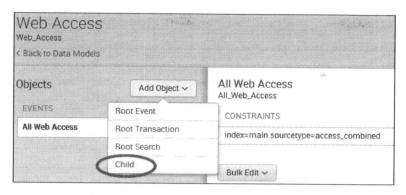

14. The **Add Child Object** screen will be displayed. Enter `Success` in the **Object Name** field and in the **Additional Constraints** box, enter the search syntax `status_category="Success"`. Click on **Preview** to confirm that the results are displayed, and then click on **Save** to save the new child object type.

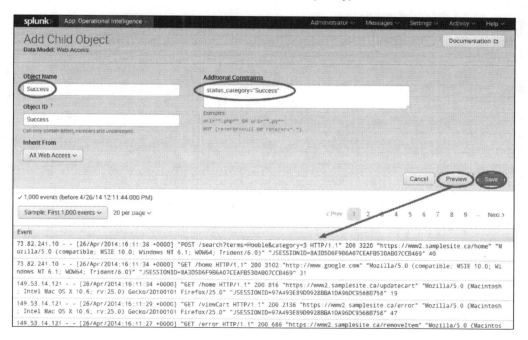

15. After saving the object, you will be back in the Data Model Editor and the new **Success** child object will be seen underneath the root level **All Web Access** event object. Click on the **All Web Access** event object, and then repeat steps 13 and 14, adding another child object type named `Error` with **Additional Constraints** of `status_category="Client Error" OR status_category="Server Error"`.

16. Once complete, you should see two child objects named **Success** and **Error** underneath the root event object named **All Web Access**.

Our initial data model is now complete—congrats!

How it works...

In this recipe, you started off by creating a new data model for our web access dataset. After the initial data model was created, you added a root-level event object type, named **All Web Access** that will sit at the top of the object hierarchy. This event object allows for simple constraints and you created an object constraint that constrained the object to only web access logs. Following this, you added object attributes to the object, consisting of all the autoextracted fields that Splunk already knew about, in addition to an evaluated expression attribute to categorize the various status codes in the event data. You then used this newly created **status_category** evaluated attribute to create child object types for **Success** and **Error** events.

Behind the scenes, Splunk is essentially creating a Splunk search to report on the dataset that is being modeled. The constraint provided essentially tells Splunk what data to look at and the attributes are basically the fields within the data that Splunk will search. The **Success** and **Error** child object types inherit all the attributes and constraints from their parent **All Access Logs** object and act as further filters for the backend search that Splunk creates.

There's more...

Once data models are built, they provide the search time mapping needed by the Pivot tool for reporting. However, it is also possible to view the underlying dataset mapped by data models and their objects using the Splunk search interface.

Searching data models using the search interface

The Splunk `datamodel` command allows for the searching of the dataset mapped by data models and their associated objects directly from the Splunk search interface. In order to be used, the command must be the first command used in your Splunk search.

Navigate to the search bar in the **Operational Intelligence** application and enter the following search to see a list of all the data models in the application:

```
| datamodel
```

If we have multiple data models, you can filter to just the **Web Access** data model, by entering the following search:

```
| datamodel Web_Access
```

The data returned is in JSON format and you are able to expand out the `objectNameList` to see all the objects within the data model. To see data related to the **All Web Access** object, enter the following search:

```
| datamodel Web_Access All_Web_Access
```

Here you can actually see the underlying search that has been written by Splunk for the data model Object—it is pretty large! It might be large, but it is not that complicated. There are actually a lot of renames and `evals` taking up most of the search, which give a rather intimidating appearance.

To search the data in this object, enter the following search:

```
| datamodel Web_Access All_Web_Access search
```

Notice how all the data is now displayed and all the object attributes you declared in the object type are represented as fields in the field sidebar. All these fields begin with the name of the object, in this case, `All_Web_Access.fieldname`, which is not terribly useful, so we can remove this by entering the following search:

```
| datamodel Web_Access All_Web_Access search | rename All_Web_Access.*
AS *
```

Now we can basically use this data as we would use any Splunk search. So, to see all error events by `status_category`, you would enter the following search:

```
| datamodel Web_Access All_Web_Access search | rename All_Web_Access.*
AS * | search is_Error=1 | stats count by status_category
```

So why would you want to take this search approach over searching the data directly? Well you can actually use data models to do a bit of heavy lifting for you in terms of correlating datasets and adding additional calculated fields and so on. Therefore, there may be times when this approach to searching the data does indeed make a lot of sense. Additionally, even when data model acceleration is turned on, the `datamodel` command does not currently use the acceleration. However, the `pivot` command (more on this later), does use acceleration, but is not as useful.

For more information on the `datamodel` command, you should review the search reference at `http://docs.splunk.com/Documentation/Splunk/latest/SearchReference/Datamodel`.

See also

> ► The *Creating a data model for application logs* recipe
> ► The *Accelerating data models* recipe

Creating a data model for application logs

This recipe is similar to the first, except this time, you will create a data model for application logs. You will be using Splunk's Data Model Editor to do this and will define a number of object types, and add constraints and attributes. In order to save pages, this recipe will be lighter on screenshots than the first recipe. The first recipe should therefore be used as a reference where needed.

Getting ready

To step through this recipe, you will need a running Splunk Enterprise server, with the sample data loaded from *Chapter 1, Play Time – Getting Data In*, and the completed recipes from earlier chapters. You should have also completed the first recipe in this chapter and be familiar with navigating the Splunk user interface.

How to do it...

Follow the steps in this recipe to create the **Application** data model:

1. Log in to your Splunk server.
2. Select the **Operational Intelligence** application.
3. Select the **Settings** menu item at the top-right corner of the screen, and then select **Data models**.

4. The **Web Access** data model we created in the earlier recipe will be listed. Click on the **New Data Model** button located at the top-right corner of the screen.

5. A pop-up box will be displayed. Enter `Application` in the **Title** field and as you type, the ID will automatically populate. Ensure the selected app is **Operational Intelligence**, and then click on the **Create button**.

6. This will create an empty data model and the Data Model Editor will be displayed. Select the **Add Object** dropdown and select **Root Event**.

7. The **Add Event Object** page will be displayed. Enter `All Application` in the **Object Name** field and in the **Constraints** box, enter the search syntax `index=main sourcetype=log4j`. Once entered, click on the **Preview** button and some application log events will be displayed in the preview area. Following this, click on **Save** to save the event object type.

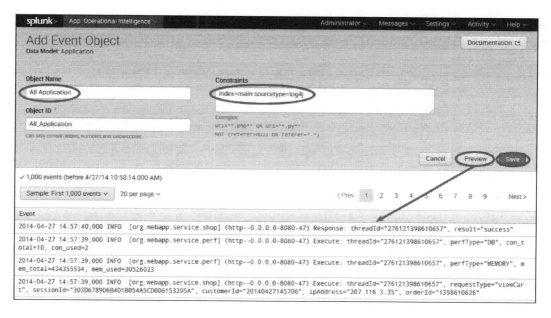

8. After saving the object type, the Data Model Editor will be displayed with the newly created **All Application** object. Some inherited attributes will be seen on the right-hand side. You will now add a few more. Click on the **Add Attribute** dropdown and select **Auto-Extracted**.

9. A pop-up box will be displayed with all the fields that Splunk has already extracted for the application logs. Check the checkbox next to the **Field** column heading at the top of the field list. Notice that all fields will then become checked. Once complete, click on **Save** and all these fields will now become attributes for the data model object.

10. You will now add a **regular expression (regex)** attribute to extract a new field called **Service** from the dataset. This regex matches a pattern in the event that relates to the different service events, either `perf`, `odbc`, or shop application events. Click on the **Add Attribute** dropdown again, but this time select **Regular Expression**:

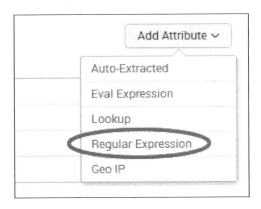

11. The **Add Attributes with a Regular Expression** screen will be displayed. In the **Regular Expression** box, enter the following search syntax:

    ```
    (?<Service>\w+)(?=\])
    ```

12. Enter `Service` in the **Field Name** field if not already automatically populated and leave all other fields with the defaults. Then click on the **Preview** button. You should see the new **Service** field populated in the preview results. Click on **Save** to save this new regular expression attribute:

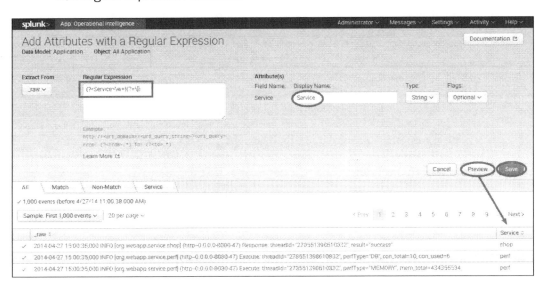

13. You will now create a number of nested child object types to help filter the different types of events within the application dataset. The following table lists all of the child objects that you should create under the **All Application Data** root event object:

Child object	Secondary child object	Tertiary child object	Constraints
Performance			Service="perf"
	Memory		perfType="MEMORY"
	DB		perfType="DB"
Database			Service="odbc"
Shop			Service="shop"
	Request		requestType=*
	Response		NOT requestType=*
		Success	result="success"
		Error	NOT result="success"

Remember, that in order to add a child object, you need to select the **Add Object** dropdown, and then select **Child**. Additionally, ensure that you preview the data as you go, to ensure you have typed the attribute names correctly and that you have the child objects under the correct parent object!

14. Once completed, your object hierarchy should resemble the following screenshot:

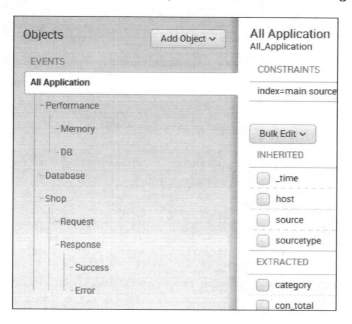

15. Finally, we will add a transaction object type to group event requests with respective event responses. Select the **Add Object** dropdown and select **Root Transaction**:

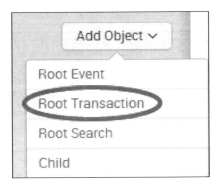

The **Add Transaction Object** screen will be displayed. Enter Transactions in the **Object Name** field. Under **Group Objects**, select to group the **Request** and **Response** child objects that we just created. Select the **threadid** object attribute in the **Group by (optional)** field and enter a maximum span of 1 hour.

16. Click on the **Preview** button and you should see the grouped transactions populated in the event results box. Click on **Save** to save this new object type:

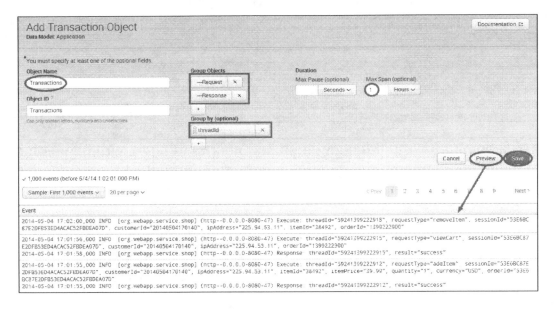

Our **Application** data model is now complete—congratulations!

How it works...

In this recipe, you started off replicating a similar path to the first recipe by creating a new data model for our application dataset. After the data model was created, you added a root-level event object type, named **All Application** that will sit at the top of the object hierarchy. This event object allows for simple constraints and you created an object constraint that constrained the object to only application logs. Following this, you added object attributes to the object, consisting of all the autoextracted fields that Splunk already knew about, in addition to a regular expression attribute to categorize the various services within the event data. You then used this newly created **Service** regular expression attribute plus other **Auto-Extracted** attributes to create several nested child objects, in order to build an object hierarchy for the **Application** data model. We also added a root level transaction object type, which grouped related application events into individual transactions based on a common **threadid**.

Behind the scenes, Splunk is essentially creating a Splunk search to report on the dataset that is being modeled. The constraints provided essentially tell Splunk what data to look at and the attributes are basically the fields within the data that Splunk will search. The child objects types inherit all the attributes and constraints from their parents and act as further filters for the backend search that Splunk creates.

See also

- ▸ The *Creating a data model for web access logs* recipe
- ▸ The *Accelerating data models* recipe

Accelerating data models

Splunk has several options for optimizing search performance, including summary indexing, report acceleration, and data model acceleration. We will cover both summary indexing and report acceleration later in this book. Data model acceleration helps to speed up reporting for the Object Attributes defined in a data model and this acceleration is leveraged by the Pivot tool when reporting.

In this next recipe, you will accelerate the data models that we just created in order to familiarize yourself with the process and enhance understanding. Ordinarily, you would only really want to use data model acceleration for reporting on extremely large datasets over a period of time.

Getting ready

To step through this recipe, you will need a running Splunk Enterprise server, with the sample data loaded from *Chapter 1, Play Time – Getting Data In*, and the completed data model recipes from earlier in this chapter. You should be familiar with navigating the Splunk user interface.

How to do it...

Perform the following steps in this recipe to accelerate the web access and **Application** data models:

1. Log in to your Splunk server.
2. Select the **Operational Intelligence** application.
3. Select the **Settings** menu item at the top-right corner of the screen, and then select **Data Models**.
4. The two data models we created in the first two recipes will be displayed. Click on **Edit** next to the **Application** data model, and then on **Edit Acceleration**.

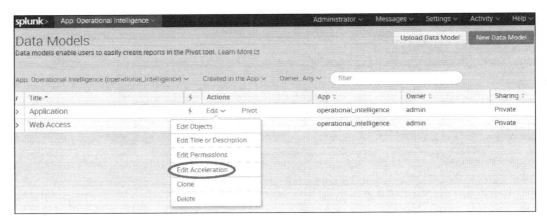

5. An **Add Acceleration** pop-up box will be displayed, informing you that private data models cannot be accelerated. Click on the green **Edit Permissions** button.

6. Change the **Display For permissions** button to **App**, and then click on **Save**.

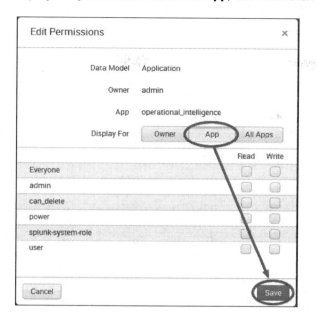

7. Repeat step 4 and this time an **Edit Acceleration** pop-up box will appear. Check the **Accelerate** checkbox, select **1 Month** in the **Summary Range** field, and then click on **Save**:

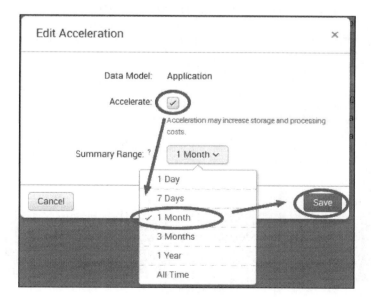

8. In the list of **Data Models**, you should now see a little yellow lightning bolt, which indicates that acceleration is now activated for the **Application** data model.

9. Repeat the previous steps to accelerate the **Web Access** data model. Once complete, both models will display the yellow lightning bolt and will also have **App** level sharing permissions:

How it works...

Once you accelerate each model, Splunk starts building acceleration summaries behind the scenes for the one month range that we selected. These summaries are built in the indexes that contain the attributes specified in each data model; in this case, the main index. The summaries are held in Splunk TSIDX files alongside the buckets of data in the index. Splunk runs an internal process to keep these summaries updated every 5 minutes and also runs a maintenance process to clean out old data every 30 minutes.

In this recipe, you accelerated both data models. However, accelerating data models does require disk space and adds additional overhead and processing, so it is only recommended on large datasets where reporting performance is less than optimal. For more information on Splunk's data model acceleration, please see http://docs. splunk.com/Documentation/Splunk/latest/Knowledge/ Acceleratedatamodels.

There's more...

Data model acceleration has its advantages, but it also has several caveats that you should be aware of. Some are as follows:

▸ Only administrators can accelerate data models and private data models cannot be accelerated.

▸ Acceleration adds overhead and requires disk space to build the acceleration summaries and maintain them on an ongoing basis. Therefore, acceleration is best used for large datasets where Pivot-based reporting performance is suboptimal.

- ▶ Once accelerated, the data model cannot be edited without first disabling acceleration. Disabling the acceleration, editing the data model, then re-enabling acceleration will likely require summaries to be rebuilt.

- ▶ Only root-level event objects and their direct child objects can be accelerated; the models we just accelerated fit this criteria.

- ▶ To keep data model acceleration as efficient as possible, indexes should be specified in the object constraints and the summary range limited to as short as possible. The larger the summary range, the greater the disk space and processing required.

Viewing data model and acceleration summary information

Splunk provides some nice summary information on each data model that is not immediately apparent from the interface. From the data model management screen that lists the available data models, you will notice a small information (**i**) column on the far left-hand side with a greater than sign (**>**) next to each model. Click on this sign, and information pertaining to the data model and acceleration summaries will be displayed, including the build status of the acceleration summary and size on disk that the summary is using. You can also force a rebuild or update of the acceleration summary.

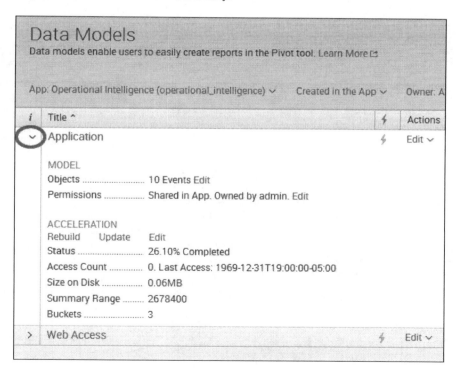

Advanced configuration of data model acceleration

In this recipe, you enabled acceleration through the user interface. However, behind the scenes, a number of configuration files can be edited directly to offer more flexibility.

Acceleration enablement, acceleration summary range, and the acceleration update frequency can be edited and/or configured in `datamodels.conf`.

The location of the data model TSIDX summaries can be changed by modifying the `tstatsHomePath` variable in `indexes.conf`.

See also

 ▸ The *Creating a data model for web access logs* recipe
 ▸ The *Creating a data model for application logs* recipe

Pivoting total sales transactions

Now that we have built a couple of data models, we can begin using Splunk's Pivot tool to search and report the data without needing to write any searches.

In this recipe, you will start to get familiarized with the Pivot interface and use it to calculate total sales transaction data. You will focus on identifying successful checkout transactions. These are important from an intelligence standpoint, as they indicate that a sale has occurred and payment has been made successfully. This data will then be populated on the **Product Monitoring** dashboard. You will be using the transaction data model object that we defined in the **Application** data model.

Getting ready

To step through this recipe, you will need a running Splunk Enterprise server, with the sample data loaded from *Chapter 1, Play Time – Getting Data In*, and the completed recipes from earlier in this chapter. You should be familiar with navigating the Splunk user interface.

How to do it...

Follow these steps in this recipe to pivot the total sales transactions:

1. Log in to your Splunk server.
2. Select the **Operational Intelligence** application.

3. Select the **Pivot** menu item from the application menu:

4. Now, select the **Application** data model, and then select the **Transactions** object:

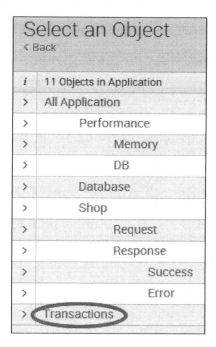

5. The **New Pivot** screen will load. Under the **Filters** section, change the time range to **Last 24 Hours**. Next, select the **+** sign to add a new filter and select **requestType** from the list of available attributes. Then select to match **requestType** of **checkout**. Click on the **Add to Table** button once complete, to add this new filter to the Pivot.

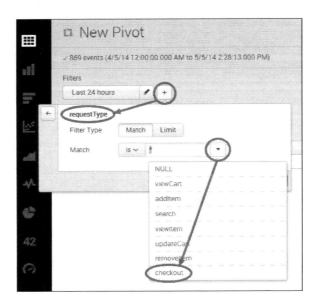

6. Add another filter where **result** matches **success**:

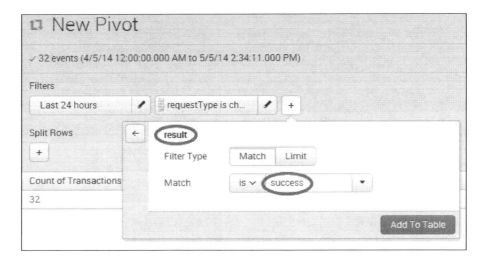

7. You should see a total count of transactions displayed. To turn this into a single value visualization, select the **Single Value Display** icon on the left-hand side of the screen.

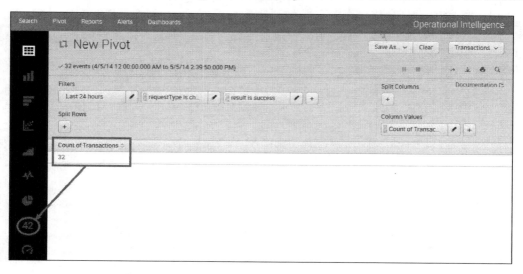

8. Locate the **Under Label** textbox on the left-hand side and enter a value of Sales Transactions. You should see this appear under the number of transactions. Then click on **Save As** and select **Dashboard Panel**:

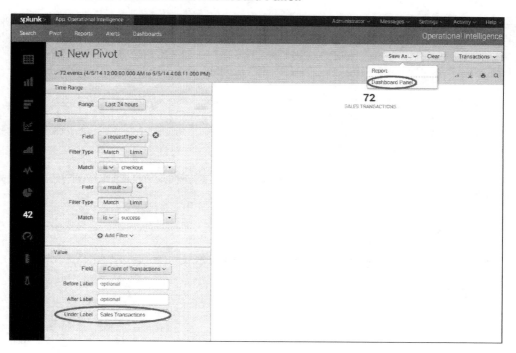

9. Select **Existing** in the **Dashboard** field and ensure **Product Monitoring** is selected. Enter `Sales Transactions` in the **Panel Title** field and click on **Save**:

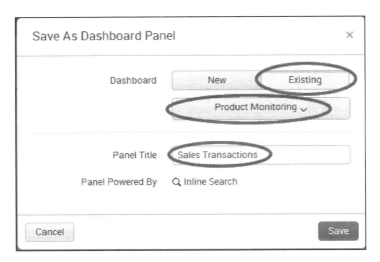

10. The single value is added to the dashboard and this recipe is complete.

How it works...

The Pivot tool allows for datasets defined in data models to be searched without the need to enter any searches into Splunk. In this recipe, you leveraged the transaction data model object, created in a previous recipe, which brings together all application requests and associated responses. You applied filters to the dataset to identify only the successful checkout transactions. Splunk then subsequently displayed the count of transactions that matched the specified filter over the selected time range and you chose to display this as single value visualization and add it to the **Product Monitoring** dashboard. Behind the scenes, Splunk uses the defined object and object attributes, together with the **Attribute** filters, to create a Splunk search, not too different from a | `stats count` type search. Splunk is then able to visualize the data in a similar way to how you visualized data from a search. When adding to the existing dashboard, Splunk identifies the inline search associated with it as a Pivot search.

There's more...

The Pivot tool provides users with a great *point and click* method for reporting and visualizing datasets, without having to get to grips with the Splunk search language. However, it is also possible to view the pivoted data using the Splunk search interface.

Pivot searching using the pivot command and search interface

The Splunk `pivot` command allows for Pivot-based searching of datasets mapped by data models directly from the Splunk search interface. The command differs from the `datamodel` command we looked at earlier in this chapter, as it can take advantage of performance gains offered by accelerated data models, whereas `datamodel` cannot. However, the `datamodel` command is more extensible, as it allows for regular Splunk search syntax following the command, whereas Pivot uses a specialized search syntax that is slightly different from the regular Splunk search syntax.

When you use the Pivot tool interface to manipulate the underlying dataset, Splunk is writing a search using the `pivot` command behind the scenes. Once you have filtered and split the data to report on as needed, you can select to **Open in Search** by clicking on the little magnifying glass in the top-right corner of the Pivot interface.

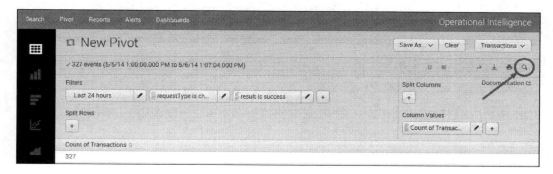

For this recipe, you will notice that the Pivot search resembles something along the lines of the following search:

```
| pivot Application Transactions count(Transactions) AS "Count of
Transactions" FILTER requestType is checkout FILTER result is
success ROWSUMMARY 0 COLSUMMARY 0 NUMCOLS 0 SHOWOTHER 1
```

As can be seen, this is a slightly different search syntax from the regular Splunk SPL that we have covered to date. Much like the `datamodel` command, the `pivot` command must be the first command of the search and is followed by the name of the data model (`Application`) and then the name of the object (`Transactions`). Following this, you must also provide a transforming function, such as `count`. However, given this specialized syntax, it is easier to use the Pivot tool to filter the data as needed to create the underlying Pivot search, than it is to write the search yourself.

For more information on the `pivot` command, you should review the search reference at `http://docs.splunk.com/Documentation/Splunk/latest/SearchReference/Pivot`.

See also

▶ The *Pivoting slowest responding web pages* recipe

▶ The *Pivoting purchases by geographical location* recipe

▶ The *Pivot charting top error codes* recipe

Pivoting purchases by geographical location

In the previous recipe, you performed a simple count of the number of successful sales transactions. In this recipe, we will expand insight into these sales by exploring where in the world sales requests are coming from. To do this, you will leverage the built-in geolocational abilities of Splunk. First, you will amend the **Application** data model to bring in geolocational object attributes. Then you will pivot off this data to map purchases by location.

Getting ready

To step through this recipe, you will need a running Splunk Enterprise server, with the sample data loaded from *Chapter 1, Play Time – Getting Data In*, and the completed recipes from earlier in this chapter. You should be familiar with navigating the Splunk user interface.

How to do it...

Follow these steps in this recipe to pivot purchases by geographic region:

1. Log in to your Splunk server.

2. Select the **Operational Intelligence** application.

3. Select the **Settings** menu item at the top-right corner of the screen, and then select **Data models**.

4. The two data models we created in the first two recipes will be displayed. Click on the **Application** data model and the Application Data Model Editor will be displayed.

5. As the data model is accelerated, you will see an error message stating that it cannot be edited. Click on the **Edit** button, and then on **Edit Acceleration**. Uncheck the **Accelerate** checkbox in the pop-up box that is displayed, and then click on **Save**:

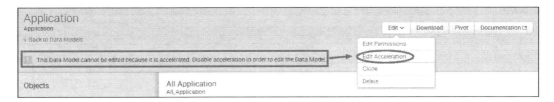

6. Ensure the **All Application** object is selected on the left. Then locate **ipAddress** from the list of **Object Attributes** and click on **Edit**:

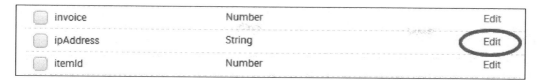

7. On the **Edit Attribute** screen that is displayed, change the type to **IPV4**, and then click on **Save**.

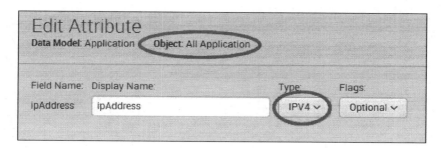

8. Back in the main Data Model Editor screen, click on **Add Attribute** and select **Geo IP** from the drop-down list.

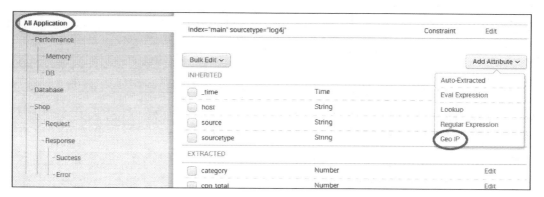

9. The **Add Geo Attributes with an IP Lookup** screen will load. You will notice a list of additional attributes that are to be added to the data model. Enter `lon`, `lat`, `city`, `region`, and `country` in the **Display Name** field for **lon**, **lat**, **City**, **Region**, and **Country** respectively. Then click on **Preview**, to preview the data, followed by **Save** if everything looks good.

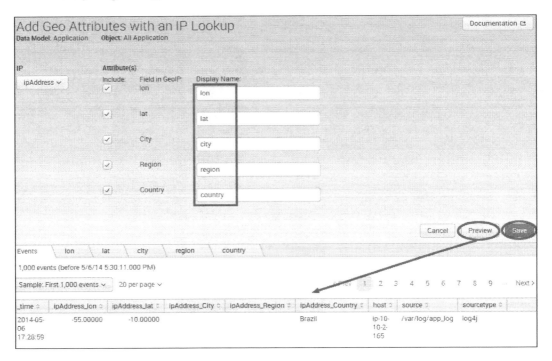

10. Back in the main Data Model Editor screen, these new attributes will be displayed as calculated attributes at the bottom of the attribute listing. You will notice that they are all marked as **Required**, which is not needed. Select all of these new attributes by checking their associated checkboxes:

11. At the top of the attribute list, click on **Bulk Edit** and select **Optional**. Once this has been done, the word **Required** will be removed from the attribute list.

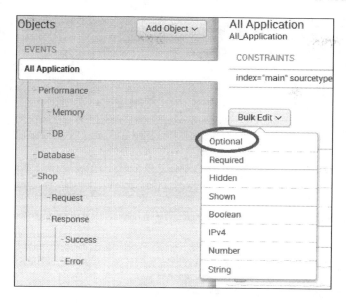

12. Now, click on the **Pivot** button at the top-right corner of the screen:

13. Select the **Request** object (a child of the **Shop** object) from the list of objects that are displayed.

14. Configure the Pivot with a time range of **Last 24 Hours** and **requestType** of **checkout**.

15. Next, select **Country** in **Split Rows**. A pop-up box will be displayed. Select **Descending** in the **Sort** field, and then click on **Add to Table**.

16. The count of checkout requests will be calculated and displayed in a table by country. To turn this into a pie chart visualization, select the **Pie Chart** icon on the left-hand side of the screen. You should now see the data represented as a pie chart with different country segments.

17. As with the previous recipe, click on **Save As** and select **Dashboard Panel**.

18. Select **Existing** in the **Dashboard** field and ensure **Product Monitoring** is selected. Enter `Sales Countries` in the **Panel Title** field and click on **Save**.

19. The pie chart is added to the dashboard and this recipe is complete.

How it works...

Splunk has a built-in external IP address lookup, which is being leveraged in this recipe. First, you specified which object attribute was an IP address. Following this, you configured a number of Geo IP object attributes for longitude, latitude, city, region, and country. Behind the scenes, Splunk passes the specified external IP address attribute into an internal lookup database that returns the values of these additional Geo IP object attributes. We chose not to make these required attributed (as is default), because not every event mapped by our **Application** data model contains an IP address field. As you defined these fields at the root event object level in the data model hierarchy, the attributes are available to other child objects in the hierarchy. Following this, you pivoted off the checkout requests, which contain an IP address and these IPs were then mapped to countries and reported on in the Pivot tool.

See also

▸   The *Pivoting slowest responding web pages* recipe

▸   The *Pivot charting top error codes* recipe

▸   The *Pivoting total sales transactions* recipe

Pivoting slowest responding web pages

In the past couple of recipes, we worked with the **Application** data model and added some additional reports to the **Product Monitoring** dashboard related to sales and customer location. In the next couple of recipes, you will begin to look at the operational health of our environment and begin creating an **Operational Monitoring** dashboard.

The response time of a web application is one of the most important factors in determining overall user experience and high response times could lead to lost customers, who are not prepared to deal with slow loading web pages.

In this recipe, you will use the Pivot tool to table the response times for the various web pages on our web application and identify the pages that are taking longest to load. You will add this report to a new **Operational Monitoring** dashboard.

Getting ready

To step through this recipe, you will need a running Splunk Enterprise server, with the sample data loaded from *Chapter 1, Play Time – Getting Data In*, and the completed recipes from earlier in this chapter. You should be familiar with navigating the Splunk user interface.

How to do it...

Perform the following steps to pivot search for the slowest responding web pages:

1.   Log in to your Splunk server.

2.   Select the **Operational Intelligence** application.

3.   Select the **Settings** menu item at the top-right corner of the screen, and then select **Data models**.

4.   The two data models we created in the first two recipes will be displayed. Click on the **Web Access** data model and the Web Access data model editor will be displayed.

5.   As this data model is likely to be accelerated, you will need to click on the **Edit** button, then select **Edit Acceleration**, and uncheck the **Accelerate** checkbox, as we did in the previous recipe with the **Application** data model.

6. If you scan through the list of object attributes for the **All Web Access** data model, you will see there is no `ResponseTime` attribute. This data is in the underlying dataset but is not autoextracted by Splunk and therefore, not in the list. Click on the **Add Attribute** button and select **Regular Expression**:

7. The **Add Attributes with a Regular Expression** screen will be displayed. In the **Regular Expression** box, enter the following regex syntax that will identify the value in the event relating to the response time:

    `(?i)^(?:[^"]*"){8}\s+(?P<ResponseTime>.+)`

8. Enter `ResponseTime` in the **Field Name** field if not already automatically populated and change **Type** to **Number**. Then click on the **Preview** button. You should see the new **ResponseTime** field populated in the preview results. Click on **Save** to save this new **Regular Expression** attribute.

9. Next, click on the **Pivot** button at the top-right corner of the screen and select the **All Web Access** object in the list of available objects. The Pivot tool will then load.

10. Using the Pivot interface, select a filter of **Last 24 Hours**. Next select `uri_path` in the **Split Rows** field. Select **Descending** in the **Sort** field, specify **Max Rows** value of `10`, and then click on the **Add To Table** button.

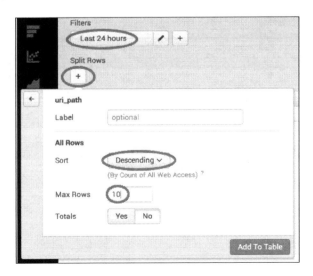

11. Splunk will now display a count of records by Web Application pages. Change the **Column Values** attribute to the newly extracted `ResponseTime` attribute and select a value of **Average** from the available list of operator values, then click on the **Update** button.

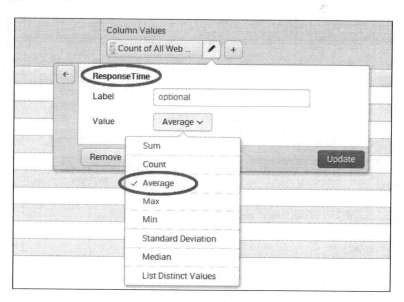

12. The results will now display the web application pages together with their average response times, sorted in a descending order:

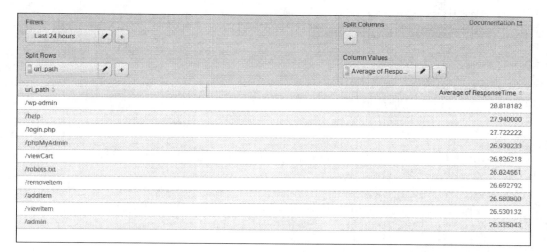

13. This provides a good level of insight, but doesn't indicate how things change over time. To plot these results by time, click and hold the `uri_path` box under **Split Rows** and drag it over to **Split Columns**. You will notice the results are now transposed and the web pages now appear as columns, rather than rows. Pretty cool!

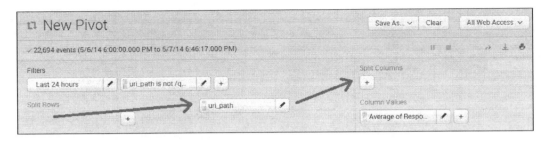

14. Next, select **_time** in the **Split Rows** field and choose **Hours (2011-01-31 23:00)** from the **Periods** drop-down list. Then click on the **Add To Table** button:

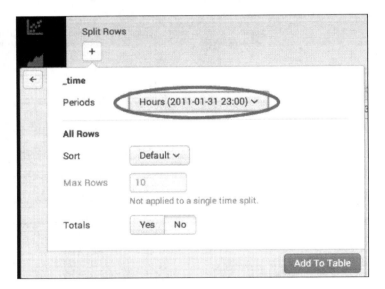

15. The data will now display rows representing each hour and the average response time for each page during that hour.

16. This is not terribly useful information when displayed in tabular form; so, click on the Column Chart icon on the left-hand side of the screen. Next, find the **Color** section and choose stacked in the **Stack Mode** field. Following this, click on the **Save as** button and select **Dashboard Panel**:

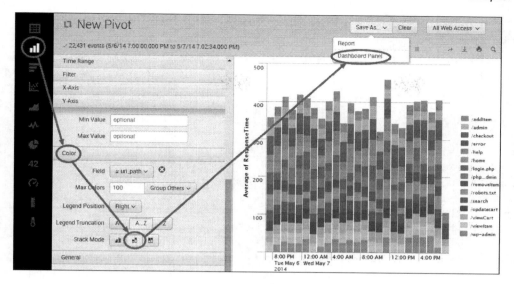

17. In the pop-up box, create a new dashboard named `Operational Monitoring` and ensure that **Permissions** field is set to **Shared in App**. Finally, enter `Page Response Times` in the **Panel Title** field and click on the **Save** button.

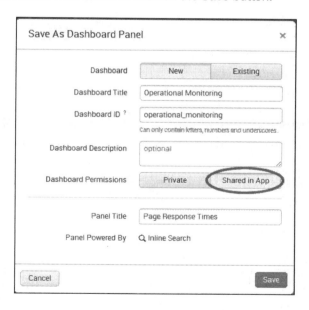

18. The visualization will be saved to the new dashboard and the recipe is now complete.

How it works...

In this recipe, you explored some additional features of Splunk's Pivot tool. In order to pivot off data related to response time, you had to add this attribute to the underlying **Web Access** data model. Selecting to pivot off the **All Web Access** object filtered the dataset to the data defined within the object constraints; in this case only web access event data. When you began setting up the Pivot in step 9, you initially split the rows by `uri_path` and chose to sort the rows in a descending order, keeping only 10 rows. This is very similar to performing a `| top uri_path` search at the end of a filtered Splunk search, where only the top 10 results are displayed. When you changed the **Column Value** to average `ResponseTime`, Splunk summed the total response time for all events specific to each web page and then calculated an average response time, similar to doing a `| stats avg(ResponseTime) by uri_path` search at the end of a filtered search. Following this step, you added the additional element of time to the dataset, taking a snapshot of average response times by web page for each hour. This is similar to doing a `| timechart span=1h avg(ResponseTime) by uri_path` at the end of a filtered search. Finally, you visualized this data as a stacked bar chart. This is a good way to present the data visually, as each block in each stack on the chart represents the average response time for a given web page. It is then very easy to compare all the pages together over a given time frame. Pages that take longer to load than others, will have a bigger block in the stack.

See also

▸ The *Pivot charting top error codes* recipe

▸ The *Pivoting purchases by geographical location* recipe

▸ The *Pivoting total sales transactions* recipe

Pivot charting top error codes

In this final recipe, you will use the Pivot tool to chart the top error codes over time. Error codes from web application logs generally fall into two main categories, client-side errors and server-side errors. Plotting the error codes over time will help identify which errors are occurring, the types of errors, and when they occur.

While this recipe is slightly less technical to implement than the previous recipe, it will serve to reinforce understanding and less instruction will be provided.

Getting ready

To step through this recipe, you will need a running Splunk Enterprise server, with the sample data loaded from *Chapter 1, Play Time – Getting Data In*, and the completed recipes from earlier in this chapter. You should be familiar with navigating the Splunk user interface.

How to do it...

Follow these steps to pivot chart the top error codes:

1. Log in to your Splunk server.
2. Select the **Operational Intelligence** application.
3. Select the **Pivot** menu item from the application menu.
4. Select the **Web Access** data model and the **Error** object.
5. Configure the Pivot interface such that **Filters** is set to **Last 24 Hours, Split Rows** is set to **_time, Periods** under **_time** is set to **Hours (2011-01-31 23:00)**, **Split Columns** is set to **status**, and **Column Values** is set to **Count of Error**.

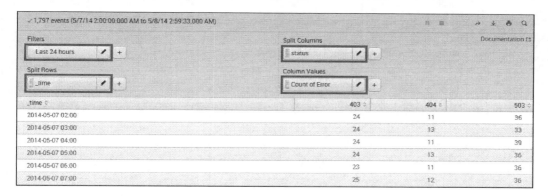

6. You should see a count by status codes over 1-hour time periods. Select the **Line Chart** icon to visualize this data as a line chart. Each error code will be represented as a different colored line on the chart. Save this chart with a title of **Web Error Codes** to the **Operational Monitoring** dashboard that we created in the previous recipe.

How it works...

This recipe further familiarized you with the Pivot interface. Directly selecting the **Error** data model object filtered the data to just web access data containing errors, due to the constraints defined within the object. From here, you leveraged Pivot to count status codes over time in 1 hour increments. This is similar to doing a `| timechart span=1h count by status` search at the end of a filtered search. Selecting to visualize this data on a line chart helps to easily identify the various status codes over time and can clearly illustrate error spikes or increases over a specific time period.

See also

- ▶ The *Pivoting slowest responding web pages* recipe
- ▶ The *Pivoting purchases by geographical location* recipe
- ▶ The *Pivoting total sales transactions* recipe

Summary

The key takeaways from this chapter are as follows:

- ▶ Data models allow Splunk datasets and associated knowledge to be mapped for use by the Pivot tool
- ▶ Data models contain objects of different types, constraints, and attributes
- ▶ Data models can be accelerated to speed up Pivot searching over the underlying dataset mapped by the model
- ▶ Data models power the Pivot tool and allow dynamic reports and visualizations to be built without the need to write any searches
- ▶ The Pivot tool allows for simple point and click, drag-and-drop, and slicing and dicing of modeled data
- ▶ Pivot is suitable for less technical users, but leveraging the Splunk SPL directly is more powerful and advanced

6
Diving Deeper – Advanced Searching

In this chapter, we will cover some of the more advanced search commands available within Splunk. You will learn about:

- ▶ Calculating the average session time on a website
- ▶ Calculating the average execution time for multi-tier web requests
- ▶ Displaying the maximum concurrent checkouts
- ▶ Analyzing the relationship of web requests
- ▶ Predicting website-traffic volumes
- ▶ Finding abnormally sized web requests
- ▶ Identifying potential session spoofing

Introduction

In the previous chapter, we learned about Splunk's new data model and Pivot functionality and how they can be used to further intelligence reporting. In this chapter, we will return to Splunk's SPL, diving deeper and making use of some very powerful search commands to facilitate a better understanding and correlation of event data. You will learn how to create transactions, build subsearches and understand concurrency, leverage field associations, and so on.

Looking at event counts, applying statistics to calculate averages, or finding the top values over time only provide a view of the data limited to one angle. Splunk's SPL contains some very powerful search commands that provide the ability to correlate data from different sources and understand or build relationships between the events. Through the building of relationships between datasets and looking at different angles of the data, you can better understand the impact one event might have over another. Additionally, correlating related values can provide a much more contextual value to teams when reviewing or analyzing a series of data.

Identifying and grouping transactions

Single events can be easily interpreted and understood, but these single events are often part of a series of events, where the event might be influenced by preceding events or might affect other events to come. By leveraging Splunk's ability to group associated events into transactions based on field values, the data can be presented in a way in which the reader understands the full context of an event and gets to see what led up to this point. Building transactions can also be useful when needing to understand the time duration between the start and finish of specific events or calculating values within a given transaction and comparing them to the values of others.

Converging data sources

Context is everything when it comes to building successful operational intelligence, and when you are stuck analyzing events from a single data source at a time, you might be missing out on rich contextual information that other data sources can provide. With Splunk's ability to converge multiple data sources using the `join` or `append` search commands and search across them as if they are a single source, you can easily enrich the single data source and understand events from other sources that occurred at, or around, the same time.

For example, you might notice there are more timeouts than usual on your website, but when you analyze the website access log, everything appears normal. However, when you look at the application log, you notice that there are numerous failed connections to the database. Even so, by looking at each data source individually, it is hard to understand where the actual issue lies. Using Splunk's SPL to converge the data sources will allow for both the web access and application logs to be brought together into one view, to better understand and troubleshoot the sequence of events that might lead to website timeouts.

Identifying relationships between fields

In the operational intelligence world, the ability to identify relationships between fields can be a powerful asset. Understanding the values of a field, and how these values might have a relationship with other field values within the same event, allows you to calculate the degree of certainty the values will provide in future events. By continually sampling events as they come in over time, you can become more accurate at predicting values in events as they occur. When used correctly, this can provide a tremendous value in being able to actively predict the values of fields within events, leading to a more proactive incident or issue identification.

Predicting future values

Understanding system, application, and user behavior will always prove to be extremely valuable when building out any intelligence program; however, the ability to predict future values can provide values more immense than simple modeling actions. The addition of predictive capabilities to an Operational Intelligence program enables the ability to become more proactive to issue identification, forecast system behavior, and plan and optimize thresholds more effectively.

Imagine being able to predict the amount of sessions on your website, amount of purchases of a specific product, response times during peak periods, or general tuning alerting thresholds to values that are substantiated rather than taking an educated guess. All of this is possible with predictive analytics; by looking back over past events, you can better understand what the future will hold.

Calculating the average session time on a website

In the previous chapters, we created methods to assess various values that show how consumers interact with our website. However, what these values did not outline is how long consumers spend on our website. By leveraging Splunk's more powerful search commands, we can calculate the average session time of consumers interacting with our website, which can act as supporting information when articulating data such as engagement rates, resource requirements, or consumer experience.

In this recipe, you will write a Splunk search to calculate the average time of a session on the website over a given period of time. You will then graphically display this value on a dashboard using the single value visualization.

Getting ready

To step through this recipe, you will need a running Splunk Enterprise server, with the sample data loaded from *Chapter 1, Play Time – Getting Data In*. You should be familiar with navigating the Splunk user interface.

How to do it...

Follow the steps in this recipe to calculate the average session time on a website:

1. Log in to your Splunk server.
2. Select the **Operational Intelligence** application.

3. Ensure the time range picker is set to **Last 24 Hours**, and type the following search into the Splunk search bar. Then, click on the magnifying glass icon or hit *Enter*:

```
index=main sourcetype=access_combined | transaction
JSESSIONID | stats avg(duration) AS Avg_Session_Time
```

4. Depending on your Splunk server, this might take a little while to run. Splunk will return a single value representing the average duration in seconds for a session on the website.

5. Click on the **Visualization** tab.

6. Since there are a number of visualizations within Splunk, the single value visualization might not be displayed by default within the **Visualization** tab. Click on the dropdown listing the visualization types, and select **Single Value**:

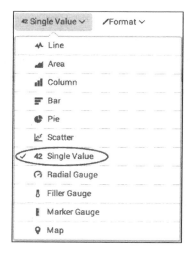

7. You should now see the value represented as the single value visualization.

8. Let's add more context to the visualization. Click on **Format**. Enter `Avg Session Time:` in the **Before Label** and `secs` in the **After Label** textbox. Click on **Apply** to save these labels:

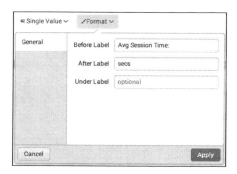

9. Your single value visualization should now look similar to the following example:

10. Let's save this search as a report. Click on **Save As** and choose **Report** from the drop-down menu:

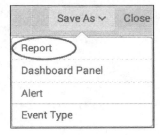

11. In the **Save As Report** window that appears, enter `cp06_average_session_time` as the title, and click on **Save**:

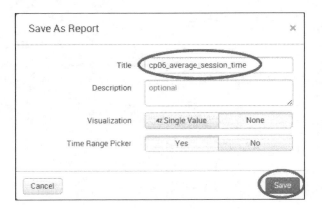

12. You will receive confirmation that your report has been created. Now, let's add this report to a dashboard. In the next window, click on **Add to Dashboard**:

13. You will create a new dashboard for this report. On the **Save As Dashboard Panel** screen, ensure **New** is selected and enter `Session Monitoring` as the dashboard title. Select **Shared in App** for the dashboard permissions and **Report** to power the panel by a report. Finally, click on **Save** to create the dashboard:

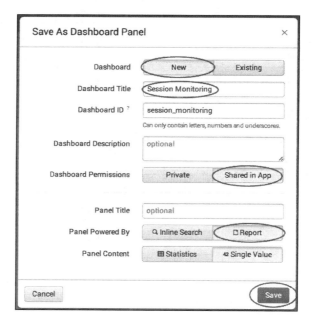

14. The report is saved and a new **Session Monitoring** dashboard is created. You can now choose to click on **View Dashboard** to see your newly created dashboard with the average session time report.

How it works...

Let's break down the search piece by piece:

Search fragment	Description
`index=main` `sourcetype=access_combined`	You should be familiar with this search from the recipes in previous chapters. It is used to return events from the website access log.
`| transaction JSESSIONID`	Using the `transaction` command, we group events together based on their given `JSESSIONID` to form a single transaction. The `JSESSIONID` field is chosen as each visitor to the website is given a random session identifier whose value is stored in this field. One of the fields created by the `transaction` command is the `duration` field. The `duration` field represents the amount of time, in seconds, between the first and last events in the transaction.
`| stats avg(duration) AS` `Avg_Session_Time`	Using the `stats` command, we calculate the average value of the `duration` field. Using the `AS` operator, we rename the resulting field that is created with the given value to something more readable, for example, `Avg_Session_Time`.

There's more...

The `transaction` command provides many parameters to control the way in which transactions are grouped. Using the `startswith` and `endswith` parameters, you can control what marks the start and end of a transaction based on data inside the events. Using the `maxspan`, `maxpause`, or `maxevents` parameter, you can control the constraints around how long a transaction will be, the amount of time between events before splitting it into a new transaction, or the total number of events within a transaction.

Where possible, using the parameters available for the `transaction` command is highly encouraged. Using the `transaction` command without any other parameter can result in a processing intensive (and inefficient) search that takes a while to run.

Starts with a website visit, ends with a checkout

To mark where a transaction begins and ends, you can make use of two parameters available within the `transaction` command, called `startswith` and `endswith`, respectively. In the following example, we modify the search in the recipe to include the `startswith="GET /home"` and `endswith="checkout"` parameters. This constrains the `transaction` command to only group events together with a general website request when the first event begins and the last event is a request to checkout. Any other event, or transaction, that does not meet these criteria will be discarded and not included in the returned results:

```
index=main sourcetype=access_combined  | transaction JSESSIONID
startswith="GET /home" endswith="checkout" | stats avg(duration)
AS Avg_Session_Time
```

By making use of these parameters, you can be more explicit on what gets treated as a transaction or focus on specific groupings of data.

Defining maximum pause, span, and events in a transaction

Three more very useful parameters available, apart from the `transaction` command, are `maxpause`, `maxspan`, and `maxevents`. These parameters allow you to apply more constraints around the duration and size of transactions and can be used individually or all together for even more precise constriction.

Adding the `maxpause=30s` parameter to the search in the recipe tells the `transaction` command that there must be no pause between events greater than 30 seconds, otherwise the grouping breaks. By default, there is no limit:

```
index=main sourcetype=access_combined | transaction JSESSIONID
maxpause=30s | stats avg(duration) AS Avg_Session_Time
```

Adding the `maxspan=30m` parameter to the search in the recipe tells the `transaction` command that when building the transaction, the first and last events cannot be greater than 30 minutes, otherwise the grouping breaks. By default, there is no limit:

```
index=main sourcetype=access_combined | transaction JSESSIONID
maxspan=30m | stats avg(duration) AS Avg_Session_Time
```

Adding the `maxevents=300` parameter to the search in the recipe tells the `transaction` command that when building the transaction, the total number of events contained within cannot be greater than 300, otherwise the grouping breaks. By default, the value is 1,000:

```
index=main sourcetype=access_combined | transaction JSESSIONID
maxevents=300 | stats avg(duration) AS Avg_Session_Time
```

As mentioned, all of these parameters can be combined to create an even more constrained transaction for specific use cases. Here is an example of a transaction that starts with a home page request, ends with a checkout, is no longer than 30 minutes, has no events where there is a pause greater than 30 seconds, and the maximum number of events contained within is 300:

```
index=main sourcetype=access_combined | transaction JSESSIONID
startswith="GET /home" endswith="checkout" maxpause=30s
maxspan=30m maxevents=300 | stats avg(duration) AS
Avg_Session_Time
```

 For more information on the `transaction` command, visit `http://docs.splunk.com/Documentation/Splunk/latest/SearchReference/Transaction`.

See also

▶ The *Calculating the average execution time for multi-tier web requests* recipe

▶ The *Displaying the maximum concurrent checkouts* recipe

Calculating the average execution time for multi-tier web requests

With components existing at many different layers to provide varying functionalities, web applications are no longer as straightforward as they once were. Understanding the execution time for a web request across the entire application stack, rather than at a single layer, can be extremely beneficial in correctly articulating the average time that requests take to execute in their entirety. This can lead to identification of issues in relation to increasing website response times.

In this recipe, you will write a Splunk search to calculate the average execution time of a web request that traverses not only the website access logs but also application logs. You will then graphically display this value on a dashboard using the single value visualization.

Getting ready

To step through this recipe, you will need a running Splunk Enterprise server, with the sample data loaded from *Chapter 1, Play Time – Getting Data In*. You should also complete the recipes in previous chapters and be familiar with navigating the Splunk user interface.

How to do it...

Follow the steps in this recipe to calculate the average execution time for multi-tier web requests:

1. Log in to your Splunk server.
2. Select the **Operational Intelligence** application.
3. Ensure the time range picker is set to **Last 24 Hours**, and type the following search into the Splunk search bar. Then, click on the magnifying glass icon or hit *Enter*:

    ```
    index=main sourcetype=access_combined | join JSESSIONID
    usetime=true earlier=false [ search index=main
    sourcetype=log4j | transaction threadId maxspan=5m | eval
    JSESSIONID=sessionId ] | stats avg(duration) AS
    Avg_Request_Execution_Time
    ```

4. After a little while, Splunk will return a single value representing the average execution time in seconds for a complete web request on the website.
5. Click on the **Visualization** tab.
6. Since there are a number of visualizations within Splunk, the single value visualization might not be displayed by default within the **Visualization** tab. Click on the dropdown listing the visualization types, and select **Single Value**:

7. You should now see the value represented as the single value visualization.

8. Let's add more context to the visualization. Click on **Format**. Enter `Avg Request Execution:` in the **Before Label** and `secs` in the **After Label** textbox, as shown in the following screenshot. Click on **Apply** to save these labels:

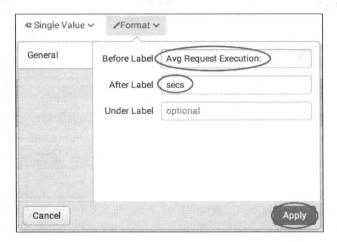

9. Your single value visualization should now look similar to the following example:

10. Let's save this search as a report. Click on **Save As**, and choose **Report** from the drop-down menu:

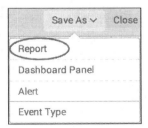

11. In the **Save As Report** window that appears, enter `cp06_average_request_execution_time` as the title, and click on **Save**:

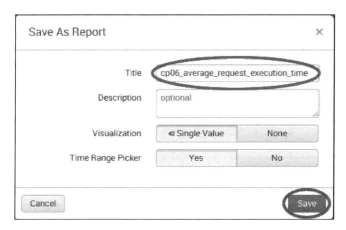

12. You will receive a confirmation that your report has been created. Now, let's add this report to a dashboard. In the next window, click on **Add to Dashboard**:

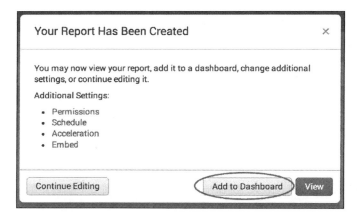

13. You will now add this to the dashboard that was created in the previous recipe named **Session Monitoring**. In the **Save As Dashboard Panel** window, click on the **Existing** button beside the **Dashboard** label. From the drop-down menu that appears, select **Session Monitoring**. For the **Panel Powered By** field, click on the **Report** button. Finally, click on **Save**:

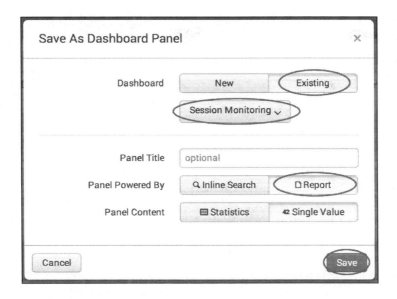

14. Click on **View Dashboard** to see the panel that's been added to your **Session Monitoring** dashboard.

15. Now, let's arrange the panels so they are side by side. Click on **Edit** and choose **Edit Panels** from the drop-down menu:

16. Now, drag the newly added panel so that both single value visualizations are on the same line, as shown in the following screenshot. When finished, click on **Done**:

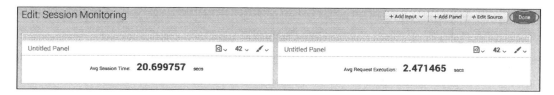

How it works...

Let's break down the search piece by piece:

Search fragment	Description
`index=main` `sourcetype=access_combined`	You should be familiar with this search from the recipes in previous chapters. It is used to return events from the website access log.
`| join JSESSIONID` `usetime=true earlier=false` `[ search index=main` `sourcetype=log4j |` `transaction threadId` `maxspan=5m	eval` `JSESSIONID=sessionId]`	Using the `join` command, we execute a subsearch to return matching events from the web application log. The `JSESSIONID` field is used as the unique value to join the events on. Within the subsearch, we leverage the `transaction` command to group all application events together based on their `threadId`, which is a unique value for each function execution. The `maxspan` parameter is used with the assumption that application events common to the transaction will all be within 5 minutes of each other. Then, we create a field named `JSESSIONID` using `eval` because it does not exist within the web application events, which has a field named `sessionId` instead. By creating this field, the join will work properly as it knows how to associate the events. The `usetime` and `earlier` parameters passed to the `join` command tell it to limit matches to only those events that come after the originating web access event. This ensures that only web application events that occurred after the website access log event will be returned, since we know the natural method of execution for our application requires a user interaction with the website before the application will trigger a function execution.

Search fragment	Description
`| stats avg(duration) AS Avg_ Request_Execution_Time`	Using the `stats` command, we calculate the average value of the duration field, since this field has been carried through by the use of the `transaction` command within the subsearch. Using the `AS` operator, we rename the resulting field that is created with the given value to something more readable, for example, `Avg_Request_Execution_Time`.

There's more...

In this recipe, you used the `join` command to join an inner subsearch with an outer main search. This is similar to a join in a SQL database. Another command that is similar to join is `append`. The `append` command allows you to string two different searches together, such that the results of the second search will be appended to the results of the first search. The maximum value is obtained from `append` if the searches you append together share common fields; use of the `eval` command or implementation of **Common Information Model** (**CIM**) can help with this.

> For more information on `join`, visit `http://docs.splunk.com/Documentation/Splunk/latest/SearchReference/Join`.
>
> For more information on the `append` command, visit `http://docs.splunk.com/Documentation/Splunk/latest/SearchReference/Append`.

While both the `join` and `append` commands can be useful, they are not the most efficient commands. This is because both commands execute multiple searches instead of just one. Often, the `stats` or `transaction` command can be used in creative ways to avoid using `join` or `append`, and to increase search performance as a result.

Calculating the average execution time without using a join

Often, there are many ways to write a search that results in providing the same or similar insight. While there is nothing wrong with the search used in this recipe, we can amend the search so that it does not use the `join` command. An example search might be as follows:

```
index=main sourcetype=access_combined OR sourcetype=log4j
| eval action=substr(uri_path,2) | eval
action=lower(if(isnull(action),requestType,action))
| eval JSESSIONID=if(isnull(JSESSIONID),sessionId,JSESSIONID)
| transaction threadId, JSESSIONID, action maxspan=1m
| stats avg(duration) AS Avg_Request_Execution_Time
```

Here, we search both the web access and application logs in the same search. We evaluated a new field called action using similar field values found in the web access (uri_path) and application logs (requestType). For example, a checkout web request generates a checkout application request. Using the transaction command, we transact all events across both sourcetypes that share a session ID, thread ID, or our new action field. We also make the assumption that our requests do not take longer than a minute to execute, and subsequently, we set a maxspan of one minute. Setting this tightened criteria will make the transaction command more efficient. Splunk will now group all web requests and subsequent application events related to the web requests together into transactions, with durations calculated for each. We then apply the same stats command to work out the average request execution time. This might actually provide a more accurate execution time as we incorporate the timestamp of the web access logs into the transaction duration.

See also

▶ The *Calculating the average session time on a website* recipe

▶ The *Displaying the maximum concurrent checkouts* recipe

▶ The *Analyzing the relationship of web requests* recipe

Displaying the maximum concurrent checkouts

Typically, when analyzing web requests, events often overlap with one another due to multiple users issuing requests concurrently. By identifying these overlapping requests, and further understanding the concurrency of events, you will gain a clearer picture of the true demand for both resources and consumer demands.

In this recipe, you will write a Splunk search to find the number of concurrent checkouts over a given period of time. You will then graphically display this value on a dashboard using the line chart visualization.

Getting ready

To step through this recipe, you will need a running Splunk Enterprise server, with the sample data loaded from *Chapter 1, Play Time – Getting Data In*. You should also complete the earlier recipes in this chapter and be familiar with navigating the Splunk user interface.

How to do it...

Follow the steps in this recipe to identify the number of concurrent checkouts over a given period of time:

1. Log in to your Splunk server.

2. Select the **Operational Intelligence** application.

3. Ensure the time range picker is set to **Last 24 Hours**, and type the following search into the Splunk search bar. Then, click on the magnifying glass icon or hit *Enter*:

    ```
    index=main sourcetype=access_combined | transaction
    JSESSIONID startswith="GET /home" endswith="checkout"
    | concurrency duration=duration | timechart max(concurrency) AS
    "Concurrent Checkouts"
    ```

4. After a short while, Splunk will return the values associated with the maximum concurrent checkout's split in 30-minute durations.

5. Click on the **Visualization** tab.

6. Since there are a number of visualizations within Splunk, the line chart visualization might not be displayed by default within the **Visualization** tab. Click on the dropdown listing the visualization types, and select **Line**:

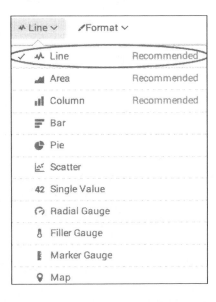

7. You should now see the value represented as the line chart visualization.

8. Let's add more context to the visualization and correct some values. Click on **Format**, and then click on the **Y-Axis** tab. Click on the drop-down **Title** menu and choose **Custom**. Enter Count as the title, and click on **Apply** to apply the changes:

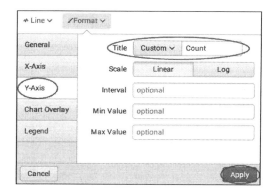

Your line chart visualization should now look similar to the following example:

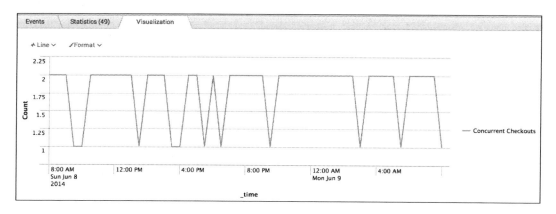

9. Let's save this search as a report. Click on **Save As**, and choose **Report** from the drop-down menu:

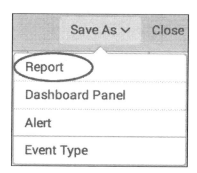

10. In the pop-up box that appears, enter `cp06_concurrent_checkouts` in the **Title** field, and then click on **Save**:

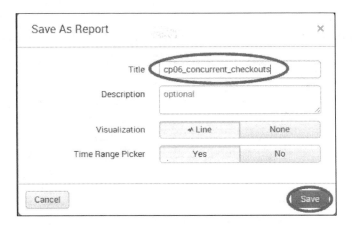

11. You will receive a confirmation that your report has been created. Now, let's add this report to a dashboard. In the next window, click on **Add to Dashboard**:

12. You add this report to the **Session Monitoring** dashboard that was created in an earlier recipe. In the **Save As Dashboard Panel** pop-up box, click on the **Existing** button beside the **Dashboard** label. From the drop-down menu that appears, select **Session Monitoring**. Enter `Maximum Concurrent Checkouts` in the **Panel Title** field, and ensure the panel is powered by **Report**. Then, click on **Save**:

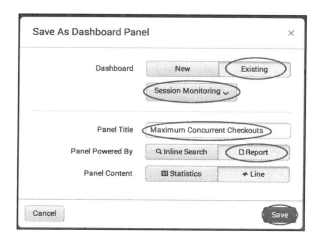

13. You can now click on **View Dashboard** to see the panel on your **Session Monitoring** dashboard.

How it works...

Let's break down the search piece by piece:

Search fragment	Description
`index=main` `sourcetype=access_combined`	You should be familiar with this search from the earlier recipes in this chapter. It is used to return events from the website access log.

`| transaction JSESSIONID`
`startswith="GET /home"`
`endswith="checkout"`
	Using the `transaction` command, we group events together, based on their given `JSESSIONID`, to form a single transaction and apply transaction parameters so that events start with a `GET` request for the main page and end with `checkout`.

Search fragment	Description
`| concurrency duration=duration`	The `concurrency` command is used to find the concurrent number of events, given a duration value, which occurred at the same start time. The `duration` field being used here is generated by the use of the `transaction` command. A field named `concurrency` will be created by the `concurrency` command, and this will store the value of concurrent events.
`| timechart max(concurrency) AS "Concurrent Checkouts"`	The `timechart` command is leveraged to plot the maximum values of the `concurrency` field over the given period of time. The `AS` operator is leveraged to rename the field to a more readable value, for example, `Concurrent Checkouts`.

The `concurrency` command is a useful way of calculating concurrent events without using too much logic. In this recipe, you were able to use the command to identify the maximum amount of concurrent checkouts throughout the day.

 For more information on the `concurrency` command, visit `http://docs.splunk.com/Documentation/Splunk/latest/SearchReference/Concurrency`.

See also

▶ The *Calculating the average execution time for multi-tier web requests* recipe
▶ The *Analyzing the relationship of web requests* recipe
▶ The *Predicting website-traffic volumes* recipe

Analyzing the relationship of web requests

To better understand the events occurring within a web application environment, you need to start building relationships between the pieces of data within events. By leveraging these relationships, efforts can become more targeted on the events requiring attention and a more proactive stance on issue identification can be taken. Imagine being able to say with confidence that when a certain page is requested, it will have a status of 404, or when a specific product is added to a cart, the service becomes unresponsive. Having this type of relationship capability added into your Operational Intelligence application opens up a vast array of possibilities when performing event analysis.

In this recipe, you will write a Splunk search to analyze the relationship of web requests between the status of the request and the pages where the request originated from over a given period of time. You will then add this table as a panel to a dashboard.

Getting ready

To step through this recipe, you will need a running Splunk Enterprise server, with the sample data loaded from *Chapter 1, Play Time – Getting Data In*. You should also complete the earlier recipes in this chapter and be familiar with navigating the Splunk user interface.

How to do it...

Follow the steps in this recipe to analyze the relationship of web requests over time:

1. Log in to your Splunk server.
2. Select the **Operational Intelligence** application.
3. Ensure the time range picker is set to **Last 24 Hours**, and type the following search into the Splunk search bar. Then, click on the magnifying glass icon or hit *Enter*:

```
index=main sourcetype=access_combined NOT status=200 |
associate uri status supcnt=50 | table Description
Reference_Key Reference_Value Target_Key
Top_Conditional_Value
```

4. Splunk will return the results in a tabular format similar to the following example:

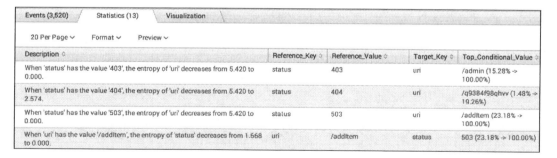

Description ⬦	Reference_Key ⬦	Reference_Value ⬦	Target_Key ⬦	Top_Conditional_Value ⬦
When 'status' has the value '403', the entropy of 'uri' decreases from 5.420 to 0.000.	status	403	uri	/admin (15.28% -> 100.00%)
When 'status' has the value '404', the entropy of 'uri' decreases from 5.420 to 2.574.	status	404	uri	/q9384f98qhvv (1.48% -> 19.26%)
When 'status' has the value '503', the entropy of 'uri' decreases from 5.420 to 0.000.	status	503	uri	/addItem (23.18% -> 100.00%)
When 'uri' has the value '/addItem', the entropy of 'status' decreases from 1.668 to 0.000.	uri	/addItem	status	503 (23.18% -> 100.00%)

5. Let's save this search as a report. Click on **Save As** and choose **Report** from the drop-down menu:

6. In the pop-up box that appears, enter `cp06_status_uri_relationships` in the **Title** field, and click on **Save**:

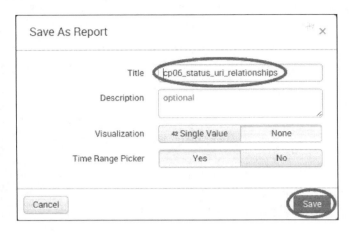

7. You will receive a confirmation that your report has been created. Now, let's add this report to our **Session Monitoring** dashboard we created earlier in this chapter. In the next window, click on **Add to Dashboard**:

8. In the **Save As Dashboard Panel** pop-up box, click on the **Existing** button beside the **Dashboard** label. From the drop-down menu that appears, select **Session Monitoring**. Enter Status and URI Relationships in the **Panel Title** field, ensure the panel is powered by **Report**, and then click on **Save**:

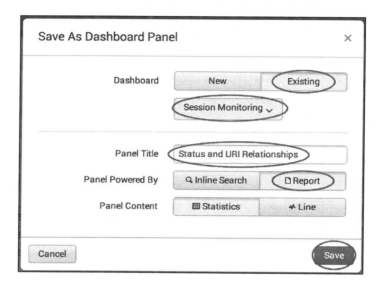

9. You can now click on **View Dashboard** to see the panel that has been added to the **Session Monitoring** dashboard.

How it works...

In this recipe, you used the associate command to find relationships between the status and uri fields in the web access events. The associate command works by calculating a change in entropy based upon field-pair values. It is able to provide a prediction of a field value based upon another field value.

Let's break down the search piece by piece:

Search fragment	Description
index=main sourcetype=access_combined NOT status="200"	You should be familiar with this search from the earlier recipes in this chapter. However, we added search criteria to not return any event where the status field is equal to 200 (success).

Search fragment	Description
`| associate uri status supcnt=50`	The `associate` command is used to identify correlations between the `uri` and `status` fields. The `associate` command creates multiple new fields. The fields `Reference_Key`, `Reference_Value`, and `Target_Key` are used to indicate the fields being analyzed. The `supcnt` parameter is used to specify the minimum number of times the `"reference key=reference value"` combination must appear. The fields `Unconditional_Entropy`, `Conditional_Entropy`, and `Entropy_Improvement` contain the entropy that was calculated for each pair of field values. The `Description` field provides a more easily readable summarization of the result.
`| table Description Reference_Key Reference_Value Target_Key Top_Conditional_Value`	The `table` command is used last to format the output of the results. Here, we chose to display only a few of the available fields generated by the `associate` command.

Examining the tabulated results in more detail, we selected to display the `Description`, `Reference_Key`, `Reference_Value`, `Target_Key`, and `Top_Conditional_Value` fields. The `Description` field provides a textual description in the following format:

```
"When the 'Reference_Key' has the value 'Reference_Value', the
entropy of 'Target_Key' decreases from Unconditional_Entropy to
Conditional_Entropy."
```

Taking a row from the results table, when the `Reference_Key` field is equal to the `Reference_Value` field, then the `Target_Key` field is most likely to be the `Top_Conditional_Value` field. For example, a `status` code of X might most likely have a `uri` value of Y.

It is highly recommended that you review the documentation for the `associate` command as there is quite a bit to it and some of the concepts are fairly complex. The documentation is available at `http://docs.splunk.com/Documentation/Splunk/latest/Searchreference/Associate`.

There's more...

The `associate` command does not require that you explicitly pass field names to it, so when starting out with your event data, it is best to just call the command without any parameters and explore the results that are returned. At times, this can prove to be most useful, as you will likely identify relationships that you might previously not have thought of.

Analyzing relationships of DB actions to memory utilization

The `associate` command is most useful to analyze events related to system resource utilization. It can be leveraged to understand if there is any relationship between the type of DB action being executed by the web application and the current memory utilization. The following search will group events together into transactions based on their given `threadId`, and then compile relationships between the `dbAction` and `mem_user` fields using the `associate` command:

```
index=main sourcetype=log4j | transaction threadId | associate
supcnt=50 dbAction mem_used
```

This can be most beneficial when trying to understand how function calls have an impact on resource utilization by drawing out direct relationships of the values.

See also

▶ The *Displaying the maximum concurrent checkouts* recipe

▶ The *Predicting website-traffic volumes* recipe

▶ The *Finding abnormally sized web requests* recipe

Predicting website-traffic volumes

In any environment, the capability to predict events provides immense value. In many cases, predictive analytics involves looking back over past events to predict what might occur in the future with a certain degree of confidence. When applied to the operational intelligence space and used correctly, predictive analytics can become a key asset that is more heavily relied on by teams rather than any other part of an Operational Intelligence program. For example, imagine having the ability to know the appropriate thresholds to set to alert key staff of impending issues, the capability to understand that a problem is beginning to occur even before it does, or simply being able to predict what consumers will purchase and ensuring the items are in stock. These examples just scratch the surface on use cases for predictive analytics.

In this recipe, you will write a Splunk search to predict website traffic volumes over a given time period. You will then graphically represent these values on a dashboard using a line chart.

Getting ready

To step through this recipe, you will need a running Splunk Enterprise server, with the sample data loaded from *Chapter 1, Play Time – Getting Data In*. You should be familiar with navigating the Splunk user interface.

How to do it...

Follow the steps in this recipe to predict website traffic volumes over a given period of time:

1. Log in to your Splunk server.

2. Select the **Operational Intelligence** application.

3. Ensure the time range picker is set to **Last 24 Hours**, and type the following search into the Splunk search bar. Then, click on the magnifying glass icon or hit *Enter*:

   ```
   index=main sourcetype=access_combined | timechart span=1h
   count | predict count
   ```

4. Splunk will return the resulting calculations in a tabular format in 1-hour intervals.

5. Click on the **Visualization** tab.

6. Since there are a number of visualizations within Splunk, the line chart visualization might not be displayed by default within the **Visualization** tab. Click on the dropdown listing the visualization types and select **Line**:

7. You should now see the value represented as line chart visualization, which is similar to the following example:

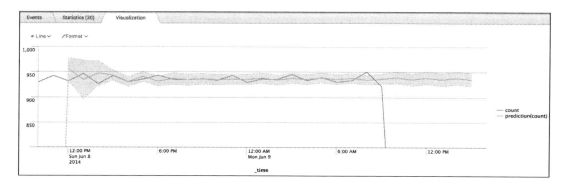

8. Let's save this search as a report. Click on **Save As** and choose **Report** from the drop-down menu:

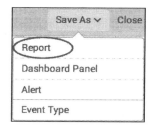

9. A **Save As Report** pop-up box will appear. Enter cp06_website_traffic_ prediction in the **Title** field, and then click on **Save**:

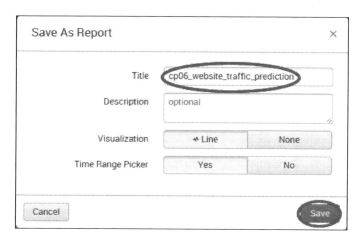

10. You will receive a confirmation that your report has been created. Now, let's add this report to a dashboard. In the next window, click on **Add to Dashboard**:

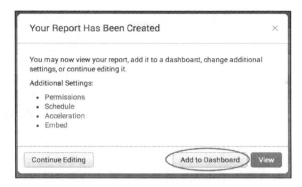

11. You will create a new dashboard for this report. On the **Save As Dashboard Panel** pop-up screen, make sure **New** is selected. Enter `Predictive Analytics` in the **Dashboard Title** field. Ensure the dashboard permissions are set to **Shared in App**. Enter `Website Traffic Volume Predictions` as the panel title and ensure the panel is powered by **Report**. Then, click on **Save** to create the dashboard:

12. You can now click on **View Dashboard** to view your newly created **Predictive Analytics** dashboard.

How it works...

Let's break down the search piece by piece:

Search fragment	Description
`index=main` `sourcetype=access_combined`	You should now be familiar with this search from the earlier recipes. It is used to return events from the website access log.
`| timechart span=1h count`	The `timechart` command simply performs a count of events in 1-hour intervals. This produces the total count in a tabular form.
`| predict count`	The `predict` command is used to look back over the given dataset and generate three new fields: `prediction`, which is the predicted future value for the given data point, `upper95`, which is the upper-confidence interval, and `lower95`, which is the lower-confidence interval. The confidence intervals specify the percentage of predictions that are expected to fail. The default value is `95%` but can be adjusted as needed.

There's more...

Predictive analytics can be applied to many different aspects of operational intelligence. The following are a few more short examples of other ways that Splunk's `predict` command might be leveraged to provide operational insight.

Predicting the total number of items purchased

The `predict` command can be used to analyze the number of items being purchased from a website, therefore ensuring that the right amount of product is always stocked. The Splunk search will be written as shown:

```
index=main sourcetype=log4j requestType=checkout | timechart
span=1h sum(numberOfItems) as count | predict count
```

Here, we simply look for all of the checkout events within the web application log and create a time chart of the sum of items purchased in 1-hour intervals. Then, we pipe the results into the `predict` command.

Predicting the average response time of function calls

Predicting the average response time of function calls can allow you to better tune your alerting thresholds if, or when, a function call falls outside the acceptable range. This can allow teams to better prioritize and hone in on issues as they occur or even when they begin to occur. The Splunk search will be written as shown:

```
index=main sourcetype=log4j | transaction threadId | timechart
span=1h avg(duration) as avg_duration | predict upper98=high
lower98=low avg_duration
```

Here, we must first calculate the duration of a function call by using the `transaction` command to group the events by `threadId`. Next, the `timechart` command will calculate the average duration by 1-hour intervals, and rename the field to `avg_duration`. Then, the results are piped to the `predict` command, where we have specified an upper and lower `98%` confidence interval in which predictions are expected to fail.

> For more information on the `predict` command, visit `http://docs.splunk.com/Documentation/Splunk/latest/SearchReference/Predict`.

See also

▶ The *Analyzing the relationship of web requests* recipe

▶ The *Finding abnormally sized web requests* recipe

▶ The *Identifying potential session spoofing* recipe

Finding abnormally sized web requests

The identification of abnormalities within events can prove to be valuable for many reasons; it can lead to the identification of a resource issue, highlight malicious activities hidden within high volumes of events, or simply detect users attempting to interact with the application in a way they were not designed to. When building an Operational Intelligence application for your website, the ability to detect abnormal activities should be at the top of your list. Frequently, after issues are identified, remediated, and due diligence has been done, it is common to see that some abnormality in the system or application was an early identifier of the cause. Capitalize on these opportunities to capture the abnormalities and triage them accordingly.

In this recipe, you will create a Splunk search to highlight abnormal web requests based on the size of the request over a given time period. You will then present all findings in a tabular format.

Getting ready

To step through this recipe, you will need a running Splunk Enterprise server, with the sample data loaded from *Chapter 1, Play Time – Getting Data In*. You should also complete the earlier recipes in this chapter and be familiar with navigating the Splunk user interface.

How to do it...

Follow the steps in this recipe to identify abnormally-sized web requests:

1. Log in to your Splunk server.

2. Select the **Operational Intelligence** application.

3. Ensure the time range picker is set to **Last 24 Hours**, and type the following search into the Splunk search bar. Then, click on the magnifying glass icon or hit *Enter*:

   ```
   index=main sourcetype=access_combined | eventstats
   mean(bytes) AS mean_bytes, stdev(bytes) AS stdev_bytes |
   eval Z_score=round(((bytes-mean_bytes)/stdev_bytes),2) |
   where Z_score>1.5 OR Z_score<-1.5 | table _time, clientip,
   uri, bytes, mean_bytes, Z_score
   ```

4. Splunk will return the results in a tabulated form, similar to the following example:

_time	clientip	uri	bytes	mean_bytes	Z_score
2014-06-09 12:06:21	220.86.20.99	/updatecart?orderId=1402315548&item=1000015&qty=2	3448	2000.294712	1.67
2014-06-09 12:05:23	126.175.137.157	/viewItem?item=4728475	585	2000.294712	-1.63
2014-06-09 12:04:40	83.15.197.56	/home	566	2000.294712	-1.65
2014-06-09 12:04:40	118.216.156.33	/checkout?orderId=1402315442&paymentId=264751402315442	3494	2000.294712	1.72
2014-06-09 12:04:37	118.216.156.33	/viewCart	521	2000.294712	-1.70
2014-06-09 12:04:22	118.216.156.33	/addItem?item=1000016&qty=1	672	2000.294712	-1.53
2014-06-09 12:04:17	118.216.156.33	/addItem?item=1000014&qty=1	3395	2000.294712	1.61

5. Let's save this search as a report. Click on **Save As** and choose **Report** from the drop-down menu:

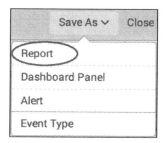

6. In the **Save As Report** pop-up box that appears, enter `cp06_abnormal_web_request_size` as the title, and then click on **Save**:

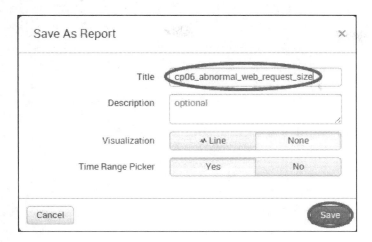

7. You will receive a confirmation that your report has been created. Now, let's add this report to the **Session Monitoring** dashboard you created earlier in this chapter. In the next window, click on **Add to Dashboard**:

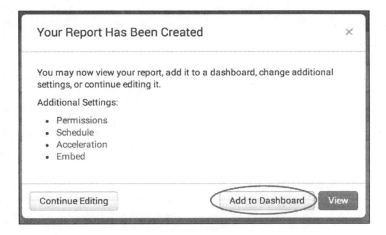

8. In the **Save As Dashboard Panel** pop-up box, click on the **Existing** button beside the **Dashboard** label, and then select **Session Monitoring** from the drop-down menu. Enter `Abnormal Web Requests by Size` in the **Panel Title** field and ensure it is powered by **Report**. Then, click on **Save**:

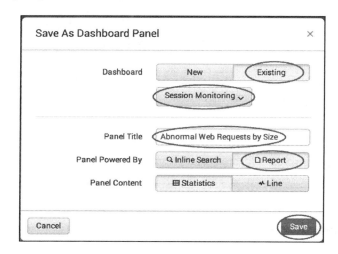

9. You can now click on **View Dashboard** to see your newly added panel.

How it works...

Let's break down the search piece by piece:

Search fragment	Description
`index=main sourcetype=access_combined`	You should now be familiar with this search from the earlier recipes. It is used to return events from the website access log.
`| eventstats mean(bytes) AS mean_bytes, stdev(bytes) AS stdev_bytes`	The `eventstats` command is used to calculate the mean value and standard deviation of bytes over a given time period. The resulting values are added as new fields to each event.
`| eval Z_score=round(((bytes-mean_bytes)/stdev_bytes),2)`	Using the `eval` command, we calculate a new field called `Z-score` for each event and round it to two decimal places. The `Z-score` field associated with each event will enable us to understand the amount and direction of variation from what is normal.

Search fragment	Description
`| where Z_score>1.5 OR Z_score<-1.5`	Using the `where` command, we filter for only those Z-scores that are deemed to be too far away from what is normal. This numeric threshold should be tuned as you get a better understanding of your data and events. As a standard best practice, 1.5 is used here. The higher the values, the more extreme the abnormalities will become.
`| table _time, clientip, uri, bytes, mean_bytes, Z_score`	The `table` command is used here to format the output of our search to make it more easily understandable.

You can make use of the `predict` command to look at previous events and to provide a better insight into the most accurate threshold values used to filter Z-scores.

There's more...

In this recipe, we looked at the use of the `eventstats` command with some general statistics applied to isolate events that might deviate too far from what is considered normal. There are a few other prebuilt commands that Splunk has to perform similar tasks. We will cover these commands in the following sections.

The anomalies command

The `anomalies` command is used to look for events based on the values of a field and return only the values that you won't expect to find. As the `anomalies` command is running, it assigns an unexpectedness score to each event, and the event is only considered unexpected if the unexpectedness score breaches the defined threshold. In the following example, we use the `anomalies` command to assess the bytes field within our website access logs, and we define a threshold of unexpectedness at `0.03`. The `table` and `sort` commands are just to make data presentation a little bit nicer:

```
index=main sourcetype=access_combined | anomalies field=bytes
threshold=0.03 | table unexpectedness, _raw | sort -unexpectedness
```

The results that are returned will be those that the `anomalies` command deems to be unexpected events. The algorithm that scores the events is proprietary to Splunk, but a short description can be found on the Splunk documentation site for the `anomalies` command.

For more information on the `anomalies` command, visit `http://docs.splunk.com/Documentation/Splunk/latest/SearchReference/Anomalies`.

The anomalousvalues command

The `anomalousvalues` command provides yet another means to find irregular or uncommon search results. It will look at the entire event set for the given time range, take into consideration the distribution of values, and then make a decision on whether a value is anomalous. In the following example, we use the `anomalousvalues` command against the website access logs and set a probability threshold of `0.03` that must be met:

```
index=main sourcetype=access_combined | anomalousvalue
pthresh=0.03
```

The results that are returned will be those that the `anomalousvalues` command deems to be anomalous.

 For more information on the `anomalousvalues` command, visit `http://docs.splunk.com/Documentation/Splunk/latest/SearchReference/Anomalousvalue`.

The cluster command

The `cluster` command provides a method to cluster similar events together, making it easier for you to identify outliers. Outliers are those events that are part of very small clusters or are on their own; all other events are a part of large-sized clusters. In the following example, we use the `cluster` command against the website access logs to identify any potential outlier. The `showercount` parameter is used to ensure the size of each cluster displayed. The `table` and `sort` commands are just to make data presentation a little bit nicer:

```
index=main sourcetype=access_combined | cluster showcount=t |
table cluster_count _raw | sort +cluster_count
```

The results that are returned will be sorted with the smallest cluster being listed first. Additional filtering, such as `NOT status=200`, can be applied to the event search to further filter out false-positives and allow for proper prioritization of event investigation.

 For more information on the `cluster` command, visit `http://docs.splunk.com/Documentation/Splunk/latest/SearchReference/Cluster`.

See also

- ▶ The *Predicting website-traffic volumes* recipe
- ▶ The *Identifying potential session spoofing* recipe

Identifying potential session spoofing

Sometimes, the most common website-operational issues relate to malicious users operating on the site or attempting malicious activities. One of the simpler and more common activities is to attempt to spoof the session identifier to that of a legitimate one in the hope that a session can be hijacked. Typically, web applications are built for proper session handling, but mistakes can be made, and even the best web applications can fall victim to simple session spoofing or hijacking. Understanding the impact that this can have on the operation of the website, we will leverage a common command we used throughout this chapter to identify any potential malicious use and flag it for investigation.

In this recipe, you will write a Splunk search to aid in the identification of potential session spoofing over a given period of time. The results will be presented in a tabular format and added to a dashboard.

Getting ready

To step through this recipe, you will need a running Splunk Enterprise server, with the sample data loaded from *Chapter 1, Play Time – Getting Data In*. You should also complete the earlier recipes in this chapter and be familiar with navigating the Splunk user interface.

How to do it...

Follow the steps in this recipe to identify potential session spoofing activity:

1. Log in to your Splunk server.
2. Select the **Operational Intelligence** application.
3. Ensure the time range picker is set to **Last 24 Hours**, and type the following search into the Splunk search bar. Then, click on the magnifying glass icon or hit *Enter*:

   ```
   index=main sourcetype=access_combined | transaction
   JSESSIONID | eval count_of_clientips=mvcount(clientip) |
   where count_of_clientips > 1 | table _time,
   count_of_clientips, clientip, JSESSIONID | sort
   count_of_clientips
   ```

4. Splunk will return the results in a tabular format.

5. Let's save this search as a report. Click on **Save As** and choose **Report** from the drop-down menu:

6. In the **Save As Report** pop-up box that appears, enter `cp06_potential_session_spoofing` in the **Title** field, and then click on **Save**:

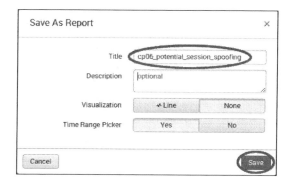

7. You will receive a confirmation that your report has been created. Now, let's add this report to the **Session Monitoring** dashboard you created earlier in this chapter. In the next window, click on **Add to Dashboard**:

8. In the **Save As Dashboard Panel** pop-up box, click on the **Existing** button beside the **Dashboard** label and select **Session Monitoring** from the drop-down menu. Enter `Potential Session Spoofing` in the **Panel Title** field and ensure the panel is powered by **Report**. Then, click on **Save**:

9. You can now click on **View Dashboard** to see your newly added panel.

It is best practice to save these types of searches as *alerts* so that you are automatically notified at the time a security incident occurs. It will help to lessen the impact of any potential repercussions due to malicious activity.

How it works...

In this recipe, you wrote a search to detect spoofed sessions. Essentially, the search looks for where a single session identifier (`JSESSIONID`) is associated with multiple client IP addresses over the given time range of 24 hours. Understandably, in almost all cases, a session identifier will only come from a single client IP address. So, if there are sessions that have multiple IPs, then this can very well detect spoofing of a session. Results will only be displayed where there is more than one client IP associated with a specific session.

Let's break down the search piece by piece:

Search fragment	Description
`index=main` `sourcetype=access_combined`	You should now be familiar with this search from the earlier recipes. It is used to return events from the website access log.
`| transaction JSESSIONID`	Using the `transaction` command, we group events together based on their given `JSESSIONID` to form a single transaction.

`| eval`
`count_of_clientips=mvcount`
`(clientip)`
	Using the `eval` command, we create a new field called `count_of_clientips`, which is populated by the output of the `mvcount` function. The `mvcount` function is responsible for providing a count of the values contained within a multivalued field.

`| where count_of_clientips` `> 1`	Using the `where` command, we tell Splunk to only return events where the value of the `count_of_clientips` field is greater than 1.

`| table _time,`
`count_of_clientips,`
`clientip, JSESSIONID`
	The `table` command is used here to format the output of our search to make it more easily understandable.

`| sort count_of_clientips`	The `sort` command is used to sort the results based on the values stored within the field named `count_of_clientips`.

There's more...

Besides presenting the data sorted based on the count of client IPs that were associated with a given session identifier, logic can be applied to ensure events that meet specific criteria and are raised higher in the list when compared to others.

Creating logic for urgency

Not all session spoofing is alike, and therefore, it needs to be responded to differently according to the urgency associated with the event. For example, a session might be spoofed, but this session is not in the midst of any purchasing, and therefore, the potential financial loss to either the website or the consumer is extremely low. Another session is spoofed in the middle of making over $1,000 in purchases, and therefore, the potential financial loss to the parties involved is substantial.

You can build some common logic into your search based upon given values to increase the urgency associated with an event. In the following example, we bring together the website access and web application logs to enhance the amount of information we have access to. We then set up specific conditions that increase the urgency based on the values stored within the given events:

```
index=main sourcetype=access_combined
| join JSESSIONID usetime=true earlier=false [ search index=main
sourcetype=log4j | transaction threadId | eval
JSESSIONID=sessionId ]
| transaction JSESSIONID
| eval count_of_clientips=mvcount(clientip) | where
count_of_clientips > 1
| eval cost_urgency=if(itemPrice>=1000,"2","1")
| eval frequency_urgency=case(count_of_clientips=="2","1",
count_of_clientips=="3","2",1=1,"3")
| eval urgency=cost_urgency + frequency_urgency
| table _time, count_of_clientips, clientip, JSESSIONID
| sort urgency
```

In this example, we join the field values from the web application log with the website access log, and then build a transaction of the session identifiers within the website access log. Next, we count the number of `clientip` values associated with each unique session identifier and ensure that only events with more than one `clientip` are returned. We now add further logic to say that if the `itemPrice` field value is greater than or equal to $1,000, then the `cost_urgency` field value will be raised to 2, otherwise it will remain at 1. The next piece of logic looks at the number of `clientip` fields associated with the unique session identifier and assigns a value to `frequency_urgency` accordingly. The values of `cost_urgency` and `frequency_urgency` are then added together to form the overall urgency value. The tabulated results are then sorted based on the overall urgency, allowing teams to focus more clearly on the most important incidents.

See also

- ▶ The *Predicting website-traffic volumes* recipe
- ▶ The *Finding abnormally sized web requests* recipe

Summary

The key takeaways from this chapter are as follows:

- There are many ways to analyze data aside from looking at events individually
- Adding contexts to events by converging data sources provides immense value
- Building transactions leads to a better understanding of user, system, and application behavior
- Using statistics to assess abnormalities in your events can lead to a more proactive issue identification
- Predictive analytics provides more conclusive evidence to assist with resource planning and threshold tuning

7
Enriching Data – Lookups and Workflows

In this chapter, we will learn how to augment and enrich the data within Splunk. You will learn about:

- ▸ Looking up product code descriptions
- ▸ Flagging suspicious IP addresses
- ▸ Creating a session state table
- ▸ Adding hostnames to IP addresses
- ▸ Searching ARIN for a given IP address
- ▸ Triggering a Google search for a given error
- ▸ Creating a ticket for application errors
- ▸ Looking up inventory from an external database

Introduction

In the previous chapter, you continued to improve your Splunk search and analytical skills by creating more advanced searches that leveraged more of the deep analytical commands to gain more operational intelligence from the data contained within the logs. In this chapter, you will leverage Splunk's lookup functionality to enrich these results with the data found outside of the logs. You will also use Splunk's workflow functionality to perform some simple actions on the data that you discovered.

Lookups

Lookups are used to enrich log data with additional data not found in the log events themselves. They allow you to key off one or more fields in the event data and add additional fields to this data. These additional fields are commonly added by looking up the specified fields in a static CSV-based lookup table and then bringing back additional fields associated with that specific entry in the table. However, lookups can also be a lot more dynamic, leveraging Python scripts or directly looking up fields in an external database table. Lookup tables can also contain time fields to allow for time-based lookups in a given time period.

While external lookups using Python scripts are usually dynamic in nature, you might think that CSV-based lookups would only be useful for types of data such as HTTP status codes that never change over time (well, maybe every once in a while). However, Splunk can be used to populate CSV lookups using the output of a search and saving this as a lookup table. This technique can provide many different possible uses, from identifying trends to creating various aging reports. In this chapter, you will build and populate a number of lookups and leverage a dynamic scripted lookup.

Workflows

When working with events being returned by Splunk, there are often times where there is a need to perform a subsequent operation in order to get more details. Sometimes, performing another search within Splunk is enough, but at other times, you might need to send this data to an external system for further processing.

Splunk provides a feature known as workflow action that can be configured to provide different options, depending on what fields are present in your search results. There are two types of workflow actions currently available: the ability to open a link to a web-based resource and the ability to execute an additional search within Splunk. The link action can be used to search for data in popular search engines or link to other internal resources such as helpdesk tools or change management systems. The search action can be used to initiate more complex searches than you can get with a chart or table drilldown. In this chapter, you will build both link- and web-based workflow actions.

DB Connect

Splunk DB Connect is a Splunk supported application for Splunk Enterprise that lets you enrich and combine your log data with external database data. Using DB Connect, you can directly query external databases using SQL from Splunk directly and return the results to Splunk. These results can be combined with other log data, converted to local lookups, or indexed into Splunk. DB Connect also allows for external database lookups to enrich your log data with additional information while it is being searched. At the end of this chapter, we will install DB Connect and pull in inventory data from an external database.

Ok, enough of discussion; let's get started!

Looking up product code descriptions

Log data can be filled with identification numbers, short codes, error numbers, or other values that don't always make the information easy to read or understand quickly.

This recipe will show you how to add a lookup table to your Operational Intelligence application so that when a product code field is present in an event, a description field can automatically be added and populated with the full description of that product.

Getting ready

To step through this recipe, you will need a running Splunk Enterprise server, with the sample data loaded from *Chapter 1, Play Time – Getting Data In*. You should be familiar with navigating the Splunk user interface.

How to do it...

Follow the steps in this recipe to create an automatic product code lookup:

1. Create a new file called `productdescriptions.csv` using your favorite text editor on your local computer and add the following lines, taking care to ensure that the commas are typed correctly:

   ```
   itemId,itemName,itemDescription
   4728475,Rolux Navigator,Stylish mens watch with metal band
   38492,Rolux Sportsman,Mens sport watch with timer
   1000014,Ripple BookPro 13,13 inch laptop - 5PB HDD/200GB RAM
   1000015,Ripple Jukebox 500,Portable music player - 984 hour
   battery life
   1000016,Poku Castbox,Video streaming device - HDMI compatible
   1000017,Ripple Jukebox 300,Music streaming device 300GB storage
   capacity
   1000020,Ripple MyPhone 8,The latest phone from Ripple - 8 inch
   with 8TB of storage capacity
   ```

2. You can alternatively use the `productdescriptions.csv` file that is provided.

3. Save the file in a location that is easily accessible from your web browser.

4. Log in to your Splunk server.

5. Select the **Operational Intelligence** application.

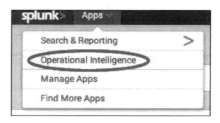

6. Click on the **Settings** menu, and then select the **Lookups** menu item.

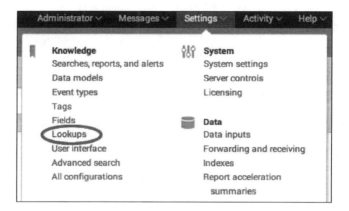

7. Click on **Lookup table files**.

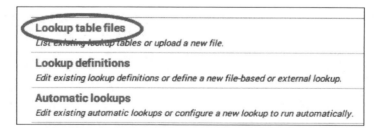

8. Click on **New**.

9. Select the destination app as **operational_intelligence**.

10. Click on the **Choose File** button (it may be different depending on your browser or operating system) and select your `productdescriptions.csv` file.

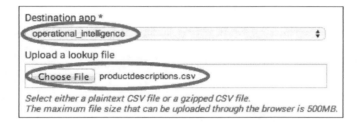

As the file is much smaller than the maximum 500 MB file size, we are able to upload it via the GUI without any issue.

 Larger files can be uploaded through the backend filesystem to `$SPLUNK_HOME/etc/apps/operational_intelligence/lookups`.

11. In the **Destination filename** field, enter `productdescriptions.csv` and then click on **Save**.

12. Now, we need to define our lookup in Splunk.

13. Click on **Lookups**.

14. Click on **Lookup definitions**.

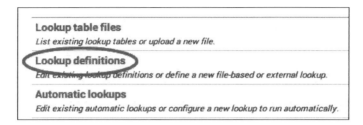

15. Click on **New**.

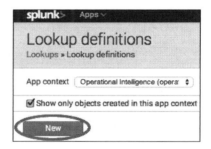

16. In the **Name** field, enter Product_Descriptions, set the **Type** field to **File-based**, and select the **productdescriptions.csv** file in the **Lookup file** field. Then, click on **Save**.

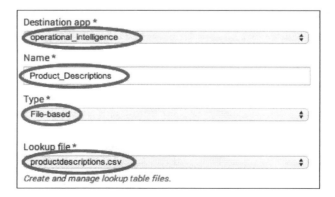

17. Finally, we are going to automate the lookup such that the lookup is performed automatically when searching for the `log4j` sourcetype. Click on **Lookups** again.

18. This time, click on **Automatic lookups**.

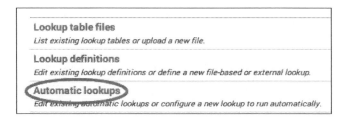

19. Click on **New**.

20. Select **operational_intelligence** in the **Destination app** field, and enter `Product_Descriptions` in the **Name** field.

21. In the **Lookup table** dropdown, select **Product_Descriptions**:

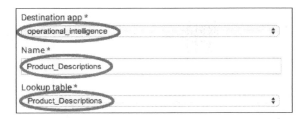

22. Select **sourcetype** in the **Apply to** field and enter `log4j` in the **named** field.

23. Enter `itemId` in both fields for **Lookup input fields**.

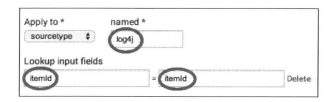

24. Set `itemDescription` to `ProductDescription` and `itemName` to `ProductName` in the **Lookup output fields**.

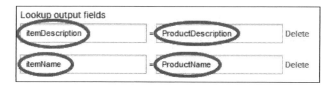

25. Click on **Save**.

26. Click on **Apps** and select the **Operational Intelligence** app.

27. In the search bar, enter the following search over **Last 24 hours**:

```
index=main sourcetype="log4j" itemId=* | table itemId
ProductDescription, ProductName
```

28. It should now display the **ProductDescription** and **ProductName** entries for each field.

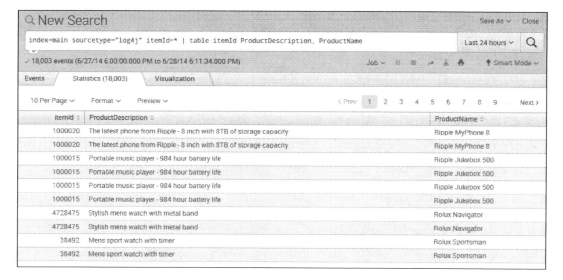

How it works...

When you issue a search in Splunk, it checks its configuration to see if there are any lookups defined. If it finds a lookup that matches the appropriate host, source, or sourcetype for the events returned in the search, it will take the input fields that are defined and match them against the data in the lookup file and the fields in the events. If the field values match, it will add the output fields from the lookup table to the events as the new fields using the fieldnames as configured in the lookup.

There are many different configurations possible with lookup tables. For example, it is possible to have input field matches on more than one field, and you can have the output fields overwrite the fields that already exist in the search results.

In this recipe, we chose to implement an automatic lookup. Automatic lookups negate the need to explicitly use the `lookup` command in your search but can carry a performance cost. For example, every search of the `log4j` sourcetype will now perform this product lookup automatically, whether we need the fields and associated values returned from the lookup or not.

> Automatic lookups are only recommended where it makes sense to do so and where every search of that sourcetype, source, or host would benefit from the automatic lookup.

There's more...

As with most configurations in Splunk, there is more than one way to do something. While the product lookup can be configured via the web interface, it can also be performed manually.

Manually adding the lookup to Splunk

Lookups don't have to be added just via the web interface. The lookup files can be manually uploaded to the Splunk server and the configuration can be manually added to the lookup configuration.

1. Upload your `productdescriptions.csv` file to `$SPLUNK_HOME/etc/apps/operational_intelligence/lookups` (create the `lookups` directory if required)

2. Add the following stanza to `$SPLUNK_HOME/etc/apps/operational_intelligence/local/transforms.conf` (create the `transforms.conf` file if required):

   ```
   [Product_Descriptions]
   filename = productdescriptions.csv
   ```

3. Add the following stanza to `$SPLUNK_HOME/etc/apps/operational_` `intelligence/local/props.conf` (create the `props.conf` file if required):

```
[log4j]
LOOKUP-Product_Descriptions = Product_Descriptions itemId
AS itemId OUTPUTNEW itemDescription AS ProductDescription,
itemName AS ProductName
```

See also

▸ The *Flagging suspicious IP addresses* recipe

▸ The *Creating a session state table* recipe

▸ The *Looking up inventory from an external database* recipe

Flagging suspicious IP addresses

Any server that receives requests from clients will always be a potential target for someone to try and exploit by initiating an attack. Attacks can come in many different forms, and over time, it is important to keep a history of the originating source of the attack. So, we can monitor the behavior and patterns more closely and potentially use this data to block access as needed.

In this next recipe, you will learn how to store the source IP addresses of clients, who based on their request behavior are to be flagged as suspicious IPs.

Getting ready

To step through this recipe, you will need a running Splunk Enterprise server, with the sample data loaded from *Chapter 1, Play Time – Getting Data In*. You should be familiar with navigating the Splunk user interface.

How to do it...

Follow the steps in this recipe to create a lookup table of malicious IP addresses:

1. Log in to your Splunk server.

2. Select the **Operational Intelligence** application.

3. In the search bar, enter the following search over a time range of **Last 7 days**, and press *Enter* or click on the search icon to execute the search:

```
index=main sourcetype="access_combined" status=403 | stats
count by clientip | eval suspect="1" | outputlookup
createinapp=true suspect_ips.csv
```

4. A tabulated list of IPs that contain the three columns of **clientip**, **count**, and **suspect** will be displayed. Click on the **Save as** link and select **Report**.

5. Enter cp07_suspect_ips in the **Title** field.

6. Select **None** in the **Visualization** field and **No** in the **Time Range Picker** field. Then, click on **Save**.

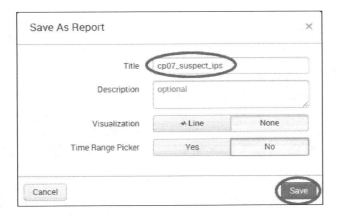

7. Click on the **Schedule** link.

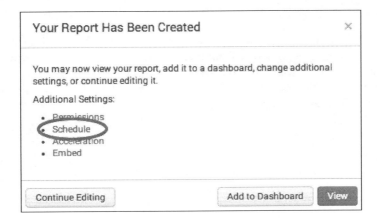

8. Check the **Schedule Report** box.

9. In the **Schedule** dropdown, select **Run every hour**.

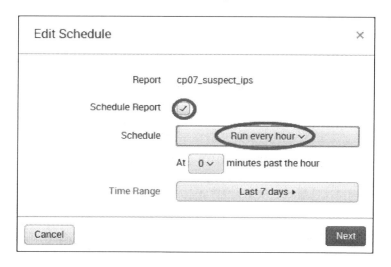

10. Click on **Next** and then on **Save**.

11. Now, let's leverage the new `suspect_ips.csv` lookup to identify all the web access events from the IP addresses that are suspect. In the search bar of the **Operational Intelligence** application, enter the following search over **Last 24 hours**:

```
index=main sourcetype=access_combined | lookup
suspect_ips.csv clientip AS clientip OUTPUTNEW suspect AS
suspect | where suspect=1
```

12. You will now see all the web access events filtered to only show the `clientip` addresses that were in the `suspect_ips.csv` lookup file.

How it works...

In this recipe, you identified the clients associated with web requests that have a status code of 403 over the past 7 days and wrote these IP addresses to a lookup file. Status code 403 means the `clientip` address in question has attempted to access something that is forbidden. When writing the lookup, you evaluated a new field called `suspect` and gave every entry a value of 1. This `suspect` field will be used as a flag to filter data later on.

When the initial search is executed, it leverages the `outputlookup` command, which writes data to a lookup file that you specify in the search (in this case, a file called `suspect_ips.csv`). The `outputlookup` command takes several arguments, as shown in the following table:

Argument	Value
`<filename>` or `<tablename>`	This tells Splunk where to insert the lookup data. If the name matches an existing lookup stanza in the `transforms.conf` configuration, then it will use that location; otherwise, it will create a new file with the filename specified. This field is required.
`append`	This will tell Splunk to append the table data to the end of the file. Otherwise, it will just overwrite the file with new data.
`max`	This limits the number of rows that Splunk will populate in the lookup table.
`create_empty`	This can be `true` (default) or `false`. If `true`, then when there is no data to output, Splunk will still create a zero-byte file. If `false`, then when there is no data to output, Splunk will not create a file, and if the file already exists, it will delete it.
`createinapp`	This tells Splunk to create the lookup file in the app context in which the search was run. If not specified, then the lookup table is created in the system location.

The inline `outputlookup` command is a convenient way to create lookup tables or maintain lookup tables since the lookup file was created following the execution of the search. You then saved the search and scheduled it to run every hour. By doing this, the search will run hourly and rewrite the lookup file each hour with up-to-date data. As a result, the suspect IP listing will be continually updated and maintained.

Once this was done, you wrote a new search to leverage the lookup file you just created and filter the `access_combined` events to only those events that contain a `suspect=1` field value. The search leverages the `lookup` command to match `clientip` in the data with `clientip` in the `suspect_ips.cvs` lookup file. The lookup file then enriches the data by adding a `suspect=1` field/value pair where `clientip` matches. You were then able to use this new data in the search to filter the results to only events that contained a `suspect=1` field/value.

This recipe scratches the surface of how lookups can be used in a powerful way. In this recipe, you were able to filter your results using the data that was not present in the source but rather the data that you enriched the source data with using a lookup.

> In this recipe, you wrote a search to look back over 7 days but then had the schedule of the search running hourly. This works fine in our example dataset but might be considered inefficient. Report acceleration or summary indexing can be used for efficiency gains. Review _Chapter 9, Speed Up Intelligence – Data Summarization_, for more information on this.

There's more...

As with most configurations in Splunk, there is more than one way to do something. While the product lookup can be configured via the web interface, it can also be performed manually.

Modifying an existing saved search to populate a lookup table

You can modify an existing saved search via a configuration file to populate a lookup table by adding the following code to the search stanza in any of your `savedsearches.conf` files:

```
action.populate_lookup = 1
action.populate_lookup.dest = <string>
```

The `<string>` value can either be the path to a `*.csv` file or the name of an existing lookup table definition in the `transforms.conf` file.

Alternatively, you can also just use the Splunk GUI and amend the saved search to include the `outputlookup` command and required parameters.

See also

- ▸ The *Looking up product code descriptions* recipe
- ▸ The *Creating a session state table* recipe
- ▸ The *Looking up inventory from an external database* recipe

Creating a session state table

In this recipe, you will learn how to leverage lookups to maintain a state table that will capture the first time a session was seen and continually update the existing session's information accordingly. You can use this to determine if a session has gone stale and has been abandoned or if someone is trying to hijack an old session.

Getting ready

To step through this recipe, you will need a running Splunk Enterprise server, with the sample data loaded from *Chapter 1, Play Time – Getting Data In*. You should be familiar with navigating the Splunk user interface.

How to do it...

Follow the steps in this recipe to create a state table of sessions:

1. Log in to your Splunk server.

2. Select the **Operational Intelligence** application.

3. In the search bar, enter the search and select to run it over **Last 15 minutes**:

```
index=main sourcetype="access_combined" | eval
firsttime=_time | eval lasttime=_time |  stats
last(firsttime) as firsttime, first(lasttime) as lasttime
by JSESSIONID | outputlookup createinapp=true
session_state.csv
```

4. You should see a tabulated list by session ID, listing the **firsttime** and **lasttime** columns. Splunk will also have created a lookup named `sessions.csv` as a result of the search.

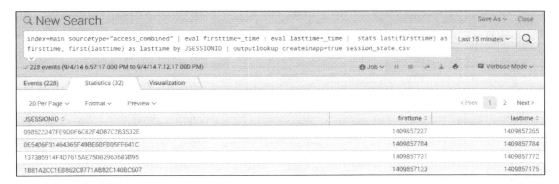

5. Next, amend the query slightly as follows and rerun the search over **Last 15 minutes** again:

```
index=main sourcetype="access_combined" | eval
firsttime=_time | eval lasttime=_time | fields JSESSIONID
firsttime lasttime | inputlookup session_state.csv
append=true | stats last(firsttime) as firsttime,
first(lasttime) as lasttime by JSESSIONID | outputlookup
createinapp=true session_state.csv
```

6. You should see a very similar (if not the same) list of times and session IDs. Now, let's save this search as a report. Click on the **Save As** link and select **Report**.

7. Enter `cp07_session_state` as the title, and then click on **Save**.

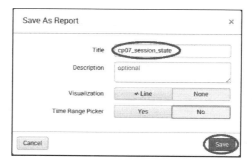

8. Click on the **Schedule** link.

9. Check the **Schedule Report** box.

10. In the **Schedule** dropdown, select **Run on Cron Schedule**, and then enter */15 * * * * in the **Cron Expression** field. This cron schedule means that the saved report will run every 15 minutes. Then, click on **Next** and then on **Save**.

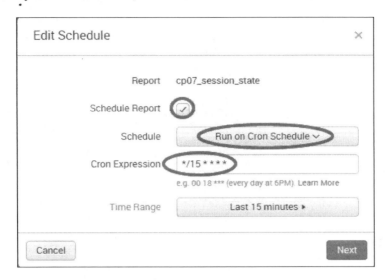

11. The state table is now created and will periodically update every 15 minutes. Let's now view the table. Enter the following search in the search bar of the **Operational Intelligence** application:

```
|inputlookup session_state.csv
| eval firsttime_daysago=round((now()-firsttime)/60/60/24)
| eval lasttime_daysago=round((now()-lasttime)/60/60/24)
| convert ctime(firsttime), ctime(lasttime)
| table JSESSIONID firsttime, firsttime_daysago, lasttime,
lasttime_daysago
```

12. You should be presented with a session table, listing the first time the session was seen, how many days ago the first time was, the last time the session was seen, and how many days ago the last time was.

How it works...

This recipe is designed to maintain some form of state about the sessions being used within the application we are monitoring. The data we are capturing includes both the first time the session ID was detected and also the last time the session ID was detected. A lookup table is used to maintain the up-to-date states of the sessions over time and will be a lot faster to search than trying to search for all the sessions over time.

In this recipe, we initially started with two searches: the first search was used to create the lookup file as this did not exist, and the second search was the search that we chose to save and schedule. This second search brings in the existing lookup table we created in the first search, which is why the first search was performed.

As the first and second searches are similar, let's explain how the second search works with the help of the following table:

Search fragment	Description
`index=main sourcetype="access_combined"`	This tells Splunk to find all of the web server logs in the main index.
`| eval firsttime=_time	eval lasttime=_time`	Here, we use the `eval` command to evaluate `firsttime` and `lasttime`. In this case, both times will be using the `_time` field in the event, which is the timestamp of the event.
`| fields JSESSIONID firsttime lasttime`	Next, we declare that we only want to use the `JSESSIONID`, `firsttime`, and `lasttime` fields.
`| inputlookup session_state.csv append=true`	Next, we leverage the `inputlookup` command to bring in the existing `session_state.csv` lookup file (created in the one-time first search). The results of this will be appended to the existing results of the search.
`| stats last(firsttime) as firsttime, first(lasttime) as lasttime by JSESSIONID`	Here, we leverage the `last()` and `first()` functions of the `stats` command to find the oldest `firsttime` date (using `last`) and the most recent `lasttime` date (using `first`), and list these two fields using `JSESSIONID`. This will ensure that we keep a copy of the oldest date as the first time the session was seen and the most recent date as the last time the session was seen.
`| outputlookup createinapp=true session_state.csv`	Finally, we write back to the `session_state.csv` lookup using the `outputlookup` command. This will replace the old file with a new one that contains the results of our search.

As this search is scheduled to run every 15 minutes and look back over the past 15 minutes, it will build up a large table of session IDs in time. This can be very useful for tracking purposes.

 You might want to amend the lookup population search to drop session IDs that have a `firsttime` date older than a certain number of days so that the lookup does not keep filling up forever.

Once the lookup was saved and scheduled, the final part of the recipe involved putting together a search that leveraged `inputlookup` to view the data in the lookup file. You evaluated new fields to calculate the number of seconds between the present time (using `now()`) and both the `firsttime` and `lasttime` field's epoch values. The `convert` command and `ctime` function were then leveraged to display the `firsttime` and `lasttime` fields in a readable timestamp format rather than displaying the epoch seconds.

See also

- ► The *Flagging suspicious IP addresses* recipe
- ► The *Adding hostnames to IP addresses* recipe
- ► The *Searching ARIN for a given IP address* recipe

Adding hostnames to IP addresses

In this recipe, you will learn how to add hostnames to IP addresses in the log data by leveraging external lookups. There are many times where a hostname value can be more valuable than an IP address, and it can provide an easier identifier around what clients are connecting to your application. Many ISP-based connections can be very identifiable by the format of their hostnames, which can help you identify potential malicious activity.

Getting ready

To step through this recipe, you will need a running Splunk Enterprise server, with the sample data loaded from *Chapter 1, Play Time – Getting Data In*. You should be familiar with navigating the Splunk user interface.

How to do it...

Follow the steps in this recipe to lookup hostnames for given IP addresses:

1. On your Splunk server, create a new `transforms.conf` file at `$SPLUNK_HOME/etc/apps/operational_intelligence/local/transforms.conf`. If one already exists, then you can just edit the existing file.

2. Add the following text to the file and save it:

   ```
   [dnsLookup]
   external_cmd = external_lookup.py host ip
   fields_list = host, ip
   ```

3. Return to the Splunk web interface and select the **Operational Intelligence** application.

4. In the search bar, enter the following search:

```
index=main sourcetype="access_combined" | lookup dnslookup
clientip
```

5. Hit your *Enter* key, and the search should start; wait for some results to show.

6. You should now see a `clienthost` field in your data.

How it works...

The external lookup used in this recipe is bundled with Splunk. When the script is called at search time, a lookup table is created in the memory to facilitate the passing back of content, just as if it had been read from a CSV file on the server. Multiple columns are in the table and can be mapped to in order to have the lookup enrich your data with the appropriate new field/values from the table. In this case, we passed the `clientip` to the script, the IP is looked up using DNS, and `clienthost` returned.

External lookup commands provide a mechanism to look up data in real time. This is useful when a local lookup data table becomes too large or the data becomes stale too quickly. As external lookups are just scripts, they can also be used to call out to your custom applications or services to provide a very simple integration. Other examples for external lookups could involve looking up more data about specific product codes or order information.

Note that as an external script is generally used to access third-party systems, there can be a delay in the time it takes to return search results, or the script might place additional load on the third-party systems.

 Currently, Splunk only supports Python scripts to be used for external lookups.

There's more...

In this recipe, we leveraged a DNS lookup to convert IP addresses into hostnames. We did this by calling the lookup in the search directly using the `lookup` command. However, you might wish to automate this and have the IP/host translation done automatically for a given sourcetype, host, or source.

Enabling automatic external field lookups

To enable DNS lookups to occur automatically on the web server logs, add the following code to the `$SPLUNK_HOME/etc/apps/operational_intelligence/local/props.conf` file. If there is no `props.conf` file, then you will need to create one.

```
[access_combined]
LOOKUP-dns = dnsLookup clientip OUTPUTNEW clienthost AS
resolved_hostname
```

See also

▶ The *Flagging suspicious IP addresses* recipe

▶ The *Creating a session state table* recipe

▶ The *Searching ARIN for a given IP address* recipe

Searching ARIN for a given IP address

IP addresses, on their own, can only give a tiny glimpse into their association, where they are from, or what they are for. You might be able to determine if an IP is from a private range, what asset it belongs to, or if it is from a well-known server, but in many cases, you might not know much about the IPs in question.

In this recipe, you will learn how to leverage Splunk's workflow functionality to search an IP address in your events against the **ARIN (American Registry for Internet Numbers)** database to look up more useful information about the IP in question, such as who the IP address is assigned to.

Getting ready

To step through this recipe, you will need a running Splunk Enterprise server, with the sample data loaded from *Chapter 1, Play Time – Getting Data In*. You should be familiar with navigating the Splunk user interface.

How to do it...

Follow the steps in this recipe to create a workflow action ARIN search for a given IP address:

1. Log in to your Splunk server.
2. Select the **Operational Intelligence** application.
3. Click on the **Settings** menu.

4. Click on the **Fields** menu option.

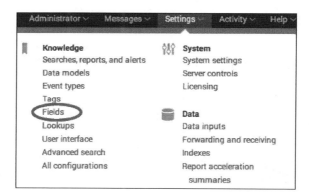

5. Click on the **Workflow actions** link.

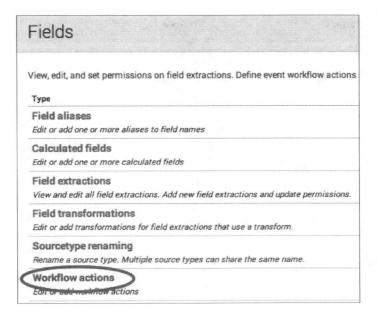

6. Click on **New**.

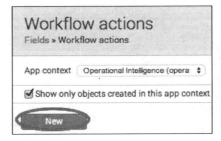

7. Ensure that the destination app is the **operational_intelligence** app.

8. Enter `ARIN_Lookup` in the **Name** field. This name must not contain any spaces or special characters. It will be used as the internal name of the action and is not the text that will be made visible.

9. Enter `Lookup $clientip$ in ARIN` in the **Label** field. The label is the text that will appear in the workflow dropdown. It can contain a field name enclosed with dollar signs, which will be replaced with the value of that field in the event.

10. Enter `clientip` in the **Apply to the following fields** field.

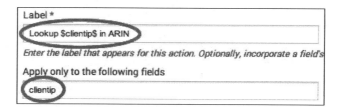

11. In the **Show action in** dropdown, select **Both**, and in the **Action Type** dropdown, select **link**.

12. In the **URI** field under **Link configuration**, enter `http://whois.arin.net/rest/ip/$clientip$` and ensure that the **Link method** field is set to **get**.

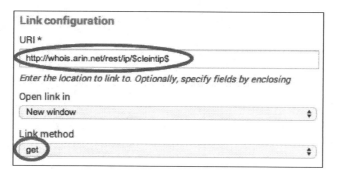

13. Click on **Save** to finish creating the workflow action.

14. Let's now test the workflow action and see what it does. In a new search bar of your **Operational Intelligence** app, enter the following search over **Last 15 minutes**:

```
index=main sourcetype=access_combined
```

15. Once the results are displayed, click on the little arrow next to an event, and then click on the **Event Actions** button. You will see an option in the dropdown to run the ARIN search on the `clientip` address.

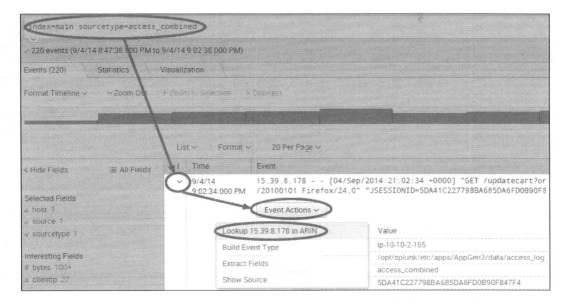

16. Clicking on this option in the dropdown will open a new tab in the browser; this tab passes the IP address to `arin.net` and performs a `whois` lookup. The results from `arin.net` will be displayed.

How it works...

When your search results are rendered in the event listing, Splunk will match the returned fields and event types with the workflow actions you have configured and present the dropdown workflow actions as required. In this case, the `clientip` field was matched with the ARIN workflow action you created.

The basic GET link method used in this recipe will insert the variable value into the URI for the user to click on. In this case, the `$clientip$` field variable inserts the IP address into the ARIN query URI, such that the IP is passed within the URI when it is clicked on. Other link methods are available and covered in other recipes in this chapter.

Workflow actions can be made to appear in both the **Event Actions** drop-down menu and **Action** column in the row specific to the field in the event that the workflow action is set to work with.

By utilizing the field name substitution in the label and the URI, you can dynamically create a full assortment of workflow actions to enable your users to link to other internal or external resources.

There's more...

While workflow actions can be a convenient way to link to external resources based on the presence of certain fields in your events, you sometimes require more control when particular workflow actions are displayed.

Limiting workflow actions by event types

Edit the workflow action that you created in this recipe, and in the **Apply only to the following event types** box, you can add in a comma-separated list of the event type names that this workflow action will be limited to.

> For more information on event types, see the Splunk documentation at
> `http://docs.splunk.com/Documentation/Splunk/latest/`
> `Knowledge/Abouteventtypes`.

See also

- ▸ The *Creating a ticket for application errors* recipe
- ▸ The *Triggering a Google search for a given error* recipe
- ▸ The *Adding hostnames to IP addresses* recipe

Triggering a Google search for a given error

Many times, you will run across data in your events that you might not fully understand. For example, logs typically contain error codes that can be cryptic to figure out. You can use a lookup table to translate these error codes into something meaningful, if this makes sense. However, you can also create a workflow action to search the Internet for codes that, perhaps, you do not need to look up that often. Looking at what the greater web community has posted has certainly saved many an administrator a sleepless night.

This recipe will show you how to build a workflow action that will allow you to take the status code from a search in Splunk and have it initiate a search in Google with the Google search terms already populated.

Getting ready

To step through this recipe, you will need a running Splunk Enterprise server, with the sample data loaded from *Chapter 1, Play Time – Getting Data In*. You should be familiar with navigating the Splunk user interface.

How to do it...

Follow the steps in this recipe to create a workflow action that allows you to trigger a Google search for the error codes in your events:

1. Log in to your Splunk server.
2. Select the **Operational Intelligence** application.
3. Click on the **Settings** menu.

4. Click on the **Fields** menu option.

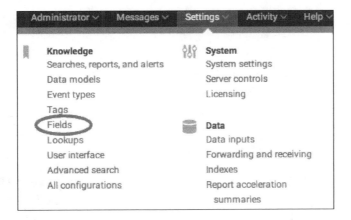

5. Click on the **Workflow actions** link.

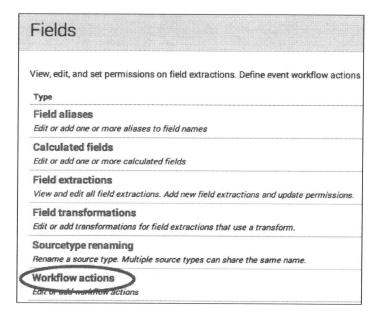

6. Click on **New**.

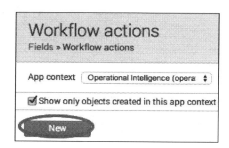

7. Ensure that the destination app is the **operational_intelligence** app.

8. Enter `Google_Search` in the **Name** field. This name must not contain any spaces or special characters. It will be used as the internal name of the action and is not the text that will be made visible.

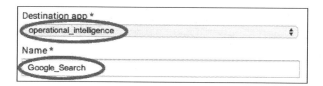

9. Enter `Google HTTP Status $status$` in the **Label** field. The label is the text that will appear in the workflow dropdowns. It can contain a field name enclosed with dollar signs, which will be replaced with the value of that field in the event.

10. Enter `status` in the **Apply only to the following fields** box.

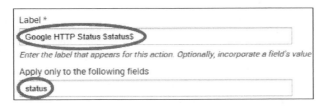

11. In the **Show action in** dropdown, select **Both**, and in the **Action type** dropdown, select **link**.

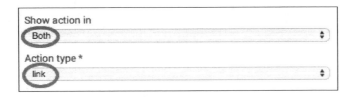

12. In the **URI** field under **Link configuration**, enter `http://google.com/search?q=http%20status%20$status$` and ensure that the **Link method** field is set to **get**.

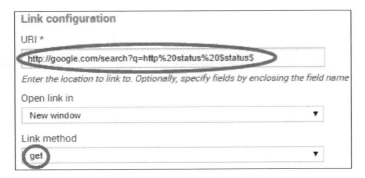

13. Click on **Save** to finish creating the new workflow action.

14. Let's now test the workflow action and see what it does. In a new search bar of your **Operational Intelligence** app, enter the following search over **Last 15 minute**s:

    `index=main sourcetype=access_combined`

15. As in the previous recipe, once the results are displayed, click on the little arrow next to an event, and then click on the **Event Actions** button. You will see an option in the dropdown to run the Google search on the status code in the event.

16. Clicking on this option in the dropdown will open a new tab in the browser that passes the status code to `google.com`, and a Google search is then performed for the status code in question.

How it works...

This recipe is similar to the previous recipe. When your search results are rendered in the event listing, Splunk will match the returned fields and event types with the workflow actions you have configured and present the dropdown workflow actions as required. In this case, the status field was matched with the Google workflow action you created.

The basic `GET` link method used in this recipe will insert the variable value into the URI for the user to click on. In this case, the `$status$` field variable inserts the HTTP status code into the Google search query URI such that the status code is passed within the URI when it is clicked on.

By utilizing the field name substitution in the label and the URI, you can create a full array of dynamically named workflow actions that can be generated to enable your users to link to other internal or external resources.

There's more...

While workflow actions can be a convenient way to link to external resources based on the presence of certain fields in your events, it is possible to link data to external resources in other ways.

Triggering a Google search from the chart drilldown options

Workflow actions work well when you are in an event-based view, but sometimes, you might wish to perform a Google search when looking at data within a visualization. By adding some minor tweaks to the SimpleXML in a chart element, you can have the chart linked to Google as well.

```
<drilldown>
<link target="_blank">
http://google.com/search?q=$row.sourcetype$
</link>
</drilldown>
```

You can replace `$row.sourcetype$` with the correct chart variable you need to pass to your Google search.

See also

▶ The *Creating a ticket for application errors* recipe

▶ The *Searching ARIN for a given IP address* recipe

▶ The *Adding hostnames to IP addresses* recipe

Creating a ticket for application errors

When errors or other notable events are detected in your application events, you might wish to carry out some further investigation or remediation measures. Often, this involves creating a ticket in a system to assign and track progress.

This recipe will show you how you can take error code data from your search results in Splunk and have it open a ticket in your helpdesk system, using a Splunk workflow action. Of course, there are tons of different ticketing systems in use out there, and there isn't a one-size-fits-all approach. So, while the principles of this recipe are sound, you might need to configure things slightly differently to work with the ticketing system in use within your own business.

Getting ready

To step through this recipe, you will need a running Splunk Enterprise server, with the sample data loaded from *Chapter 1, Play Time – Getting Data In*. You should be familiar with navigating the Splunk user interface.

How to do it...

Follow the steps in this recipe to set up a workflow action that allows us to generate a ticket when errors are detected:

1. Log in to your Splunk server.
2. Select the **Operational Intelligence** application.
3. Click on the **Settings** menu and then on the **Fields** menu option.

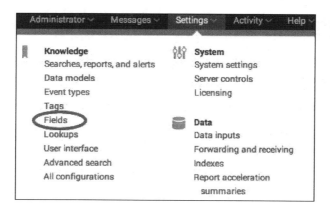

4. Click on the **Workflow actions** link.

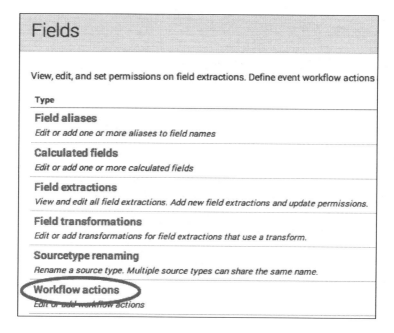

5. Click on **New**.

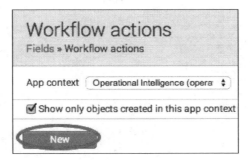

6. Ensure that the destination app is the **operational_intelligence** app.

7. Enter `Open_JIRA_Issue` in the **Name** field. This name must not contain any spaces or special characters. It will be used as the internal name of the action and is not the text that will be made visible.

8. Enter `Open JIRA Issue for $errorCode$` in the **Label** field. The label is the text that will appear in the workflow dropdowns. It can contain a field name enclosed with dollar signs, which will be replaced with the value of that field in the event.

9. Enter `*` in the **Apply to the following fields** field.

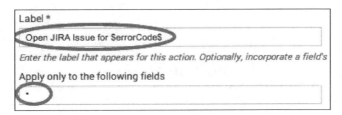

10. In the **Show action in** dropdown, select **Both**, and in the **Action type** dropdown, select **link**:

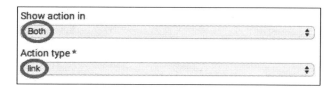

11. In the **URI** field under **Link configuration**, enter `http://127.0.0.1:8000/jira/issue/create`.

12. Select **Post** in the **Link method** dropdown:

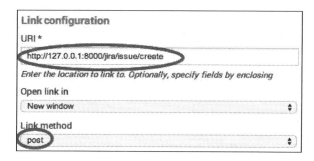

13. Enter `error` in the first **Post arguments** field and `$errorCode$` in the second field.

14. Click on **Save**.

 When creating workflow actions that you wish to share with other users, make sure that you update the permissions. More information on permissions can be found at `http://docs.splunk.com/Documentation/Splunk/latest/Knowledge/Manageknowledgeobjectpermissions`.

How it works...

This recipe is somewhat theory based and will not work with our sample data as, first, we do not have an `errorCode` field in our dataset, and secondly, the workflow action configuration will need to point to your own ticketing system. However, this recipe works in a very similar way to the other recipes in this chapter that use workflow actions to improve the integration with external resources. The difference with this recipe is that it uses an HTTP `POST` method to submit data to the external system. When configuring a `POST` request, you need to specify the field names and values within the body of the request. This differs from the simple `GET` method that does everything via the query string. `POST` requests are useful when you are sending a larger number of fields or a larger amount of data .Some browsers or web servers cannot handle sending that much data using a `GET` request. In this case, you might wish to *post* a number of different fields to the ticketing system.

This recipe showed how tickets can be generated using a workflow action. However, often, tickets can be generated based upon an e-mail being sent, containing the information needed. Splunk's native alerting functionality can be used to do this automatically when an alert is triggered. Additionally, the `sendresults` command on the Splunk apps site might also be useful.

There's more...

Workflow actions can also be configured at the backend rather than using the Splunk GUI. To do this, you will need to create/edit the `workflow_actions.conf` file in the application's local directory.

Adding a workflow action manually in Splunk

You can manually add a workflow action to Splunk by updating the configuration files directly. To add our action to open a ticket for application errors, add the following code to `$SPLUNK_HOME/etc/apps/operational_intelligence/local/workflow_actions.conf`:

```
[Open_JIRA_Issue]
display_location = both
fields = *
label = Open JIRA issue for $errorCode$
link.method = post
link.postargs.1.key = error
link.postargs.1.value = $errorCode$
link.target = blank
link.uri = http://127.0.0.1:8000/jira/issue/create
type = link
```

See also

▶ The *Triggering a Google search for a given error* recipe

▶ The *Searching ARIN for a given IP address* recipe

Looking up inventory from an external database

In this recipe, you will install and leverage DB Connect to search an external database's product inventory table. You will then pull this data back into Splunk and turn it into a local lookup that harvests the data once per day. This product inventory table will be used in the next chapter.

[DB Connect has a dedicated Splunk manual that can be found at `http://docs.splunk.com/Documentation/DBX/latest/DeployDBX`.]

Getting ready

To step through this recipe, you will need a running Splunk Enterprise server, with the sample data loaded from *Chapter 1, Play Time – Getting Data In*. You should be familiar with navigating the Splunk user interface.

Additionally, it is recommended that you have one of the following supported databases installed:

▶ DB2

▶ MS SQL

▶ MySQL

▶ Oracle

▶ Sybase

▶ HyperSQL

▶ PostgreSQL

▶ H2

▶ SQLite

▶ Adaptive Server Enterprise v15.7 Developer Edition

DB Connect might work with other databases and data stores using the generic ODBC driver provided with the application, but this is **not** guaranteed.

How to do it...

Follow the steps in this recipe to generate a local Splunk lookup using data from an external database and DB Connect:

1. In your database application, create a new database called `productdb`, and within the database, create a new table called `productInventory`. Insert the contents of the provided `productInventory.csv` file into the new database table. The new table will resemble the following screenshot:

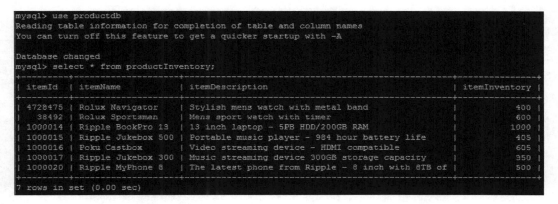

2. Once the DB table is built, you need to install the DB Connect application in order to connect to it. From the drop-down application menu, select **Find More Apps**.

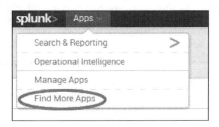

3. Search for the Splunk DB Connect application, and then, select it to install it. You will have to enter your Splunk.com account credentials after hitting the **Install free** button.

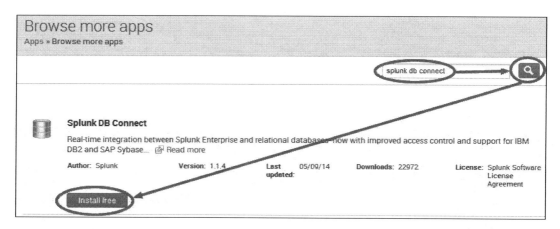

> If your environment has no Internet access, you can download the DB Connect application from the Splunk app store at `http://apps.splunk.com/app/958`. Once it is downloaded, you can upload and install the application to your Splunk environment by selecting **Manage Apps** from step 2.

4. When prompted, select to restart Splunk, and DB Connect will continue its installation.

5. After logging back in, you will see a DB Connect **Install successful** message. Click on the **Set up now** button.

6. On the next screen, we will leave the default settings as they are. If you are connecting to a large amount of data, the heap size might need to be increased, as this will allocate more memory and result in faster performance.

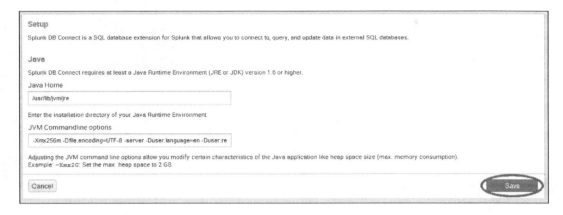

7. Click on the **Settings** menu on the top-right corner, and then, click on the new option called **External Databases**.

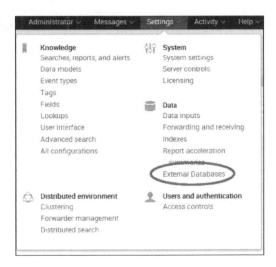

8. Click on the **New** button, and you will be presented with a configuration screen. Enter `productdb` as the name and enter all other details on the configuration screen to connect to your specific `productdb` database, using your database username and password.

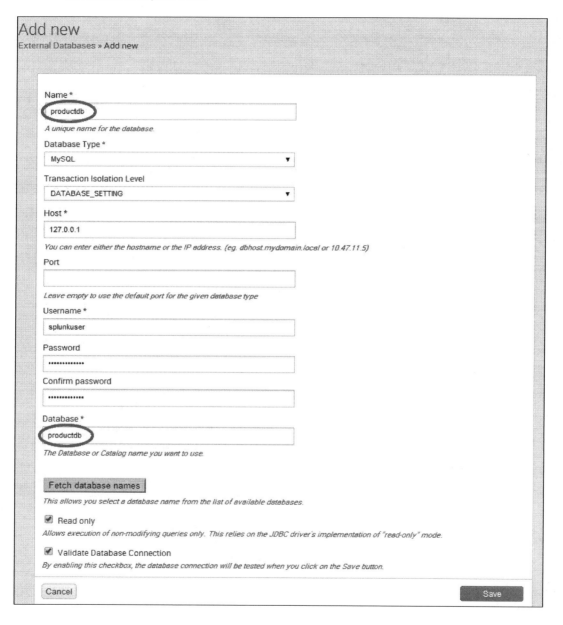

If you receive an error message about missing drivers, you might need to install the JDBC driver for the database you are using. For example, the MySQL JDBC driver is not installed by default. The process to install the driver is simple and is well documented at `http://docs.splunk.com/Documentation/DBX/latest/DeployDBX/Installdrivers`. Once the driver is installed, you will need to restart Splunk and return to this configuration screen.

9. After saving, the new database connection will be created and displayed.

Name ⇕	Database Type ⇕	Transaction Isolation Level ⇕	Host ⇕	Port ⇕	Database ⇕	Additional JDBC Parameters ⇕	Sharing ⇕	Status ⇕	Actions
productdb	mysql	DATABASE_SETTING	127.0.0.1		productdb		App | Permissions	Enabled | Disable	Clone | Delete

10. Return to the **Operational Intelligence** application from the application dropdown, and enter the following search in the search bar:

    ```
    | dbquery productdb limit=1000 "select * from
    productInventory;"
    ```

11. The contents of the `productdb` table should now be displayed inside Splunk.

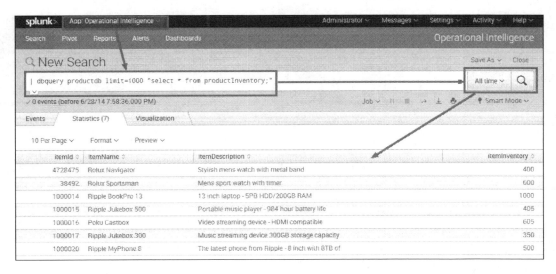

12. Amend the search as follows in order to save the database data as a local lookup inside Splunk:

```
| dbquery productdb limit=1000 "select * from
productInventory;" | outputlookup productInventory.csv
```

13. Run this new search to create the lookup. Then, save it as a report and name it `generate_productInventory_dblookup`.

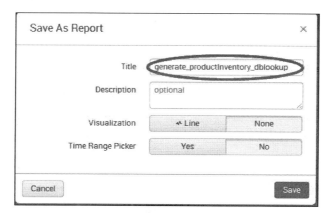

14. Click on the **Save** button, and on the next screen, select the **Schedule** link and set **Schedule** to **Run every day**.

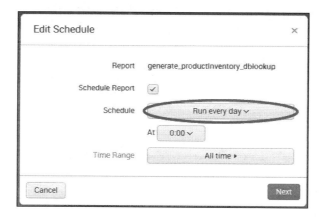

15. Click on the **Next** button, and then, on the next screen, hit the **Save** button to save the report. This search will now pull the inventory data back from our product database once per day and turn it into a local lookup for use in Splunk.

How it works...

DB Connect enables real-time integration between Splunk and traditional relational databases. In this recipe, you installed the DB Connect application and configured it to talk to a product inventory table in your external `productdb` database. When installed, DB Connect sets up something called a Java Bridge Server that is essentially a **Java Virtual Machine** (**JVM**) that is constantly running in the background. The Java Bridge Server helps speed up connectivity to external databases by allocating memory and caching a lot of the metadata associated with the database tables. Once the `productdb` database was configured through DB Connect, you were able to execute standard SQL inside a Splunk search and return the contents of the `productInventory` table to Splunk. Once the data is in Splunk, it is treated the same as any other data inside of Splunk, and you were able to very easily turn the data into a local lookup using the `outputlookup` command.

There's more...

In this recipe, we chose to pull the data out of the database and create a lookup locally in Splunk. This is likely to be a best practice approach, as it is unlikely that you would want users constantly polling your database directly. However, rather than creating the lookup locally, DB Connect does also allow you to look up data in the database directly. In addition, DB Connect is able to monitor external database tables and index content into Splunk as it is written to the table.

Use DB Connect for direct external DB lookups

Rather than creating the lookup locally inside Splunk, as we did with this recipe, Splunk DB Connect allows you to create a lookup table that uses an external database table as its source. If you navigate to the **Lookups** screen (**Settings | Lookups**), you will notice a new line item called **Database lookups**. This was added when DB Connect was installed.

Clicking on **Add new** allows you to add a new lookup. Give the lookup a name—in this case, we used `productInventory_dblookup`—and select the `productdb` database and the `productInventory` table. After a few seconds, the **Fill all columns** button will become active, and clicking on this button will populate all the fields in the table as lookup fields.

Add new

Lookups » Database Lookups » **Add new**

Database lookups allow you to fetch data from an external SQL database but still leveraging the splunk lookup command.

Lookup Name *

```
productInventory_dblookup
```

A unique name for the database lookup. A corresponding lookup definition will be automatically added.

Database *

```
productdb                                              ▼
```

Database Table

```
productInventory
```

Enter the database table name (double click for suggestions).

Fill all columns

Fill all columns for the given table.

Lookup Fields

Please specify the fields/columns that are supported by this lookup

itemId	Delete
itemName	Delete
itemDescription	Delete
itemInventory	Delete

Add another field

☐ Configure advanced Database lookup settings
Advanced settings allow you to specify a SQL query that is executed.

Cancel   Save

After clicking on **Save**, return to the **Operational Intelligence** search bar and execute the following search:

```
index=main sourcetype=log4j itemId=*
| lookup local=1 productInventory_dblookup itemId AS itemId
OUTPUT itemInventory AS itemInventory
```

In this search, we look for events that contain `itemId` and then use the direct database lookup to return `itemInventory` for `itemId` in the event. You should notice that `itemInventory` is populated as a new field for the event. Also notice that we used `local=1` in the previous search. This is because DB Connect database lookups are constrained only to the search head where DB Connect is installed.

This approach might have some advantages, as it gets data from the database directly, but this can also be a disadvantage. Pulling the data back on a periodic basis and creating a local lookup, as we did in the earlier recipe, will result in a lookup that performs faster and has less impact on any production database.

 DB Connect is bundled with a generic ODBC driver. This driver allows you to connect to other data stores outside of traditional RDBMS databases. For example, DB Connect can be used to connect into Hadoop and query data directly from the Hive or Hadoop vendor data products such as Cloudera Impala—very cool!

See also

▶ The *Looking up product code descriptions* recipe

Summary

The key takeaways from this chapter are as follows:

▶ Use lookup tables to add more user-friendly data to search results

▶ Create state tables that can track data over long periods of time

▶ Create workflow actions that can link to external resources that can't be added in lookup tables

▶ Automate tasks such as opening helpdesk tickets using data extracted from Splunk

▶ The DB Connect application allows for a powerful connectivity between external databases or between ODBC/JDBC data stores and Splunk

8

Being Proactive – Creating Alerts

In this chapter, we will learn about alerting capabilities within Splunk. You will learn about:

- ▶ Alerting on abnormal web page response times
- ▶ Alerting on errors during checkout in real time
- ▶ Alerting on abnormal user behavior
- ▶ Alerting on failure and triggering a scripted response
- ▶ Alerting when predicted sales exceed inventory

Introduction

Throughout the previous chapters in this book, you created a great deal of Splunk searches, including historic searches that look back over a period of time and real-time searches. In this chapter, you will learn about alerting—arguably, one of Splunk's most powerful features.

A key part of gaining complete operational intelligence is the ability to be proactive rather than reactive. Periodic, ad hoc searching of the data for certain conditions might provide some operational insight, but a better approach would be to continually monitor the data and know immediately when certain conditions are met. For example, instead of reacting to a network outage after it has occurred, it would be better to proactively look for the factors that could lead to a network outage and prevent it from occurring in the first place. It is this type of proactive approach that Splunk's alerting functionality allows for.

In this chapter, we will continue to build our Operational Intelligence application and incorporate alerting for a number of different scenarios. You will learn how to implement the different types of alerts and leverage a number of different alert actions.

About Splunk alerts

As with many features of Splunk, alerts are powered-off underlying searches. These underlying searches can either run on a schedule against historically indexed data or run against real-time data as it flows into Splunk. Alerts can then be triggered every time a search runs or when certain conditions are met as a result of the search.

Additionally, all alerting in Splunk can be throttled such that alerts do not continuously fire if similar conditions are met repeatedly, and this will be covered later in the chapter.

 Splunk has a dedicated manual for alerting, which can be found at `http://docs.splunk.com/Documentation/Splunk/latest/Alert/Aboutalerts`.

Types of alerts

There are three types of alerts, and these are detailed in the following table:

Alert	Description	Trigger	Example
Scheduled alert	This is an alert based on a historical search that runs periodically in accordance with a set schedule.	This triggers an alert whenever the results of the historic search meet a particular condition defined in the alert. It is usually less resource intensive than other alert types and used when immediate action is not required.	An example of a scheduled alert would be to trigger an alert whenever the number of web server errors exceeds 200 in any 30-minute interval.
Per-result alert	This is an alert based on a real-time search that is set to run over **All time**.	This triggers an alert every time the base search returns a result. It is useful to know immediately when a matching result is detected.	An example of a per-result alert would be to trigger an alert whenever a web server error occurs on a specified host. To avoid a flood of alerts, this can optionally be throttled to alert only once per time period, such as once per 10 minutes.

Alert	Description	Trigger	Example
Rolling-window alert	This is an alert based on real-time search that is set to run over a user-defined, rolling time window.	This triggers an alert whenever events pass through the rolling window that match the particular condition defined in the alert.	An example of a rolling-window alert would be to trigger an alert whenever there are five consecutive errors of the same type for a specific session ID within a 10-minute window, but they are optionally throttled such that only one alert for a particular session ID is sent within a 30-minute timeframe.

In this chapter, you will gain experience in creating all three types of alerts and apply them to real-world operational intelligence examples.

Trigger conditions

Alerts are triggered when the results of the search meet specific conditions. For example, you might have a condition that specifies to only alert when the count of results is greater than X. Triggering conditions are set when you set up the alert, and the following table lists the various conditions that are available:

Type	Description
Per-result	This triggers whenever a search returns a result. It is only available for real-time alerts and leveraged by the per-result alert type.
Number of results	This triggers based on the number of search results. The options include greater than, less than, equal to, and not equal to.
Number of hosts	This triggers based on the number of hosts seen. The options include greater than, less than, equal to, and not equal to.
Number of sources	This triggers based on the number of sources seen. The options include greater than, less than, equal to, and not equal to.
Custom	This triggers based on a custom search condition. Think of this as sticking a custom search at the end of the base search, for example, `search count > 20`.

Alert actions

So, what happens when an alert fires in Splunk? Well, that is up to you, as Splunk offers a number of possible actions out of the box, and these are detailed in the following table:

Action	Description
E-mail notification	This sends an e-mail to one or more specified individuals together with details of the alert that has fired. This e-mail can be substantially customized in Version 6 and is probably the most commonly used action.
Execute a script	This executes a custom script when the alert is triggered and provides a very powerful functionality. For example, you might have a script that opens a ticket in a third-party ticketing system when an alert is triggered.
RSS notification	This creates an RSS feed for all alerts that have triggered for a particular search. Users can then subscribe to this feed.
Summary indexing	This writes data from the alert to a summary index. It is best used with statistical commands.
Display in Alert manager	Splunk has a built-in Alert manager console that will list all the triggered alerts that have been selected to be displayed in the Alert manager.

Multiple alert actions can be selected for a given alert. For example, you might wish to send an e-mail and also execute a script when a particular alert is triggered.

There are commands for Splunk that will allow you to craft a search and send an e-mail directly from the search itself. These can be used in a fashion similar to alerting if the search that contains the commands is scheduled. One of these commands is `sendemail`, which is bundled with Splunk and allows search results to be sent to specified e-mail addresses. Another command is `sendresults`, which is developed by Discovered Intelligence and available for free in the Splunk app store. The `sendresults` command allows you to dynamically evaluate where to send the search results, based on the search results themselves.

Alerting on abnormal web page response times

It is important that our web application remains responsive for users. Sites that lag frequently put off users and can result in them going elsewhere or lost sales. In *Chapter 2, Diving into Data – Search and Report*, you completed a recipe that analyzes average response times over a given period. In this recipe, you will create a scheduled alert to identify response times that are abnormal (that is, not within a normal range).

Getting ready

To step through this recipe, you will need a running Splunk Enterprise server, with the sample data loaded from *Chapter 1, Play Time – Getting Data In*. You should be familiar with navigating the Splunk user interface. You should also have configured the e-mail settings on your Splunk to enable the delivery of e-mail alerts.

> Should you be running your Splunk server on a desktop PC for the purposes of this book and wondering how to configure the e-mail settings, there is a good Splunk blog posting on configuring Splunk to work with Gmail and Yahoo Mail at `http://blogs.splunk.com/tag/gmail/`.

How to do it...

Follow the steps in this recipe to create an alert that identifies abnormal response times:

1. Log in to your Splunk server.

2. Select the **Operational Intelligence** application.

3. Ensure that the time range picker is set to **Last 60 Minutes**, and type the following search into the Splunk search bar. Then, click on the magnifying glass icon or hit *Enter*:

   ```
   sourcetype=access_combined index=main | stats max(response)
   AS MAX by uri_path | join uri_path [search earliest=-25h
   latest=-24h sourcetype=access_combined index=main | stats
   avg(response) AS AVG by uri_path] | eval MAG=round(MAX/AVG)
   ```

> This search relies on data being indexed on your Splunk server 25 hours ago. If this data is not present, you might need to adjust the subsearch's `earliest` and `latest` times accordingly.

4. Once the search completes, you should see tabulated data. In the **Save As** dropdown, select **Alert**:

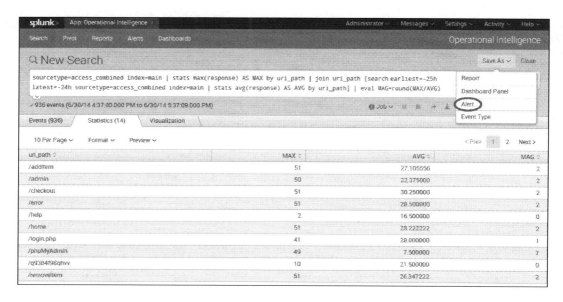

5. A pop-up box will appear. Give the alert a title of cp08_abnormal_webpage_ response. Select **Scheduled** as the alert type, and select **Run every hour** in the **Time Range** field. Select **Custom** as the trigger condition, and enter search MAG>5 in the **Custom Condition** field Then, click on **Next**.

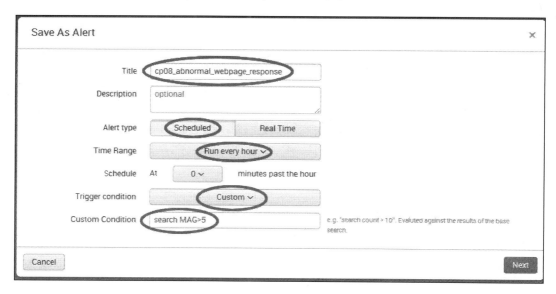

6. The alert configuration screen will be displayed. Perform the following steps on this screen:

    1. Check the **List in Triggered Alerts** checkbox.

    2. In the **Severity** dropdown, select **Medium**.

    3. Select the **Send Email** checkbox.

    4. Enter a valid e-mail address in the **To** box; this is where the alert will go.

    5. In the **Include** section, check **Link to Alert**, **Link to Results**, and **Trigger Condition**.

    6. Scroll down to **Sharing**, and in **Permissions** select the **Shared in App** option.

    7. Verify that the given details are entered correctly, and then, click on **Save**.

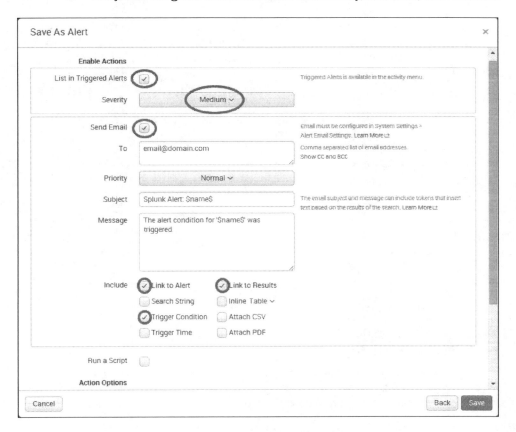

7. Click on **View Alert**. A summary screen should be displayed, and your first alert is now configured and set to run every hour in accordance with the schedule. The alert should trigger but might take some time depending on when you scheduled the alert.

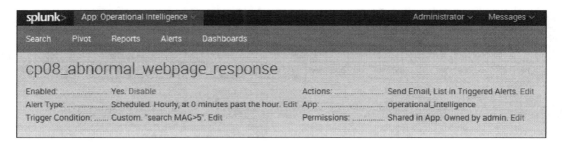

8. When the alert triggers, you should receive an e-mail similar to the following screenshot. Note that the link to the alert, the link to the results, and the trigger condition in the body of the e-mail are as specified when configuring the alert.

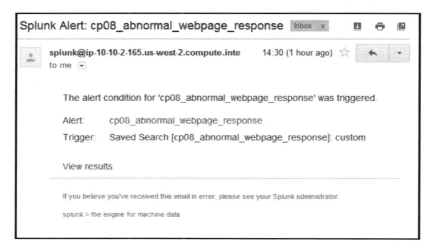

How it works...

In this recipe, you created a search to look for abnormal web page response times by creating an alert to trigger when the maximum response time in the last hour for a given web page is greater than 5 times the average response time for that page at the same time the previous day.

We selected to get the average from the same period yesterday, as the data might be abnormal today. You might wish to look back over a wider period, such as 7 days, to get a more accurate average. Alternatively, you might have a hardcoded threshold for the number of milliseconds within which a web page must respond.

Let's break the search down piece by piece.

Search fragment	Description
`index=main sourcetype=access_combined`	You should now be familiar with this search from the earlier recipes in this book.
`| stats max(response) AS MAX by uri_path`	Using the `stats` command with the `max` function, we first identify the maximum response time per web page or `uri_path` in the past hour. We name this a field `MAX`.
`| join uri_path [search earliest=-24h latest=-23h sourcetype=access_combined index=main | stats avg(response) AS AVG by uri_path]`	Using the `join` command, we join the results of another search with our results. This search looks back over the same past hour period, but 24 hours earlier. The average response time is calculated for each page and given a field name of `AVG`.
`| eval MAG=round(MAX/AVG)`	Using the `MAX` and `AVG` fields, we calculate how many times the `MAX` value is greater than the `AVG` value (that is, the order of magnitude). This then gives us a `MAG` field.
`| search MAG>5`	This is not in our actual search but represents the custom alert condition we selected for our alert. Behind the scenes, Splunk essentially adds this to the search, and if any values are returned, the alert is triggered.

There's more...

This alert used the scheduled alert type and is based on a **historical** search that runs periodically in accordance with the hourly schedule you set. In terms of alert actions, you selected to have an e-mail sent out each time the alert is triggered and also for the triggered alert to appear in the Alert manager inside Splunk.

Viewing triggered alerts in Splunk's Alert manager

Assuming that an alert has been triggered, you can view the alert in the Alert manager by clicking on the **Activity** drop-down menu in the top-right corner of the screen and selecting **Triggered Alerts**.

Once the screen has loaded, you will see all of the alerts that have triggered till date. There are not too many management actions you can take on the triggered alerts, although you can delete them from the list or select to edit the underlying alert if any tweaks are needed. Clicking on **View Results** of any alert will pop open a new screen with the results of the underlying search that powers the alert. Basic filtering and search capability are also provided for the triggered alerts in the list.

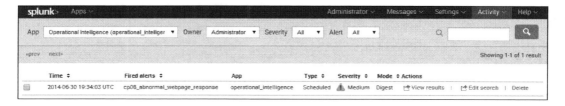

See also

▸ The *Alerting on errors during checkout in real time* recipe

▸ The *Alerting on abnormal user behavior* recipe

▸ The *Alerting on failure and triggering a scripted response* recipe

Alerting on errors during checkout in real time

A very powerful feature of Splunk is the ability to trigger alerts based on specific conditions in real-time events. From the perspective of operational intelligence, real-time alerting provides the ability to be notified of something that requires immediate action. Real-time alerting in Splunk is based upon an underlying real-time search.

In this recipe, you will create a real-time alert that will trigger anytime there is an error during the checkout stage of our online store. The checkout stage in the purchasing process is where the payment details are submitted by the customer and our sales transactions ultimately occur. Errors here can result in lost sales revenue and lost customers. It is, therefore, important to immediately understand if errors occur such that they can be remediated as soon as possible.

Getting ready

To step through this recipe, you will need a running Splunk Enterprise server, with the sample data loaded from *Chapter 1, Play Time – Getting Data In*. You should be familiar with navigating the Splunk user interface. You should also have configured the e-mail settings on your Splunk server to enable the delivery of e-mail alerts.

How to do it...

Follow the steps in this recipe to create a real-time alert when checkout errors occur:

1. Log in to your Splunk server.

2. Select the **Operational Intelligence** application.

3. In the **Search** bar, enter the following search:

   ```
   index=main sourcetype=log4j
   | transaction threadId maxspan=5m
   | search requestType="checkout" result="failure"
   | stats count by requestType, threadId, sessionId,
   customerId, orderId, invoice, paymentId, numberOfItems,
   total, result
   ```

4. Change the search time period to a 5-minute window by selecting **5 minute window** from the real-time **Presets** column on the time range picker.

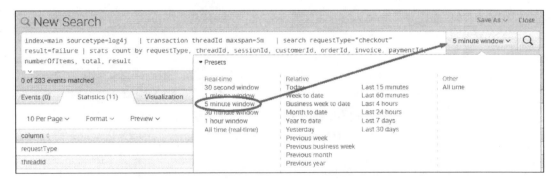

5. The search will run but might not produce any results if there are no results to display. This is OK. Click on the **Save As** dropdown and select **Alert**.

6. A pop-up box will appear. Enter `cp08_realtime_checkout_error` in the **Title** field. Select **Real Time** in the **Alert type** field and change the **Trigger condition** field to **Number of Results**. Select **Greater than** and `0` in the **Number of results is** field and then click on **Next**.

7. The alert configuration screen will be displayed. The configuration of this alert is slightly more complex than the previous recipe. Perform the following steps on this screen:

   1. Check the **List in Triggered Alerts** checkbox.

   2. In the **Severity** dropdown, select **High**; this simply classifies the alert severity in Splunk.

   3. Check the **Send Email** checkbox, as we want to send an e-mail when the alert fires.

   4. Specify an e-mail address that the alert should go to in the **To** textbox.

   5. In the **Priority** dropdown, select **High**.

   6. In the **Include** section, check **Link to Alert, Link to Results, Inline Table**, and **Trigger Time**. These settings will ensure that there are links in the e-mail to both the alert and the results in Splunk. The **Inline Table** option will tabulate the results in the e-mail body.

   7. For the **When triggered, execute actions** field, select the **For each result** option.

   8. Select the **Throttle** checkbox.

   9. In the **Suppress results containing field value** textbox, enter `threadid`.

   10. In the **Suppress triggering for** textbox, select `600` and **seconds()**.

11. For the **Permissions** field under **Sharing**, select the **Shared in App** option.

12. Verify that the given details are entered correctly, and then, click on **Save**.

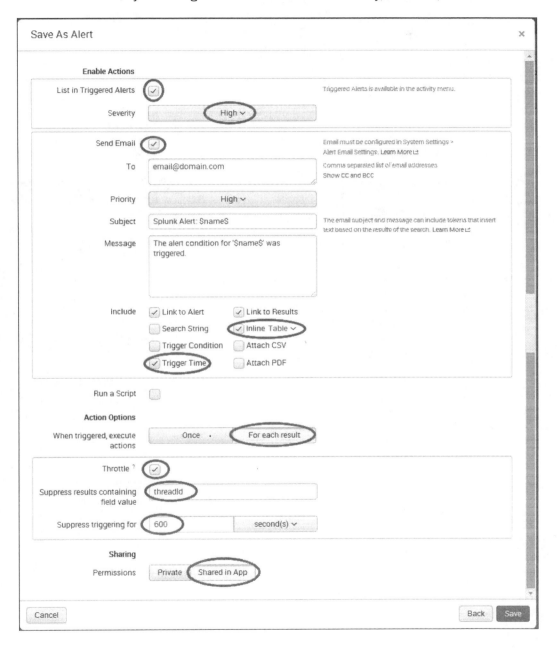

8. Click on **View Alert**. A summary screen should be displayed, and the alert is now mostly configured.

9. Unfortunately, at the time of writing this book, creating the alert in this way does not respect the 5-minute window we selected at the beginning, so we must edit the search and manually set this. This is relatively simple to do. Click on the **Settings** menu in the top-right corner, and select **Searches, reports, and alerts**.

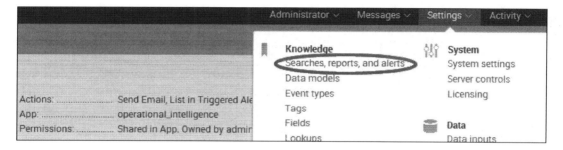

10. Search for cp08 to bring up the cp08 searches, and select the **cp08_realtime_checkout_error** search that you just created.

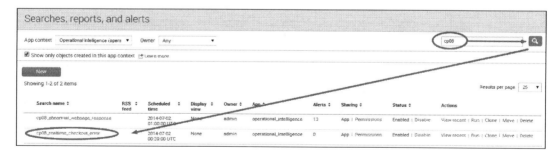

11. The details of the search will be listed. Modify the earliest time to be `rt-5m` and the latest time to be `rt-0m`. Then, click on **Save**.

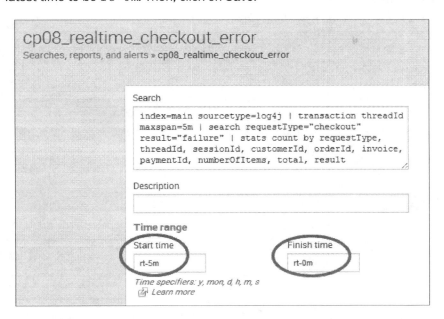

12. The search is now correctly configured and running in real time. When the alert triggers, you should receive an e-mail similar to the following screenshot. Note the **Trigger Time** and the key fields from the data are included in the e-mail body as an inline table, as specified when configuring the alert.

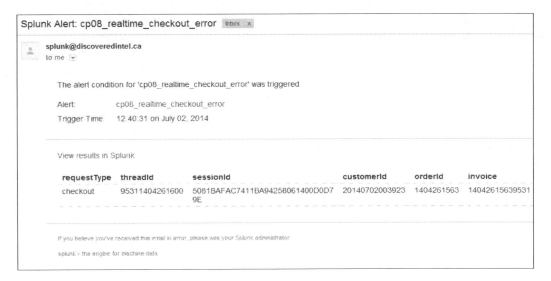

How it works...

This recipe was a little complex, so let's step through it methodically. In this recipe, we were looking at identifying checkout failures. To do this, the search looked for failure events in the application logs at the checkout stage. Specifically, we were looking for database update response failures, where payment information had been submitted to the backend application database, but a failure had been returned in the logs. The web application log events are broken into transactions known as threads. Each thread has a common `threadId` to link them together, and the events within a unique thread typically consist of requests and responses. The real-time search was set to look over a 5-minute window, as a distinct thread is unlikely to take longer than this.

Let's break down the search piece by piece.

Search fragment	Description
`index=main sourcetype=log4j`	We have selected to search the application logs in the main index.
`| transaction threadId maxspan=5m`	Using the `transaction` command, we first group all the events with the same `threadId` together into multivalued transactional events. We have selected to look over a transactional time span of 5 minutes, as our individual threads should not take any longer than this.
`| search requestType="checkout" result=failure`	Once the events are grouped into transactions by `threadId`, we search only for the threads that pertain to the checkout process. We also look for where a `failure` result is returned from the backend database update.
`| stats count by requestType, threadId, sessionId, customerId, orderId, invoice, paymentId, numberOfItems, total, result`	If/when a failure event occurs, the `stats` command is used to put the relevant field values into a nice tabulated format and eliminate duplicate values. These values are tabulated in the e-mail alert.

In this recipe, we used a rolling-window alert type and set the search to run over a 5 minute real-time rolling window. This window allows for all events in a single thread transaction to occur.

When configuring the alert, we selected the alert to trigger whenever one or more events occur that match the failure condition, as we want to be notified whenever an error occurs. We also chose to execute an action for each result, as each result will pertain to a new error. This means that if we get two errors back at once, then two alerts will be triggered, one for each error. We selected to throttle the alert on `threadId` such that an alert for a unique `threadId` values will not be triggered more than once. This throttling is sensible, as there is no need to know about the same error over and over again. We selected to throttle the alert for 600 seconds, or 10 minutes, meaning that no further alerts will be triggered for a given `threadId` for 10 minutes. However, if the error reoccurs after 10 minutes for the same `threadId`, then another alert will be triggered. In this case, `threadId` in our events are unique, so the likelihood of reoccurrence of a transaction with the same `threadId` is zero.

Within the e-mail itself, we specified to include the results as an inline table and to include the trigger time. These inclusions help make the alert a lot more actionable to the person at the receiving end. The trigger time will let the receiver know exactly when the failure event occurs, and the inline table contains key information related to the event. This helps ensure that the receiver of the alert has all the information they need to investigate, without needing to log in to Splunk and run additional searches.

> By default, only users with the admin role can run and save real-time searches, schedule searches, or create alerts. Use caution when granting users permissions to schedule their own searches and alerts, as they can write searches that are resource intensive.

There's more...

This recipe was as much about real-time alerting as it was about real-time searching. Real-time searching has limited value on its own, unless you are staring at the screen, waiting for data to come into Splunk. However, when paired with alerting, this functionality really comes into its own. Real-time searches and alerts can be more taxing on system resources than their scheduled counterparts, so care should be taken to ensure that they are efficient and delivering value. The **Jobs** screen can be helpful in understanding which real-time searches are running on your system. Additionally, alerts can be configured directly by editing a configuration file in a manner similar to editing searches.

> Indexed real-time search can be enabled to increase performance and reduce the amount of system resources used by real-time searching and alerting in Splunk. For more information on this, review the documentation at `http://docs.splunk.com/Documentation/Splunk/latest/Search/Aboutrealtimesearches`.

Building alerts via a configuration file

As alerts are just extensions of Splunk searches, the underlying configuration details related to an alert are written to the app's local directory in a file named `savedsearches.conf` alongside the search.

The `savedsearches.conf` file for our Operational Intelligence application is located at `$SPLUNK_HOME$/etc/apps/operational_intelligence/local/savedsearches.conf`.

If you open this file, you will see entries related to the two searches and alerts you have created in this chapter until now. Notice all the additional configuration fields that specify the alert criteria. If you were to copy and paste one of the searches and all the fields but give it a new name (`[name]`), it would create a duplicate alert inside Splunk. Changes made to this `.conf` file will require us to restart Splunk as with many other `.conf` file changes.

You might be wondering why you might need to configure an alert via `savedsearches.conf`. It can be useful if you want to create multiple alerts, where the alert configuration is mostly similar, but the underlying search is slightly different. Editing `savedsearches.conf` directly will likely be a lot quicker than going into the GUI and setting up each alert one by one.

Identify the real-time searches that are running

A quick and useful way to see what real-time searches are currently running on your Splunk environment is to leverage the **Jobs** screen. From the main menu in the top-right corner, click on the **Activity** dropdown and select **Jobs**.

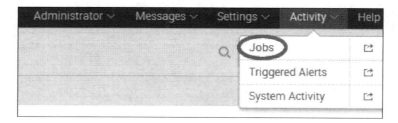

The **Jobs** screen will load. Select **Running** to view all the running jobs in the Operational Intelligence application. You will notice that the **cp08_realtime_checkout_error** search is displayed, and the **Status** column is set to **Running (100%)**. All real-time searches in Splunk will be displayed with a **Running (100%)** status, and this is a quick way of identifying them. Historical searches will increment up to 100 percent as they progress and then disappear out of the running jobs once 100 percent is reached and the search finalized. However, real-time searches will stay at 100 percent forever until they are disabled or deleted. If a restart of Splunk is performed, all real-time searches will restart automatically when Splunk comes back up.

See also

▶ The *Alerting on abnormal web page response times* recipe

▶ The *Alerting on abnormal user behavior* recipe

▶ The *Alerting on failure and triggering a scripted response* recipe

Alerting on abnormal user behavior

In this recipe, you will write a relatively simple real-time per-result type of alert to look for abnormal user behavior. The abnormal behavior you will be looking for would be successful payments that did not go through the checkout process.

Getting ready

To step through this recipe, you will need a running Splunk Enterprise server, with the sample data loaded from *Chapter 1, Play Time – Getting Data In*. You should be familiar with navigating the Splunk user interface. You should also have configured the e-mail settings on your Splunk server to enable the delivery of e-mail alerts.

How to do it...

Follow the steps in this recipe to create an alert when abnormal user behavior occurs:

1. Log in to your Splunk server.

2. Select the **Operational Intelligence** application.

3. In the **Search** bar, enter the following search over **Last 24 hours**:

   ```
   index=main sourcetype=log4j requestType=checkout
   (numberOfItems>10  OR total>3000)
   | table ipAddress, numberOfItems, total, invoice,
   customerId, paymentId, orderId
   ```

4. The search will run but might not produce any results if there are no results to display, and this is OK. As in the previous recipes, click on the **Save As** dropdown and select **Alert**.

5. A pop-up box will appear. Enter cp08_abnormal_purchase as the title of. the alert. This time, select **Real Time** in the **Alert type** field and change the **Trigger condition** field to **Per-Result**. Then, click on **Next**.

6. The alert configuration screen will be displayed. The configuration of this alert is less complex than the previous recipe, and we will leave many of the default settings as is. Perform the following steps on this screen:

   1. Check the **List in Triggered Alerts** checkbox.

   2. Check the **Send Email** checkbox.

   3. Specify an e-mail address that the alert should go to in the **To** textbox.

4. In the **Include** section, check **Link to Alert**, **Link to Results**, and **Inline Table**.

5. Do not select the **Throttle** checkbox this time.

6. For the **Permissions** field under **Sharing**, select the **Shared in App** option.

7. Verify that the given details are entered correctly, and then, click on **Save**.

7. Click on **View Alert**. A summary screen should be displayed, and the alert is now configured and running in real time.

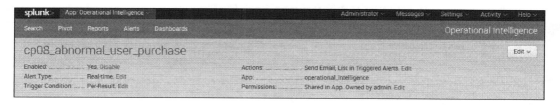

8. When the alert triggers, you should receive an e-mail similar to the following screenshot. Note that the key fields from the data are included in the e-mail body as an inline table, as specified when configuring the alert.

How it works...

This recipe revolved around a fairly simplistic search that looked for purchase events that included more than 10 items or where the total value of the purchase was greater than $3000. This might be considered abnormal in an environment where typical purchases involve two items and the total value is less than $1000. Simplicity aside, it served to illustrate how a per-result type of alert functions. Essentially, as soon as a matching result is detected, the alert is triggered. The search runs over **All time**, in real time, just waiting and watching for a matching event to come in. There was no throttling enabled, so if five matching events were to come in, then the alert will be triggered five times. A per-result type of alert would not have been suitable for the previous recipe, as the previous recipe relied on a number of events over time being transacted together.

There's more...

There are many different aspects of abnormal user behavior that you might wish to alert on, and this recipe touched on a rather obvious abnormality. For example, a more discrete user behavior might be where a successful order is made, but there is no checkout event. This might indicate unauthorized access to the backend database, where an order has been made without actually paying for it.

Alerting on abnormal user purchases without checkouts

In order to detect purchases where no checkout event exists, you will use a similar search as you did in the previous recipe (*Alerting on errors during checkout in real time*). A transactional search is required to group the entire thread together; once this has been performed, you can look for the threads that do not include a `requestType` value of checkout. The search will be as follows:

```
index=main sourcetype=log4j
| transaction threadId maxspan=5m
| search paymentReceived="Y" result="success" NOT
requestType="checkout"
| stats count by threadId, sessionId, orderId, invoice, paymentId,
result
```

You cannot use a per-result alert type for this alert, as it is transactional in nature, grouping events together over a time period. Instead, a rolling-window alert type should be used.

There are applications in the Splunk app store that leverage complex algorithms behind the scenes to help with the detection of operational anomalies and abnormal behavior.

See also

- The *Alerting on errors during checkout in real time* recipe
- The *Alerting on failure and triggering a scripted response* recipe
- The *Alerting when predicted sales exceed inventory* recipe

Alerting on failure and triggering a scripted response

By now, you have used every different type of alert available and many of the more common alert actions such as e-mailing. However, one extremely powerful alert action feature we are yet to touch upon is the ability to execute a script when an alert triggers.

In this recipe, you will create a simple real-time per-result alert that triggers when any 503 HTTP web server errors are detected. Upon triggering, the alert will execute a script that will write the details of the event to a local file on the server.

Getting ready

To step through this recipe, you will need a running Splunk Enterprise server, with the sample data loaded from *Chapter 1, Play Time – Getting Data In*. You should be familiar with navigating the Splunk user interface.

How to do it...

Follow the steps in this recipe to create an alert on failure and a scripted response:

1. The first thing to do is to write the script that Splunk will execute. Splunk is able to output a number of variables (0-8) to a script (this script will output all of them) to illustrate what each one does. An explanation of the variables follows after the recipe.

    For Unix/Linux Splunk installs, name your script `testscript.sh` and enter the following lines in the script. You can change the location that the file writes to if required.

    ```
    echo "
    `date`
    ARG0='$0'
    ARG1='$1'
    ARG2='$2'
    ARG3='$3'
    ARG4='$4'
    ARG5='$5'
    ARG6='$6'
    ARG7='$7'
    ARG8='$8'" >> "/var/tmp/splunk_testscript.log"
    ```

For Windows Splunk installs, name your script `testscript.bat` and enter the following lines in the script. You can change the location that the file writes to if required.

```
@echo off
date /T >> "c:\temp\splunk_testscript.log"
time /t >> "c:\temp\splunk_testscript.log"
echo %0 >> "c:\temp\splunk_testscript.log"
echo %1 >> "c:\temp\splunk_testscript.log"
echo %2 >> "c:\temp\splunk_testscript.log"
echo %3 >> "c:\temp\splunk_testscript.log"
echo %4 >> "c:\temp\splunk_testscript.log"
echo %5 >> "c:\temp\splunk_testscript.log"
echo %6 >> "c:\temp\splunk_testscript.log"
echo %7 >> "c:\temp\splunk_testscript.log"
echo %8 >> "c:\temp\splunk_testscript.log"
echo ***************>> "c:\temp\splunk_testscript.log"
```

2. Once the file is created, place the `testscript.sh`/`testscript.bat` file in the `$SPLUNK_HOME$/etc/apps/operational_intelligence/bin/scripts` directory. You might need to create the `scripts` directory if it doesn't exist. Ensure that file permissions are set appropriately based on the operating system you are using to allow Splunk to execute the script and write the results to the specified directory. Speak to your local administrator if you are unsure how to update these permissions

3. Log in to your Splunk server.

4. Select the **Operational Intelligence** application.

5. In the **Search** bar, enter the following search over **Last 24 hours**:

```
index=main sourcetype=access_combined status=503
```

6. The search will run but might not produce any results if there are no results to display. This is OK. As in the previous recipes, click on the **Save As** dropdown and select **Alert**.

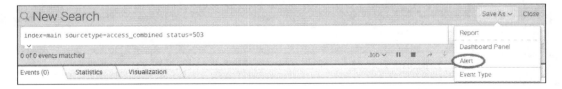

7. A pop-up box will appear. Enter `cp08_webserver_failure_script` as the title of the alert. Select **Real Time** in the **Alert type** field, and change the **Trigger condition** field to **Per-Result**. Then click on **Next**.

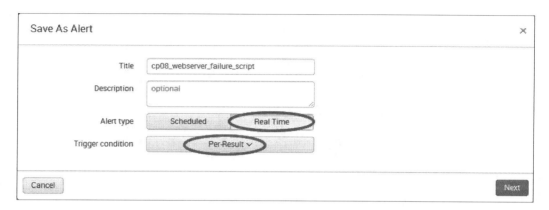

8. The alert configuration screen will display. The configuration of this alert is less complex than the previous recipe, and we will leave many of the default settings as is. Perform the following steps on this screen:

    1. Check the **Run a Script** checkbox and enter `testscript.sh` (or `testscript.bat`) in the **Filename** field.

    2. Scroll down to **Sharing**, and in **Permissions**, select the **Shared in App** option.

    3. Verify that the given details are entered correctly, and then, click on **Save**.

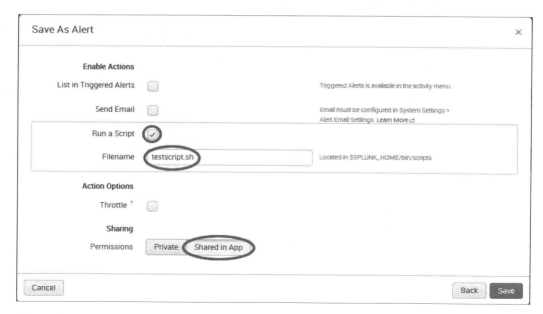

9. Click on **View Alert**. A summary screen should be displayed, and the alert is now configured and running in real time.

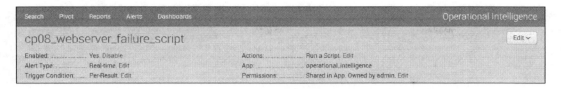

10. Navigate to the `/var/tmp` directory if on Linux or the `c:\temp` directory if on Windows. You should shortly see a `splunk_testscript.log` file; this might take 10 minutes or so to appear. Open up the log file, and you should see the details of all the alerts that have triggered.

How it works...

This was a per-result type of alert, meaning that any time a 503 error event is seen, the alert is triggered and the script executed. In this example, we wrote a simple script that wrote out details of the triggered alert to a local file on the Splunk server. Splunk can pass a number of variables to a script when an alert is triggered. The test script that you wrote in this recipe writes out every possible variable. There are eight variables in total, numbered from 0 to 8 (there is no 7), and these are listed in the following table:

Variable	Description
0	This denotes the script name
1	This denotes the number of events returned
2	This denotes the search terms
3	This denotes the fully qualified query string
4	This denotes the name of the report
5	This denotes the reason for the trigger
6	This denotes the browser URL to view the report
8	This denotes the file where the results for the search are stored

There might be times when you want to create a script that can also include the search results of the alert somewhere. In this case, you can configure your script to open the CSV file detailed in variable 8 and parse out the search results from the file.

There's more...

This recipe took a very simplistic approach to scripted alerts, simply to illustrate the functionality in a way that will work for every reader. Of course, you can get a lot more involved with the scripts that are executed when alerts are triggered. Examples of scripts might include:

 ▸ A script to pass key fields to a ticketing system; this script will then open a ticket for the triggered alert to be actioned upon by the relevant people

 ▸ A script that SSHs over to a server and restarts the web server when the web server crashes

 ▸ A script that dynamically adds firewall rules to block suspicious IP addresses

See also

 ▸ The *Alerting on errors during checkout in real time* recipe

 ▸ The *Alerting on abnormal user behavior* recipe

 ▸ The *Alerting when predicted sales exceed inventory* recipe

Alerting when predicted sales exceed inventory

In this final recipe, you will create a scheduled alert type that triggers when predicted sales are expected to exceed the levels of inventory levels on hand. This type of information is a key perspective of operational intelligence, as by knowing ahead of time that we might be running low on inventory, we might have time to order more before we actually run out.

Getting ready

To step through this recipe, you will need a running Splunk Enterprise server, with the sample data loaded from *Chapter 1, Play Time – Getting Data In*. You should be familiar with navigating the Splunk user interface and have a good command over the Splunk search language as you have completed the earlier recipes in this book. You should also have configured the e-mail settings in your Splunk server to enable the delivery of e-mail alerts.

Additionally, this chapter relies on an inventory lookup implemented in the *Looking up inventory from an external database* recipe in *Chapter 7, Enriching Data – Lookups and Workflows*. If this recipe has not been completed, you can upload the provided `productInventory.csv` file as a lookup in the Operational Intelligence application instead.

How to do it...

Follow the steps in this recipe to create an alert when predicted sales exceed inventory:

1. Log in to your Splunk server.

2. Select the **Operational Intelligence** application.

3. Ensure that the time range picker is set to **Last 60 Minutes**, and type the following search in the Splunk search bar. Then, click on the magnifying glass icon or hit *Enter*.

```
index=main sourcetype=log4j earliest=-0d@d
requestType=removeItem OR requestType=updateCart OR
requestType=addItem
[search index=main sourcetype=log4j requestType="checkout"
earliest=-0d@d | fields orderId]
| eval quantity=if(requestType="removeItem",-1,quantity)
| stats sum(quantity) AS quantity by itemId, date_hour
| stats avg(quantity) as salesRate, sum(quantity) as Sales
by itemId
| lookup productInventory.csv itemId AS itemId OUTPUT
itemInventory AS origInventory
| eval currentInventory=origInventory-Sales
| eval predictSales=round(salesRate*24)
| eval predictInventory=currentInventory-predictSales
| table itemId, origInventory, Sales, currentInventory,
salesRate, predictSales, predictInventory
```

 This search leverages a subsearch to identify `orderIds` that reached the checkout step. Subsearches work well but are limited to returning a maximum of 10,500 results. See the documentation at `http://docs.splunk.com/Documentation/Splunk/latest/Search/Aboutsubsearches` for more information.

4. You should see tabulated results relating to sales and inventory. Click on **Save As** and select **Alert**.

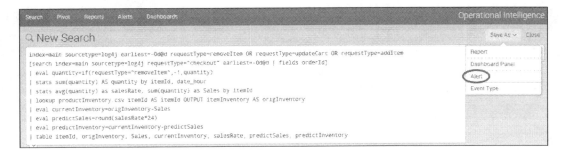

5. A pop-up box will appear. Enter `cp08_predict_sales_inventory` as the title of the alert. Select **Scheduled** in the **Alert type** field, and select **Run every hour** in the **Time Range** field. Select **Custom** in the **Trigger condition** field, and enter `search predictInventory<1` in the **Custom Condition** field. Then, click on **Next**.

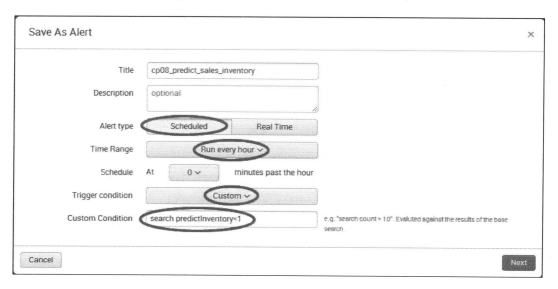

6. The alert configuration screen will be displayed. Perform the following steps on this screen:

1. Check the **List in Triggered Alerts** checkbox.

2. In the **Severity** dropdown, select **Medium**.

3. Select the **Send Email** checkbox.

4. Enter a valid e-mail address in the **To** box; this is where the alert will go to.

5. In the **Include** section, check **Link to Alert**, **Link to Results**, and **Inline Table**.

6. Scroll down to **Sharing**, and in **Permissions** select the **Shared in App** option.

7. Verify that the given details are entered correctly, and then, click on **Save**.

7. Click on **View Alert**. A summary screen should be displayed, and the alert is now configured and set to run every hour in accordance with the schedule. The alert should trigger but might take some time, depending on when you scheduled the alert.

8. When the alert triggers, you should receive an e-mail similar to the following screenshot. Note the link to the alert, the link to the results, and the actual results in the body of the e-mail as requested when configuring the alert.

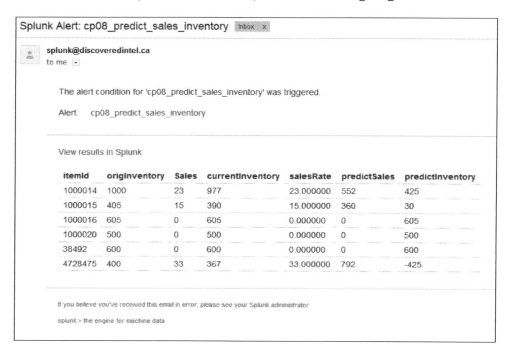

Splunk Alert: cp08_predict_sales_inventory inbox x

splunk@discoveredintel.ca
to me

The alert condition for 'cp08_predict_sales_inventory' was triggered.

Alert: cp08_predict_sales_inventory

View results in Splunk

itemId	origInventory	Sales	currentInventory	salesRate	predictSales	predictInventory
1000014	1000	23	977	23.000000	552	425
1000015	405	15	390	15.000000	360	30
1000016	605	0	605	0.000000	0	605
1000020	500	0	500	0.000000	0	500
38492	600	0	600	0.000000	0	600
4728475	400	33	367	33.000000	792	-425

If you believe you've received this email in error, please see your Splunk administrator.

splunk > the engine for machine data

How it works...

The underlying search here is a little complex. Essentially, the search looks to calculate how many sales of each item we expect to sell in the next 24 hours, based on the sales of each item since midnight on the day of the search. Once we have this data, we are able to check the inventory and calculate if we might run out of any items. The alert then triggers if the expected inventory is anticipated to be 0 or below. The search runs every hour. You should assume that the inventory lookup is refreshed each day at midnight.

Let's break the search down piece by piece.

Search fragment	Description

`index=main`
`sourcetype=log4j`
`earliest=-0d@d`
`requestType=removeItem`
`OR`
`requestType=updateCart`
`OR requestType=addItem`
	First, we search all the application logs for events related to updating the shopping cart, in this case, `removeItem`, `updateCart`, or `addItem` events. The shopping cart events give us key information about the quantities of each item that the customers are purchasing. We have selected to look back to midnight on the day of the search, using `earliest=-0d@d`.

`[search index=main` `sourcetype=log4j` `requestType="checkout"` `earliest=-0d@d	fields` `orderId]`	An inner search is used to look for only orders that actually went through to the checkout stage. A list of `orderId` is returned to the outer search that filters out any shopping cart events not related to an eventual order.

`| eval`
`quantity=if(requestType=`
`"removeItem",-`
`1,quantity)`
	The `removeItem` events do not have a quantity value, so we evaluate a quantity of `-1` for these events, as if a customer removes an item, this will reduce the quantity by 1.

`| stats sum(quantity) AS`
`quantity by itemId,`
`date_hour`
	We are left with shopping cart events relating to actual purchased orders and the quantities for each `itemId`. We are then able to use the `stats` command to sum up the quantities purchased each hour by `itemId`.

`| stats avg(quantity) as`
`salesRate, sum(quantity)`
`as Sales by itemId`
	Using the `stats` command and `avg` and `sum`, we find the overall average hourly sales rate by `itemId` and also the total number of sales for each `itemId` since midnight on the day of the search.

`| lookup`
`productInventory.csv`
`itemId AS itemId OUTPUT`
`itemInventory AS`
`origInventory`
	Using the `lookup` command, we now look up the inventory on tap for each item. Assume that this inventory is refreshed daily at midnight.

`| eval`
`currentInventory=origInv`
`entory-Sales`
	We now take the inventory for each `itemId` sold since midnight and subtract this from the inventory to get the current inventory.

`| eval`
`predictSales=round`
`(salesRate*24)`
	We now multiply the calculated average sales rate by 24 hours to get an idea of how many of each item we predict will sell over the next day.

`| eval`
`predictInventory=current`
`Inventory-predictSales`
	Once we have the predicted sales, we subtract this from the current inventory to calculate the predicted inventory in 24 hours' time.

Search fragment	Description
`| table itemId, origInventory, Sales, currentInventory, salesRate, predictSales, predictInventory`	The various evaluated fields are tabulated using the `table` command.
`| search predictInventory<1`	This is the alert condition used to trigger the alert. Should the predicted inventory for any item be `0` or less, then the alert will be triggered.

Using the previous search, we set up a scheduled alert type and set the schedule to run hourly. Should the predicted inventory for any item be `0` or less, the alert will trigger. In this case, it would go on triggering every hour until the inventory is updated, as we did not set any throttling of any kind. We selected to include the results in the e-mail; however, we could have simply included only the link to the results or attached the results as a CSV file to the e-mail.

It is likely that in a real-world situation, you would have a different way of calculating sales than looking through application logs. However, this example serves to illustrate how we can take a set of data, process it, and then use it further to help predict if anything untoward might occur in the future, based upon historical trends.

There's more...

One of the alert actions we mentioned at the beginning of this chapter is the ability to create an RSS feed of alert notifications. Unfortunately, at the time of writing this book, this is not an available action when creating an alert through the **Save As Alert** function of Splunk. However, we can implement this action by editing the alert once it is saved.

Adding an RSS feed notification action to an alert

To add an RSS feed notification to the alert you just created, click on the **Settings** menu in the top-right corner and select **Searches, reports, and alerts**.

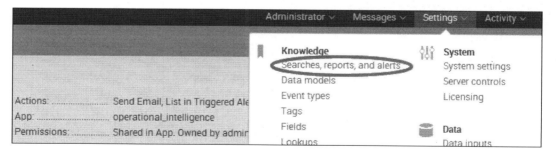

Search for `cp08` to bring up the `cp08` searches, and select the **cp08_predict_sales_inventory** search that you just created. Once the configuration screen loads, scroll down and enable the **Add to RSS** checkbox.

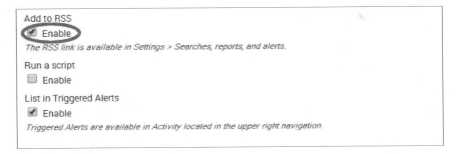

Click on **Save** and you will now see the RSS icon next to the search. Clicking on the RSS icon will take you to the feed of triggered alerts for this search.

cp08_abnormal_user_purchase		2014-07-03 01:03:00 UTC
cp08_abnormal_webpage_response		2014-07-03 02:00:00 UTC
cp08_predict_sales_inventory		2014-07-03 01:05:00 UTC
cp08_realtime_checkout_error		2014-07-03 01:03:00 UTC

See also

▸ The *Alerting on abnormal user behavior* recipe

▸ The *Alerting on failure and triggering a scripted response* recipe

Summary

The key takeaways from this chapter are as follows:

▸ There are three different types of alerts in Splunk: scheduled alerts, per-result alerts, and rolling-window alerts

▸ Alerts are based-off underlying historical or real-time searches

▸ Alerts are triggered based on user-specified conditions and can be throttled as required

▸ Alerts have a number of different actions that can be performed when an alert is triggered, including sending an e-mail and executing a script

▸ Alerts play a critical part in gaining proactive operational intelligence

▸ Alerts can be used for relatively simple use cases such as detecting errors or much more complex use cases such as predicting future sales

9
Speed Up Intelligence – Data Summarization

In this chapter, we will cover the methods that exist within Splunk to speed up intelligence. You will learn about:

- ▶ Calculating an hourly count of sessions versus completed transactions
- ▶ Backfilling the number of purchases by city
- ▶ Displaying the maximum number of concurrent sessions over time

Introduction

In *Chapter 5, Extending Intelligence – Data Models and Pivoting,* we learned all about data models and how they can be accelerated to facilitate faster Pivot reporting. Data model acceleration works by leveraging data summarization behind the scenes. In this chapter, we will take a look at two more data summarization methods within Splunk: summary indexing and report acceleration. These enable you to speed up reports or preserve focused statistics over long periods of time. You will learn how to populate summary indexes, use report acceleration, backfill summary indexes with historical data, and more.

Data summarization

Big Data is, just that, big, and even with the best infrastructure, it can be extremely time consuming to search or report over large datasets and/or very costly to store for long periods of time. Within Splunk exists data summarization features that simplify and speed up reporting over large datasets. Data summarization essentially allows for raw event datasets to be summarized to much smaller (usually statistical) datasets, which can then be searched to facilitate significantly faster reporting.

The following diagram helps to illustrate how data summarization works. In the example, we start with a large raw dataset on the left, and then create a statistical summary from it, capturing the key information. The statistical summary will be much faster to report on than the raw log data as it represents a lot less data. This summarized data can either be written into a new index or automatically captured alongside the raw event data behind the scenes by Splunk.

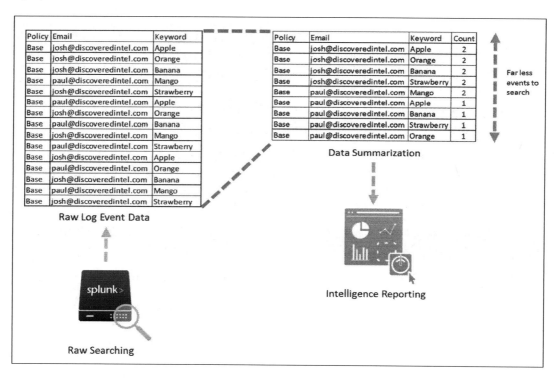

From an operational intelligence perspective, data summarization allows you to unlock the ability to quickly calculate and report on key, focused metrics, while also reducing the underlying data storage footprint.

Data summarization methods

At the time of writing this book, there are three data summarization methods in Splunk, which are listed in the following table:

Data summarization method	Description
Summary indexing	Summary indexing involves the creation of separate indexes to hold summarized event data. These indexes, instead of the index containing the raw event data, can be searched and reported on.
Report acceleration	Report acceleration creates automated summaries behind the scenes, alongside the raw event data, to facilitate faster execution of reports that have been accelerated.
Data model acceleration	Data model acceleration is similar to report acceleration in that automated summaries are created behind the scenes. However, this summarization is performed on an entire modeled set of data, rather than individual reports, and the acceleration is only realized when using Pivot.

In this chapter, we will focus on summary indexing and report acceleration since data model acceleration was covered in *Chapter 5, Extending Intelligence – Data Models and Pivoting*.

About summary indexing

Summary indexing is a simple but very useful feature within Splunk, which allows you to summarize large amounts of data into smaller subsets, based on defined search criteria. This summarized data is usually stored in a separate index from where the original data exists and is typically a lot smaller in size. Reporting over the smaller summary index rather than the original data will be a lot faster. Additionally, as the summary index is smaller, you will be able to retain data for longer periods of time, which is key for long-term trending and predictive analytics. Summary indexing is the only method to keep data longer than the retention time of the index that stores the raw events; the other summarization methods need raw events to be present.

How summary indexing helps

One of the more common operational intelligence use cases is around the generation of metrics. For example, say we want to find the average execution time of a web request for the past month. This data might come from multiple web servers and millions of events per day. So, running a report over an entire month's raw event data will likely take a long period of time simply due to the event volume.

With summary indexing, a search can be scheduled to run each day to compute the average execution time for the day, and the results can be stored in a summary index. This will result in a summary index containing roughly 30 events for a given month—a lot less than the millions of raw event records! The following month, when this same report is run, the report is merely run against the summary index that is inherently much smaller than the raw event data, resulting in a report that is computed at an exponentially faster rate than what was observed previously.

> Summary indexing of data does not count against your Splunk license as the data being used for summary indexing is almost always already indexed into Splunk.

About report acceleration

When it comes to operational intelligence, detection and response times can be critical, with delays adding to costs and potential severity. Therefore, it is likely that you will want to get to your intelligence data as fast as possible. Report acceleration allows you to speed up the time it takes to execute operational intelligence reports. Report acceleration can be thought of as a form of summary indexing, without the need to create a separate index as the summary data is stored alongside ordinary indexes.

The big difference between report acceleration and summary indexing is the way in which data is computed. Summary indexing is based on the execution of scheduled searches over a given time frame that populates summary indexes with their search results. However, report acceleration is based on the execution of acceleration-enabled scheduled searches over a given timeframe, which results in Splunk executing background processes to automatically manage the summary of data related to the search. In addition, report acceleration is self-repairing after any data interruption, whereas summary indexing is unaware if the data over a time frame is incomplete in any way or has endured gaps.

> The words search and report are used interchangeably in Splunk, but are essentially the same thing. In legacy versions of Splunk, searches that were saved and/or scheduled were known as *Saved Searches*; however, in Version 6 and above, they are known as *Reports*.

The ease of report acceleration

We earlier outlined that the one key difference between report acceleration and summary indexing is in the way in which report acceleration automatically handles the data summarization behind the scenes. Not only is this automatically computed, but Splunk also automatically identifies when searches are run, which might benefit from the already accelerated report data and make this data available to the searches; all of this is performed by the click of a button.

Calculating an hourly count of sessions versus completed transactions

From an operational intelligence standpoint, it is interesting to understand how many visitors we have to our online store and how many of these people actually purchase something. For example, if we have 1,000 people visiting a day, and only 10 people actually purchase something, this might indicate something is not quite right. Perhaps the prices of our products are too high, or the site might be difficult to use, and thus need a redesign. This information can also be used to indicate peak purchasing times.

In this first recipe, we will leverage summary indexing to understand how many sessions we have per hour versus how many actual completed purchase transactions there have been. We will plot these over a line graph going back the last 24 hours.

Getting ready

To step through this recipe, you will need a running Splunk Enterprise server, with the sample data loaded from *Chapter 1, Play Time – Getting Data In*. You should be familiar with navigating the Splunk user interface and using the Splunk search language.

How to do it...

Follow these steps in this recipe to leverage summary indexing in calculating an hourly count of sessions versus the completed transactions:

1. Log in to your Splunk server.
2. Select the **Operational Intelligence** application.
3. From the search bar, enter the following search and select to run over **Last 60 Minutes**:

```
sourcetype=log4j index=main | stats dc(sessionId) AS
Sessions, count(eval(requestType="checkout")) AS
Completed_Transactions
```

4. Click on the **Save As** dropdown and select **Report** from the list:

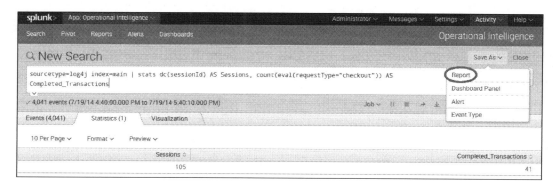

5. In the pop-up box that gets displayed, enter `cp09_sessions_transactions_summary` as the title of the report and select **No** in the **Time Range Picker** field; then, click on **Save**:

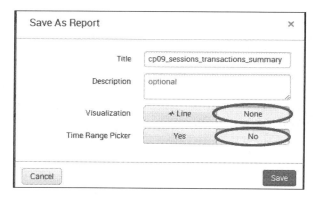

6. On the next screen, select **Schedule** from the list of additional settings:

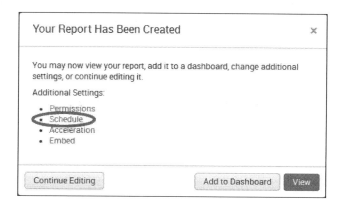

7. Select the **Schedule Report** checkbox, **Run every hour** in the **Schedule** field, and a time range of **Last 60 minutes**. Click on **Next**, and then simply click on **Save** on the next screen:

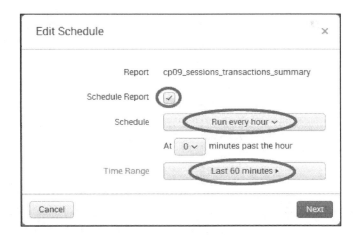

8. In order to activate summary indexing on the report that you just saved, you will need to edit the search manually. Click on the **Settings** menu at the top-right corner and select **Searches, reports, and alerts**:

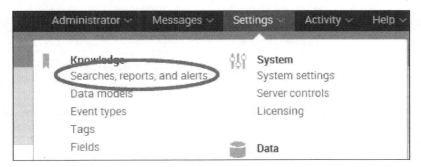

9. A list of all the saved searches will be displayed. Locate the search named **cp09_ sessions_transactions_summary**, and click on it to edit it.

10. The search editor screen will be displayed. Scroll down to the very bottom **Summary indexing** section and select the **Enable** checkbox. Ensure the default summary index called **summary** is selected, and then click on **Save**:

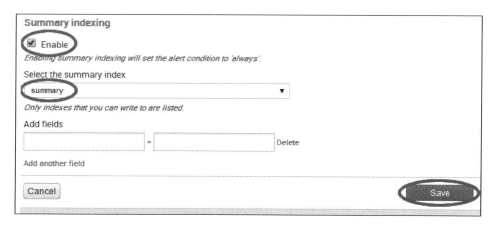

11. The search is now scheduled to run every hour, and the results are scheduled to be written to a summary index named **summary**. After 24 hours have passed, run the following search from the search bar in the **Operational Intelligence** application, with a time range set to **Last 24 hours**:

```
index=summary source="cp09_sessions_transactions_summary"
| table _time Sessions Completed_Transactions
```

12. The search will complete very fast and list 24 events, one for each hour. Select the **Visualization** tab to see the data presented as a line chart representing sessions versus completed transactions:

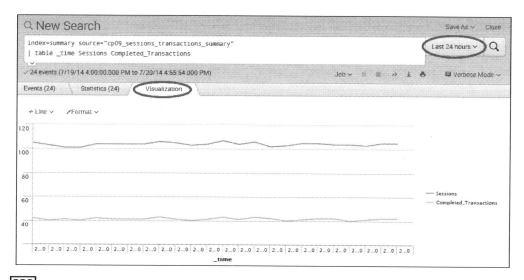

13. Let's save this as a report, and then add the report to a dashboard panel. Click on the **Save As** dropdown and select **Report**.

14. Enter `cp09_sessions_vs_transactions` in the **Title** field of the report, and ensure the **Visualization** field is set to **Line**; then, click on **Save**:

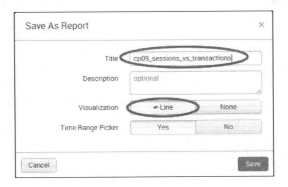

15. On the next screen, click on the **Add to Dashboard** button.

16. In the pop-up box that appears, select **New** to add a new dashboard and give it the title of `Session and Purchase Trends`. Ensure the permissions are set to **Shared in App** and give the panel we are adding a title of `Hourly Sessions vs Completed Transactions`. Ensure the panel is powered by **Report** and the panel content is set to **Line**, and then click on **Save** to create the new dashboard with the line-chart panel:

How it works...

In this recipe, you created a scheduled search that will take hourly snapshots, counting the number of unique sessions and the sessions that resulted in completed purchase transactions. Every hour the search runs, a single line item with two values is created, and the results are written to a summary index named **summary**. Returning to the search 24 hours later, you are able to run a report on the summary index to instantly see the activity over the past day in terms of sessions versus purchases. There were 24 events in the summary, one for each hour. Reporting off the summary data is a lot more efficient and faster than attempting to search across the raw data. If you wait longer, say 30 days, then you can run the report again and plot the results across an entire month. This information might then be able to provide predictive insight into the sales forecast for the next month.

There were two searches that you used for this recipe. The first search was used to generate the summary data and ran hourly. The second search was used to search and report against the summary data directly. Let's break down each search piece by piece:

Search 1 – Summary index generating search

Search fragment	Description
`sourcetype=log4j index=main`	We first select to search the application data in the main index over the past hour.
`| stats dc(sessionId) AS Sessions, count(eval (requestType="checkout")) AS Completed_Transactions`	Using the `stats` command with the distinct count (`dc`) function, we obtain the number of unique sessions in the past hour. We then use the `count` function to total the checkout requests. A checkout request indicates that a sale has gone through.

Search 2 – Reporting off the summary index

Search fragment	Description
`index=summary source="cp09_sessions_ transactions_summary"`	We first select to search the summary index. Then, within this index, we look for data with a source of `cp09_sessions_ transactions_summary`. This is the name of our saved search and is used as the source field by Splunk when writing to a summary index.
`| table _time Sessions Completed_Transactions`	We tabulate the data by time, number of sessions, and number of completed transactions.

If you search the summary data directly, you will notice that Splunk gives the summary data a `sourcetype` field value of `stash` by default. However, the source-field value for the data will be the name of the saved search. Therefore, searching by source rather than `sourcetype` is likely to be your preferred approach.

There's more...

As you can see, summary indexing is a great way to shrink down our raw dataset into just the valuable data that we need to report on. The raw dataset still exists, so we can create many summaries off the same data if we want to do so.

Generating the summary more frequently

In this recipe, the summary-generating search was set to run hourly and look back over the past hour. This results in a single event being generated per hour and written to the summary. If more granularity is required, the search can be set to run every 15 minutes; look back over the past 15 minutes, and four events per hour will be generated. As the search is now only looking back over the past 15 minutes, instead of the past hour, it will likely execute faster as there is less data to search over. For some data sources, generating the summary index data more frequently over smaller chunks of time can be more efficient.

Avoiding summary index overlaps and gaps

Care needs to be taken when creating summary index generating searches to avoid both gaps in your summary and overlaps in the data being searched.

For example, you schedule a summary index generating search to run every 5 minutes and look back over the past 5 minutes, but the search actually takes 10 minutes to run. This will result in the search not executing again, until its previous run is complete, which means it will run every 10 minutes, but only look back over the past 5 minutes. Therefore, there will be data gaps in your summary. This can be avoided by ensuring adequate search testing is performed before scheduling the search.

In another example, you schedule a summary index generating search to run every 5 minutes and look back over the past 10 minutes. This will result in the search looking back over 5 minutes of data that the previous run also looked back over. Therefore, there will be data overlaps in your summary. This can be avoided by ensuring there are no overlaps in time when scheduling the search.

Additionally, gaps can occur if you take the search head down for an extended period of time and then bring it back up. Backfilling can be used to fill in past gaps in the data, and this is discussed in the next recipe.

See also

- The *Backfilling the number of purchases by city* recipe
- The *Displaying the maximum number of concurrent sessions over time* recipe

Backfilling the number of purchases by city

In the previous recipe, you generated an hourly summary, and then, after waiting for 24 hours, you were able to report on the summary data over a 24-hour period. However, what if you wanted to report over the past 30 days or even 3 months? You would have to wait a long time for your summary data to build up over time. A better way is to backfill the summary data over an earlier time period, assuming you have raw data for this time period in Splunk.

In this recipe, you will create a search that identifies the number of purchases by city on a given day, and write this search to a summary index. You will leverage the IP location database built into Splunk to obtain the city based on IP address in the results. You will then execute a script that comes bundled with Splunk in order to backfill the summary for the previous 30 days. Following this, you will use the generated summary data to quickly report on the number of purchases by city for the past month.

Getting ready

To step through this recipe, you will need a running Splunk Enterprise server, with the sample data loaded from *Chapter 1, Play Time – Getting Data In*. You should be familiar with navigating the Splunk user interface and using the Splunk search language.

How to do it...

Follow the steps in this recipe to leverage summary indexing and to backfill the number of purchases by city:

1. Log in to your Splunk server.
2. Select the **Operational Intelligence** application.
3. From the search bar, enter the following search and select to run over **Last 24 hours**:

```
sourcetype=log4j index=main requestType="checkout"
| iplocation ipAddress | fillnull value="Unknown" City
| replace "" with "Unknown" in City
| stats count AS Purchases by City
```

4. Click on the **Save As** dropdown and select **Report** from the list:

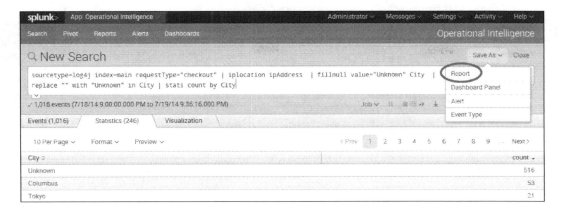

5. In the pop-up box that gets displayed, enter `cp09_backfill_purchases_city` as the title of the report and select **No** in the **Time Range Picker** field. Then, click on **Save**:

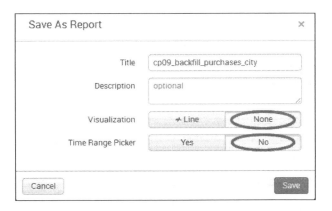

6. On the next screen, select **Schedule** from the list of additional settings:

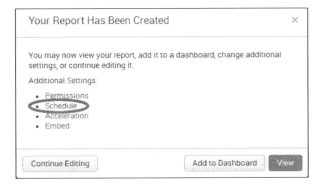

7. Select the **Schedule Report** checkbox and set **Schedule** to **Run every day** and **Time Range** to **Last 24 hours**. Click on **Next**, and then simply click on **Save** on the next screen:

8. You will be taken back to the report you just saved. Select the **Edit** dropdown, and then select **Edit Permissions** from the list:

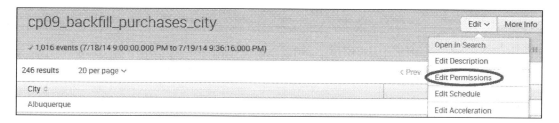

9. In the permissions pop-up box that is displayed, select the **App** option against **Display For**, and then click on **Save**:

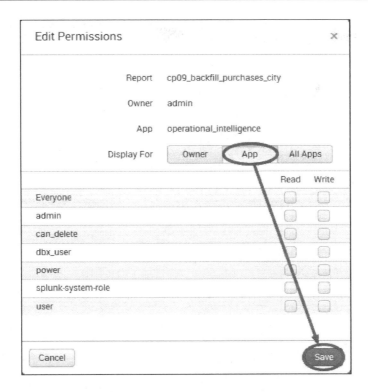

10. In order to activate summary indexing on the report that you just saved, you will need to edit the search manually. Click on the **Settings** menu at the top-right corner and select **Searches, reports, and alerts**:

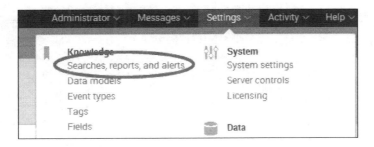

11. A list of all the saved searches will be displayed. Locate the search named **cp09_backfill_purchases_city** and click on it to edit it.

12. The search editor screen will be displayed. Scroll down to the **Summary indexing** section at the bottom, and select the **Enable** checkbox. Ensure the default summary index called **summary** is selected, and then click on **Save**:

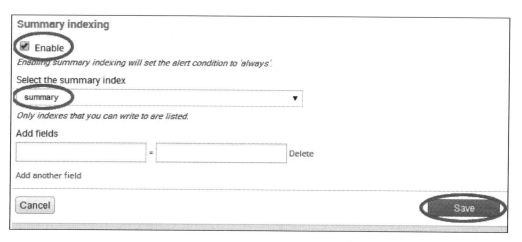

13. The search is now scheduled to run every day, and the results are written to a summary index named **summary**. Now, you will leverage the script to backfill the summary. Bring up a terminal window in Linux or open a command window in Windows.

14. From within your terminal or command window, change your working directory to `$SPLUNK_HOME/bin`.

15. From the command line, tell Splunk to backfill the summary index by executing the `fill_summary_index.py` script and supplying the required parameters. Execute the following command and change the values `admin:changeme` to the `username:password` combination of the user who populates the summary index within Splunk; an administrative login can be used here to ensure proper access to populate the summary index:

```
./splunk cmd python fill_summary_index.py -app
operational_intelligence -name cp09_backfill_purchases_city
-et -30day@day -lt now -j 8 -auth admin:changeme
```

16. In Windows, omit the `. /` at the start of the command.

17. Once the script has completed executing, run the following search from the search bar in the **Operational Intelligence** application with a time range set to **Last 30 days**:

```
index=summary source=cp09_backfill_purchases_city
City!="Unknown"
| timechart span=1d useother=F sum(Purchases) by City
```

18. The search will complete very fast and list one result per day for the last 30 days. Select the **Visualization** tab to see the data presented as a line chart representing the total purchases by day for each city over the past month:

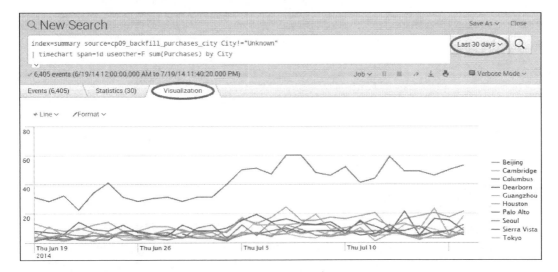

19. Let's save this chart to our **Session and Purchase Trends** dashboard that we created in the previous recipe. Click on the **Save As** dropdown and select **Report**.

20. In the pop-up box that appears, enter `cp09_purchases_city_trend` in the **Title** field and ensure **Visualization** is set to **Line**; then, click on **Save**.

21. On the next screen, select **Add to Dashboard**.

22. On the **Save As Dashboard Panel** screen, select **Existing** as the dashboard, and then select the **Session and Purchase Trends** dashboard. Give the panel the title of `Purchases by City – Last 30 Days`, ensure the panel is powered by **Report**, and content is set to **Line**. Then, click on **Save** to save the chart to the dashboard:

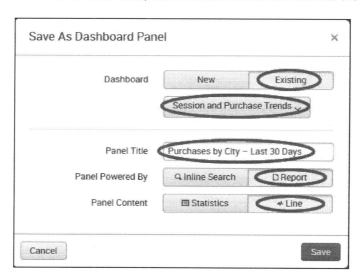

How it works...

This recipe started off by taking a similar approach to the first recipe in this chapter. You first created a search to look back over the past day for purchases by city and wrote the summarized results to a summary index. You then scheduled this search to run on a daily basis. However, rather than waiting 30 days for data to be populated, you executed a script to backfill the summary with the previous 30 days worth of data.

The bundled Splunk script inputs a number of variables, including the saved search name (`cp09_backfill_purchases_city`), the time frame that the search runs over (**Last 24 hours**), and the period of time that you wish to backfill (**Last 30 days**). Using this information, the script essentially executes the search 30 times, once for each of the 30 days, and the results of each day are written to the summary. Once the script is successfully executed, you are able to run a report across the summary index over the past 30 days to quickly see the daily purchases by city over time.

There are two searches that you used for this recipe, in addition to a script. The first search was used to generate the summary data and was run daily. The script used the first search to backfill the summary with 30 days of data. The second search was used to search and report against the summary data directly. Let's break down each search piece by piece:

Search 1 – Summary index generating search

Search fragment	Description

`sourcetype=log4j`
`index=main`
`requestType="checkout"`
	We first select to search the application data in the main index over the past day. We select to search for only events with a `requestType` of checkout.

`| iplocation ipAddress`	Using the built-in `iplocation` command, we deduce the geolocational city information from the `ipAddress` field in the data.

`| fillnull`
`value="Unknown" City |`
`replace "" with`
`"Unknown" in City`
	The `fillnull` command is used to fill in the blanks with a value of `"Unknown"`, where the `iplocation` command is unable to match a city to the IP address. The `replace` command replaces all `""` values with a value of `"Unknown"`.

`| stats count AS` `Purchases by City`	Using the `stats` command, we do a simple count to count the number of purchases by city.

fill_summary_index.py – Backfilling the summary index

Search fragment	Description
`./splunk cmd python` `fill_summary_index.py`	This is the actual command execution telling Splunk that you wish to run a command (cmd) ensuring the various Splunk environment variables are set prior to execution. Next, the command you wish to execute is specified (python). Finally, you tell Python what you wish to do; in this case, we execute the backfill script provided with Splunk, which is named `fill_summary_index.py`.
`-app` `operational_intelligence`	This parameter tells the script the name of the application under which the saved search resides. For purposes here, it will be the `operational_intelligence` application.

`-name`
`cp09_backfill_purchases_`
`city`
	This parameter tells the script the name of the saved search to run. For this execution, it will be the name of the search saved in the `cp09_backfill_purchases_city` recipe.

`-et -30day@day`	This parameter tells the script the earliest time for which results are to be returned. For purposes here, it will be 30 days.

Search fragment	Description
`-lt now`	This parameter tells the script the latest time for which it should return results. For purposes here, it will be the current time of execution.
`-j 8`	This parameter tells the script the maximum number of concurrent searches to run, which will be `8`.
`-auth admin:changeme`	This parameter tells the script which credentials to authenticate to Splunk as. In this case, it will be Splunk's default credentials, `admin:changeme`.

Search 2 – Reporting off the summary index

Search fragment	Description
`index=summary source=cp09_ backfill_purchases_city City!="Unknown"`	Firstly, we select to search the summary index. Then, we look for data with a source of `cp09_backfill_purchases_city` within this index. This is the name of our saved search and is used as the source field by Splunk when writing to a summary index. We also filter out cities with a value of `"Unknown"` to focus in on the cities that we do know about.
`| timechart span=1d useother=F sum(Purchases) by City`	Using the `timechart` command and spanning across a single day, we sum the purchases by city over 30 days. By specifying `useother=F`, we ensure that cities are not grouped together and listed as `"Other"`. This data is then perfect to use on a line chart, with each line representing a different city.

There's more...

In this recipe, you leveraged a script to help backfill the index automatically in Splunk. However, in many cases, access to the command line to execute scripts might not be permitted, and/or you won't mind doing a little bit more work to backfill a summary, if it means you can do it directly from the search bar within Splunk.

Backfilling a summary index from within a search directly

Splunk provides a way to write to a summary index directly from the search using the `addinfo` and `collect` commands. For example, using the summary-generating search in this recipe, we can modify the search to directly write to the summary index, as follows:

```
sourcetype=log4j index=main requestType="checkout" earliest=-2d@d
latest=-1d@d
 | iplocation ipAddress | fillnull value="Unknown" City
 | replace "" with "Unknown" in City
 | stats count AS Purchases by City
 | addinfo | collect index=summary
source="cp09_backfill_purchases_city" addtime=t
```

The `earliest` and `latest` field values are used to set the time range that the search should run over. In this case, we run the search over the previous day, starting 2 days ago and ending 1 day ago. We also add the `addinfo` command, which adds information that Splunk needs for summary indexing. Additionally, we use the `collect` command and specify the summary index as well as the value for the source field that is written to the summary. The source field value we use is the name of the saved search. If you execute this search, it will write a day's worth of data to the summary index. You can repeat this search, modifying the `earliest` and `latest` field values back a day each time, until you run the search 30 times and backfill the entire month. You can also use the `append` command to append 30 searches together, each with a different `earliest` and `latest` time. It is a bit uglier than the script method used in the recipe and more prone to user error, but it works.

> With summary indexing, it is very easy to write data to an index that you don't want. Perhaps, you duplicate the data or tweak your generating search to correct the results. Splunk has a `delete` command that can be used to clean out bad data from any index. However, you will likely need to have your Splunk administrator delete the data for you.

See also

▶ The *Calculating an hourly count of sessions versus completed transactions* recipe

▶ The *Displaying the maximum number of concurrent sessions over time* recipe

Displaying the maximum number of concurrent sessions over time

In the past two recipes of this chapter, you leveraged a method of data summarization called *summary indexing* to summarize data into a new index, which you then reported on. In this recipe, you will use another method of data summarization known as *report acceleration* to speed up your report times.

In this recipe, you will create a report to look for the maximum number of concurrent sessions over a time period of 30 days. This report will then be accelerated to speed up the time taken to execute the search.

Getting ready

To step through this recipe, you will need a running Splunk Enterprise server, with the sample data loaded from *Chapter 1, Play Time – Getting Data In*. You should be familiar with navigating the Splunk user interface and using the Splunk search language.

How to do it...

Follow the steps in this recipe to leverage report acceleration to display the maximum number of concurrent sessions over time:

1. Log in to your Splunk server.

2. Select the **Operational Intelligence** application.

3. From the search bar, enter the following search and select to run over **Last 7 days**:

   ```
   index=main sourcetype=log4j
   | timechart span=1m dc(sessionId) AS concurrent_sessions
   | timechart span=30m max(concurrent_sessions) AS
   max_concurrent_sessions
   ```

4. You might find that the search takes about 2-3 minutes to run if you have 7 days of generated data.

5. Click on the **Save As** dropdown and select **Report** from the list:

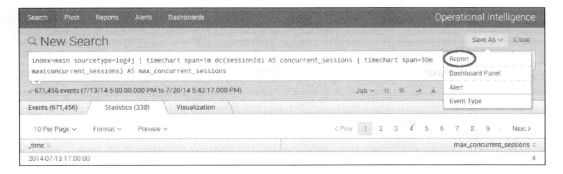

6. In the pop-up box that gets displayed, enter `cp09_maximum_concurrent_` `sessions` as the title of the report and select **No** in the **Time Range Picker** field. Then, click on **Save**:

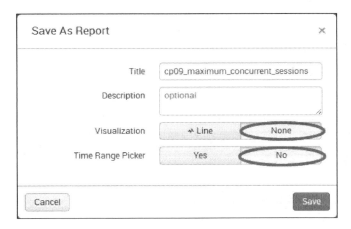

7. On the next screen, select **Acceleration** from the list of additional settings:

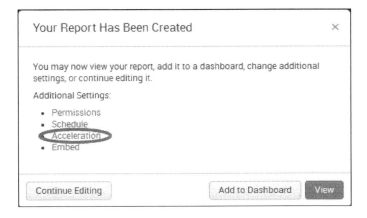

8. Select the **Accelerate Report** checkbox, set a summary range of **1 Month**, and then click on **Save**. If you see a warning about running in verbose mode, it is okay to ignore:

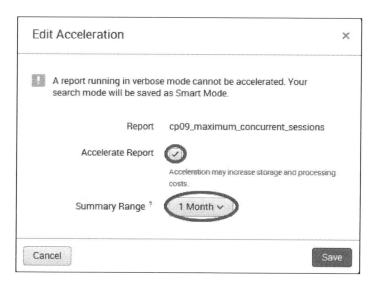

9. The report is now saved and Splunk builds the accelerated summary behind the scenes. There is no need to schedule the search. To check on the status of the summary building, click on the **Settings** menu and select **Report acceleration summaries**:

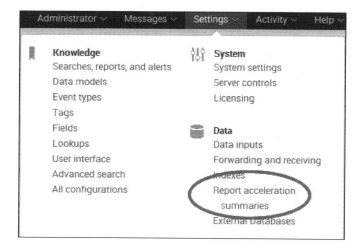

10. The list of report acceleration summaries will be displayed, and you will see the report that you just created with **Summary Status** of **Building Summary**:

11. If you do not see the summary building, try hitting refresh on the browser. Sometimes, you have to wait a bit. If you are impatient, click on the **Summary ID** value that you are monitoring and you will be taken to a screen where you can force a build by clicking on **Rebuild** . If you see a status of **Pending**, it is normal as it is telling you that an update to the summary is pending. If you see **Not enough data to summarize**, it is letting you know that there is not enough data yet to summarize properly and will wait until there is. If that occurs, consider updating **Summary Range** in the acceleration configuration to a smaller window:

12. Eventually, the report will complete the building of the summary. When it is complete, click on the **Apps** menu and select the **Operational Intelligence** app:

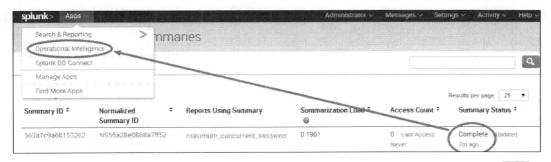

13. Once back in the app, click on **Reports**, filter on the word `maximum`, and click on **Open in Search** next to the **cp09_maximum_concurrent_sessions** report:

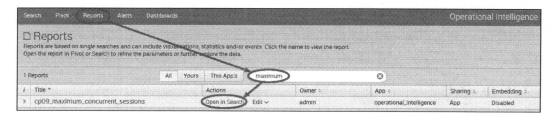

14. The report will now load in seconds. Select the **Visualization** tab to see the data presented as a line chart representing the maximum number of concurrent sessions, and select a time range of **Last 7 days**:

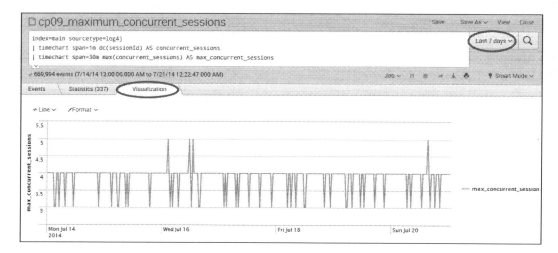

15. Let's save this chart to our **Session and Purchase Trends** dashboard that we created in the first recipe. Click on the **Save As** dropdown and select **Dashboard Panel**.

16. In the pop-up box that appears, select **Existing** in the **Dashboard** field, and then select the **Session and Purchase Trends** dashboard. Enter `Maximum Concurrent Sessions` as the title of the panel, ensure the panel is set to be powered by **Report**, ensure the panel content is set to **Line**, and click on **Save** to save the chart to the dashboard:

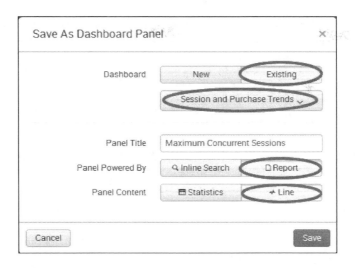

How it works...

In this recipe, you first created a search to look for concurrent sessions over time. The search has two `timechart` components to it. Let's break down the search piece by piece:

Search fragment	Description
`index=main sourcetype=log4j`	Select to search the application data in the main index.
`| timechart span=1m dc(sessionId) AS concurrent_sessions`	The first `timechart` command identifies the number of distinct (or unique) sessions in each 1-minute period.
`| timechart span=30m max(concurrent_sessions) AS max_concurrent_sessions`	The second `timechart` command takes the number of concurrent sessions that have been calculated for each minute and identifies the highest (or maximum) number in any 30-minute period.

This search is actually fairly resource intensive when searched for over an extended period of time. Running the nonaccelerated search over 7 days will likely take several minutes, mostly because Splunk performs a calculation for every minute of data for the past week. Once the report is created, you select to accelerate it over a 1-month period. Behind the scenes, Splunk creates an internal summary in line with the data itself. Once the summary is built, you return to the report and rerun it; it completes in seconds, thanks to the new acceleration. As the report is accelerated for an entire month, you can look back up to a month in the past and it will still run fast. Going forward, Splunk will periodically refresh the internal summary every 10 minutes to summarize and accelerate any new event data.

Report acceleration will only work with searches or reports that contain what is known as a **transforming** command. Examples of commonly used transforming commands are `stats`, `timechart`, `chart`, and `top`.

There's more...

Report acceleration does add some overhead as disk space is used to store the internal summary data. Splunk provides detailed information on the health of the various reports that are accelerated.

Viewing the status of an accelerated report

To investigate the details of an accelerated report, first click on the **Settings** menu, and then select **Report Acceleration Summaries**. A list of all the accelerated reports will load together with a high-level build status. Click on the report we accelerated in this recipe to drill into the details. The **Summary Details** screen provides some good insight into the accelerated report, including information such as how many times the report has been accessed, the range the report is set at, and how much data is being used by the summary.

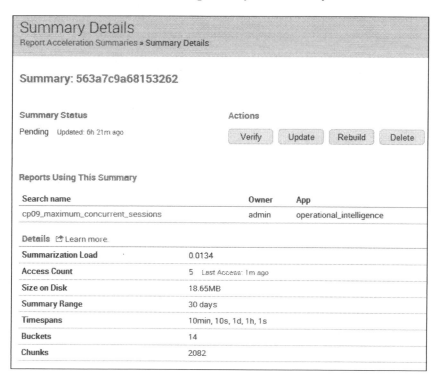

See also

▶ The *Calculating an hourly count of sessions versus completed transactions* recipe

▶ The *Backfilling the number of purchases by city* recipe

Summary

The key takeaways from this chapter are as follows:

▶ There are currently three methods of data summarization in Splunk: summary indexing, report acceleration, and data model acceleration

▶ Summary indexing can greatly improve the time taken to access key metrics computed over long periods of time

▶ Summary indexing provides a method to retain data over long periods of time with a much smaller footprint on disk space

▶ Report acceleration provides an intelligent method for automatically summarizing report data to enhance the speed of the report

▶ Report acceleration summary data is shared amongst similar reports automatically

▶ Report acceleration is self-repairing; it will automatically detect gaps in data and recompute the expected data summaries

▶ The speed at which reports are produced is a cornerstone to a successful Operational Intelligence program

10
Above and Beyond – Customization, Web Framework, REST API, and SDKs

In this chapter, we will learn how to customize a Splunk application and use advanced features of Splunk SDKs and APIs to work with the data within Splunk. You will learn about:

- ► Customizing the application's navigation
- ► Adding a force-directed graph of web hits
- ► Adding a calendar heatmap of product purchases
- ► Remotely querying Splunk's REST API for unique page views
- ► Creating a Python application to return unique IP addresses
- ► Creating a custom search command to format product names

Introduction

Throughout all of the chapters so far, we have been dealing directly with the core functionality found within Splunk Enterprise. In this chapter, we will dive into the functionality that lets us create an even more powerful interactive experience with Splunk. By leveraging the latest technology in Splunk Enterprise, we can customize the look and feel, expose our users to richer visualizations, extract knowledge and data from Splunk into our own internal applications, or build completely new applications that leverage Splunk.

Taking your Splunk experience to the next level breaks out into three areas: the web framework, the REST API, and **software development kits** (**SDKs**).

Web framework

The web framework is a core component of the Splunk 6 platform. The framework extends the abilities of Splunk to allow for more extensible development. Server-side functionality leverages the Django web framework to create a more fluid development experience. In this framework, you don't have to restart Splunk to see your changes, you can write custom handlers and URL routing, and you can create custom templates that can be used to generate client-side components. On the client side, you can leverage a custom Splunk JavaScript stack combined with HTML-based dashboards. You no longer need to do everything in SimpleXML! The SplunkJS Stack can even be downloaded as a set of libraries to be included in your applications outside of Splunk.

The full power of these technologies can be used to create the type of dashboards and reports that will meet your exact needs.

REST API

The backbone of Splunk has always been the underlying REST API. The REST API allows access to everything from configuration to ingesting data. Whether it's running one-off scripts to extract some data or automating a workflow with a third-party system, it can all be done with simple web requests to the API.

As with most of Splunk, there are also many different options and parameters that you can apply to your REST API calls in order to manipulate the output types or filter the results. Long before Splunk had the web framework, the REST API was the workhorse of integrating with Splunk and still plays a big part in this.

Software development kits (SDKs)

Over the past few years, the Splunk development team has been creating SDKs to assist developers with the creation of their own Operational Intelligence applications.

Using the SDKs, developers can easily:

- Manage and execute searches and saved searches
- Manage configuration details and user access
- Log data directly into Splunk

And many other features.

The SDKs are written to interact with the REST API and abstract the various details away to let you focus on getting the operational intelligence you need. Splunk currently has SDKs for Python, Java, JavaScript, PHP, Ruby, and C#.

OK, let's get some hands-on experience of this exciting technology!

Customizing the application's navigation

As we come to the end of this book, it is a good time to take a look at the Operational Intelligence application that you developed and add some simple customization to pull the app together from a presentation standpoint.

In this recipe, you will add custom navigation to your application to better organize the reports and dashboards.

Getting ready

To step through this recipe, you will need a running Splunk Enterprise server, with the sample data loaded from *Chapter 1, Play Time – Getting Data In*. Ideally, you should have completed all the earlier recipes in this book such that you have an Operational Intelligence application with a number of dashboards and reports contained within it. By now, you should be familiar with navigating the Splunk user interface and using the Splunk search language.

How to do it...

Follow the steps in this recipe to add some custom navigation and design tweaks:

1. Log in to your Splunk server.
2. Select the **Operational Intelligence** application.

3. Click on **Settings** and then on **User interface**.

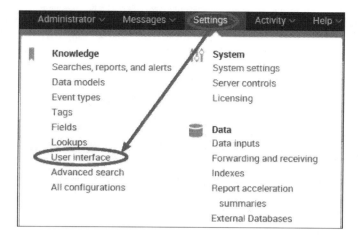

4. Click on **Navigation menus**.

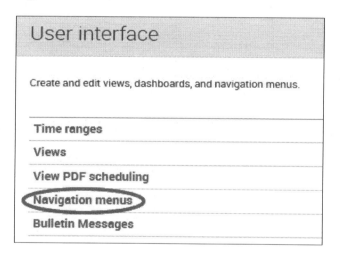

5. You should see one item in the list named **default**. Click on it.

6. You should see some existing code as follows:

```
<nav search_view="search" color="#65A637">
  <view name="search" default='true' />
  <view name="data_models" />
  <view name="reports" />
  <view name="alerts" />
  <view name="dashboards" />
</nav>
```

7. Modify the code as follows:

```
<nav search_view="search" color="#999999">
  <view name="search" default='true' />
<!--
  <view name="data_models" />
  <view name="reports" />
  <view name="alerts" />
-->
  <collection label="Sales">
    <view name="product_monitoring" />
    <view name="purchase_volumes" />
  </collection>
  <collection label="Performance">
    <view name="operational_monitoring" />
    <view name="website_monitoring" />
    <view name="session_monitoring" />
    <view name="predictive_analytics" />
  </collection>
    <collection label="Operations">
    <view name="session_and_purchase_trends" />
    <view name="web_hits" />
  </collection>
  <collection label="Visitors">
    <view name="visitor_monitoring" />
  </collection>
  <collection label="Saved Reports">
    <collection label="Chapter 1 - Play Time">
        <saved source="unclassified" match="cp01" />
     </collection>
    <collection label="Chapter 2 - Diving into Data">
        <saved source="unclassified" match="cp02" />
     </collection>
        <collection label="Chapter 3 - Dashboards
          Visualizations">
        <saved source="unclassified" match="cp03" />
  </collection>
    <collection label="Chapter 4 - Building an App">
        <saved source="unclassified" match="cp04" />
     </collection>
    <collection label="Chapter 5 - Extending Intelligence">
        <saved source="unclassified" match="cp05" />
     </collection>
      <collection label="Chapter 6 - Advanced Searching">
```

```
            <saved source="unclassified" match="cp06" />
      </collection>
      <collection label="Chapter 7 - Enriching Data">
            <saved source="unclassified" match="cp07" />
      </collection>
      <collection label="Chapter 8 - Being Proactive">
            <saved source="unclassified" match="cp08" />
      </collection>
      <collection label="Chapter 9 - Speed Up Intelligence">
            <saved source="unclassified" match="cp09" />
      </collection>
      <collection label="Chapter 10 - Above and Beyond">
            <saved source="unclassified" match="cp10" />
      </collection>
      </collection>
      <collection label="Administration">
        <a href="http://docs.splunk.com">Splunk
          Documentation</a>
        <a href="http://apps.splunk.com">Splunk Apps</a>
        <a href="http://discoveredintelligence.ca/
          getting-started-with-splunk/">Splunk Help</a>
        <view name="dashboards" />
      </collection>
  </nav>
```

You can also edit this file outside of the Splunk GUI, and it can be found in `$SPLUNK_HOME/etc/apps/operational_intelligence/default/data/ui/nav/default.xml`.

8. Once the edits have been made, click on **Save**, and then select the **Operational Intelligence** app as you did in step 2. You should now see that you have fully customized the menus of the application and also changed the navigation toolbar color to gray.

How it works...

In this recipe, you edited the navigation of the Operational Intelligence application to better organize the dashboards and reports. You also changed the color of the navigation bar from the default green to gray. Let's break down the code a bit to explain a few things.

Search fragment	Description

`<nav`
`search_view="search"`
`color="#999999">`
	This is where the color of the navigation menu bar was changed using the HEX color value for gray.

`<!--`
`  <view`
`name="data_models" />`
`  <view name="reports"`
`/>`
`  <view name="alerts" />`
`-->`
	These default views were commented out such that they do not display in the application. You can also simply delete the lines instead.

`<collection`
`label="Sales">`
`    <view`
`name="product_monitoring" />`
`    <view`
`name="purchase_volumes" />`
`  </collection>`
	Next, you added a series of collection elements that group the various views (dashboards) into categories such as sales, performance, and so on.

`<collection label="Saved`
`Reports">`
`    <collection`
`    label="Chapter 1 -`
`    Play Time">`
`        <saved`
`        source=`
`        "unclassified"`
`        match="cp01" />`
`    </collection>`
`...`
`</collection>`
	You then added a series of nested collection elements, which allow for grouping within a common group. In this case, we list all of the reports that you saved during the recipes in this book. Using the `match` parameter, we are able to match the searches by chapter name into their respective collections.
	
	Note that to display searches, we use the `saved` parameter, and earlier, we used the `view` parameter.

Search fragment	Description
```<collection label="Administration"> <a href="http:// docs.splunk.com"> Splunk Documentation</a> <a href="http:// apps.splunk.com"> Splunk Apps</a> <a href="http:// discovered intelligence.ca/ getting-started- with-splunk/"> Splunk Help</a> <view name="dashboards" /> </collection>```	Finally, you added an admin menu that lists a number of resources. To do this, you simply added the familiar HTML `href` code. As well we retain the **Dashboards** menu item for easy access to a centralized listing of all dashboards.

There's more...

This really just skims the surface of some of the customization that can be applied to a Splunk application. For example, you can implement your own CSS for the app or even use your own icons and graphics.

 Splunk has a detailed manual on advanced development, including how to modify the CSS for an app, how to change the icons and images, and how to package your application to upload it to the Splunk app store. For more information, see the documentation at `http://docs.splunk.com/ Documentation/Splunk/latest/AdvancedDev`.

Adding a force-directed graph of web hits

As you have seen from the other recipes throughout the book, we have used many of the normal everyday visualizations seen commonly in spreadsheets and presentations. As data intelligence tools such as Splunk push the boundaries of getting data into a user's hands, there is a need to deliver and represent data via new and unique visualizations.

This recipe will show you how to install the Splunk web framework and create a **force-directed graph (FDG)** of relationships between web page hits that will be populated as a new dashboard in the Operational Intelligence application.

Getting ready

To step through this recipe, you will need a running Splunk Enterprise server, with the sample data loaded from *Chapter 1, Play Time – Getting Data In*. You should be familiar with navigating the Splunk user interface and using the Splunk search language. Some basic knowledge of JavaScript is recommended.

How to do it...

Follow the steps in this recipe to add a force-directed graph that illustrates web hits:

1. Log in to your Splunk server.
2. From the top menu, select **Apps** and then select **Manage Apps**.

3. Click on **Find more apps online**.

4. In the app search field, enter Web Framework, and click on the magnifying glass button.

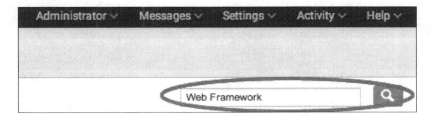

5. Find **Splunk Web Framework Toolkit** and click on the **Install free** button.

 If your Splunk server is not connected to the Internet, you will not be able to use this method to install the app. Instead, head to `http://apps.splunk.com/app/1613/`, download the app, and then click on the **Install app from file** button after completing step 2.

6. Enter your Splunk app's username and password. If you don't have an account, go to Splunk.com and register for an account.

7. Click on the **Login** button.

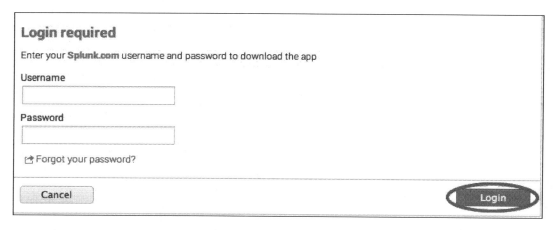

8. Splunk will need to restart. Click on the **Restart Splunk** button.

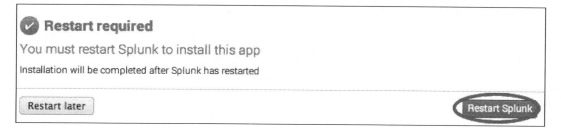

9. Once Splunk has restarted, click on **Ok** on the confirmation alert.

10. From a console window or a file explorer window, go to the `$SPLUNK_HOME/etc/apps/operational_intelligence` directory and create an `appserver` folder and then a `static` folder so that the complete path is now `$SPLUNK_HOME/etc/apps/operational_intelligence/appserver/static`.

11. Copy the `components` folder from the toolkit into the newly created `static` folder in your **Operational Intelligence** application.

   In Linux, copy the contents of the `components` folder to the `static` folder you just created in your `operational_intelligence` application:

   ```
   cp -R
   $SPLUNK_HOME/etc/apps/splunk_wftoolkit/django/splunk_wftoolkit/
   static/splunk_wftoolkit/components
   $SPLUNK_HOME/etc/apps/operational_intelligence/appserver/
   static/
   ```

 Note that `$SPLUNK_HOME` is the directory of your Splunk install, which is generally `/opt/splunk` by default in Linux.

   In Windows, copy the contents of the `components` folder in `c:\program files\splunk\etc\apps\splunk_wftoolkit\django\splunk_wftoolkit\static\splunk_wftoolkit\components` to the `static` folder you just created in your `operational_intelligence` application.

12. Log in to your Splunk server.

13. Select the **Operational Intelligence** application.

14. Click on the **Administration** menu and then click on the **Dashboards** menu item.

15. Click on the **Create New Dashboard** button.

16. In the **Create New Dashboard** window, enter `Web Hits` in the **Title** field and select **Shared in App** in the **Permissions** field.

17. Click on **Create Dashboard**.

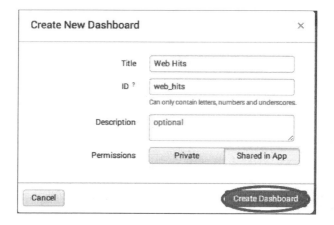

18. Click on **Done**.

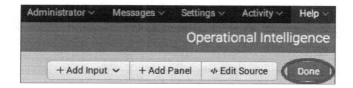

19. Click on the **Edit** button.

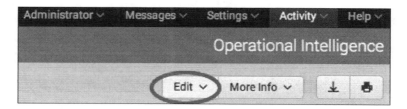

20. Click on the **Convert to HTML** menu item.

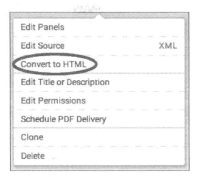

21. Click on the **Replace Current** option.

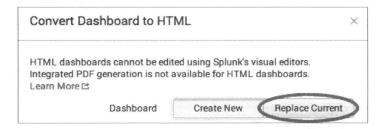

22. Click on **Convert Dashboard**.

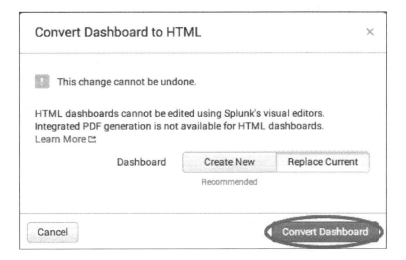

23. Click on the **Edit HTML** button.

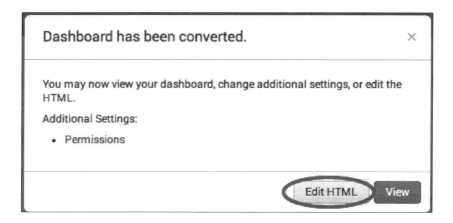

24. In the dashboard editor form, locate the HTML `<div>` tag with the `data-role="main"` value and update it to look like the following code:

```
<div class="dashboard-body container-fluid main-section-body"
data-role="main">
    <div class="dashboard-header clearfix">
        <h2>Web Hits</h2>
        <p class="description"></p>
    </div>
    <div class="dashboard-row dashboard-row1">
        <div class="dashboard-cell" style="width: 100%;">
            <div class="dashboard-panel clearfix">
                <div class="panel-element-row">
                    <div class="dashboard-element chart"
id="element1" style="width: 100%">
                        <div class="panel-head">
                            <h3>Webpage relationship</h3>
                        </div>
                        <div class="panel-body">
                        <div id="fd-chart"></div>
                        </div>
                    </div>
                </div>
            </div>
        </div>
    </div>
</div>
```

25. Locate the `require.config` statement just below in the script section and add the additional path that will help Splunk find the toolkit components. Add the app path to the `require.config` statement as follows (remember to add a comma to the preceding array item):

```
require.config({
    baseUrl: "{{SPLUNKWEB_URL_PREFIX}}/static/js",
    waitSeconds: 0, // Disable require.js load timeout
    paths:
    {
        "app": "../app"
    }
});
```

26. Locate the `require` portion of the JavaScript just below and add this item to the array (remember to add a comma to the preceding array item):

```
"app/operational_intelligence/components/forcedirected/
forcedirected"
```

27. Below the `function` statement, add `ForceDirected` (remember to add a comma to the preceding array item):

```
PostProcessManager,
UrlTokenModel,
ForceDirected
```

28. Locate the `SEARCH MANAGERS` section of the JavaScript and add the following code:

```
var search1 = new SearchManager({
    "id": "search1",
    "status_buckets": 0,
    "latest_time": "now",
    "search": " index=main sourcetype=access_combined | rex
field=referer \".*(?<sourcepage>\/.*?)$\" | stats count by
sourcepage, uri_path",
    "cancelOnUnload": true,
    "earliest_time": "-6h",
    "app": utils.getCurrentApp(),
    "auto_cancel": 0,
    "preview": true
}, {tokens: true, tokenNamespace: "submitted"});
```

29. Locate the `VIEWS: VISUALIZATION ELEMENTS` section of the JavaScript (close to the bottom of the page) and add the following code:

```
var forcegraph = new ForceDirected({
        'id' : 'fd1',
        'managerid' : 'search1',
        'el' : $('#fd-chart')
    }).render();
```

30. Click on **Save**, and you will be taken back to the dashboard.

31. After a short while, you should see the force-directed graph load on your dashboard. This shows the relationships between pages and page transitions.

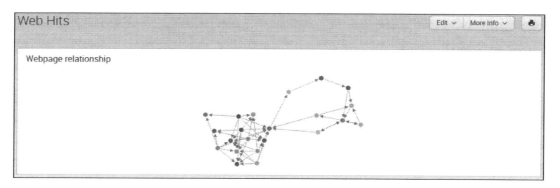

How it works...

Splunk provides the Web Framework Toolkit app to help demonstrate how different libraries can be used to create visualizations such as the force-directed graph. This app comes with prebuilt D3.js visualizations that we can use in our own apps. Force-directed graphs are visualizations that render the connectivity and clustering between objects. The typical force-directed drawing algorithm places similar objects in closer proximity to each other and unrelated objects farther apart.

In order to use the toolkit and FDG, you first had to install the necessary app and then copy the required libraries over to the Operational Intelligence application. This is useful if your app is going to be distributed as it reduces the dependency on the other apps being installed.

The dashboard needs to be in the HTML format for the FDG to be inserted, so you created an empty dashboard in SimpleXML and then converted it to HTML. You then added the HTML code that will hold the FDG and ensured that it was set with all the correct CSS classes, in order to ensure that the formatting matches the app.

The majority of the dashboard functionality comes in the JavaScript section. You first added references to the libraries that you copied into the Operational Intelligence app from the Web Framework Toolkit. You then added a search manager object that controls the searching functionality and returns the data to the graph object. Finally, you added an object that will hold the FDG and told it which HTML entity it is to be put in.

A good walkthrough of HTML can be found on the Splunk developer website at `http://dev./view/webframework-htmldashboards/SP-CAAAETK`.

Additionally, to learn more about D3.js and the types of visualizations that you can create with it, visit `http://d3js.org/`.

There's more...

Splunk is very flexible, and there are a few tweaks we can make to improve or modify the behavior of the dashboard.

Changing the time range on the search manager

The search manager JavaScript object controls and co-ordinates the search requests, and as such, it can be modified with different settings to control the different aspects of its behavior.

One of the parameters that can be easily modified is the time range. This can be done by hardcoding a new value or linking it with other controls such as dropdowns or textboxes.

To change the search time range from the previous 6 hours to the current business week, update the search manager attributes of `latest_time` and `earliest_time` as shown in the following code:

```
var search1 = new SearchManager({
    "id": "search1",
    "status_buckets": 0,
    "latest_time": "+7d@w6",
    "search": "index=main sourcetype=access_combined | rex
field=referer \".*(?<sourcepage>\/.*?)$\" | stats count by sourcepage,
uri_path",
    "cancelOnUnload": true,
    "earliest_time": "@w1",
    "app": utils.getCurrentApp(),
    "auto_cancel": 0,
    "preview": true
}, {tokens: true, tokenNamespace: "submitted"});
```

See also

- ▶ The *Adding a calendar heatmap of product purchases* recipe
- ▶ The *Remotely querying Splunk's REST API for unique page views* recipe
- ▶ The *Creating a Python application to return unique IP addresses* recipe

Adding a calendar heatmap of product purchases

As we saw in the *Adding a force-directed graph of web hits* recipe, using the D3 visualizations that come included in the Splunk Web Framework Toolkit app allow for more creative and unique representations of our data.

This recipe will show you how to create a new dashboard containing a calendar heatmap of product purchases for the past week and place it into the Operational Intelligence application.

Getting ready

To step through this recipe, you will need a running Splunk Enterprise server, with the sample data loaded from *Chapter 1, Play Time – Getting Data In*. You should be familiar with navigating the Splunk user interface and using the Splunk search language. You must also have completed the *Adding a force-directed graph of web hits* recipe in this chapter, as the Web Framework Toolkit app will be leveraged for this recipe. Some basic knowledge of JavaScript is recommended.

How to do it...

Follow the steps in this recipe to create a new dashboard that contains a calendar heatmap of purchases:

1. Log in to your Splunk server.
2. Select the **Operational Intelligence** application.

3. Click on the **Administration** menu and then click on the **Dashboards** menu item.
4. Click on the **Create New Dashboard** button.
5. In the **Create New Dashboard** window, enter Purchase Volumes in the **Title** field and select **Shared in App** in the **Permissions** field.
6. Click on **Create Dashboard**.

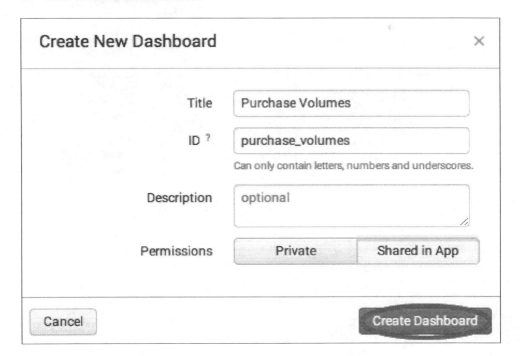

7. Click on **Done**.

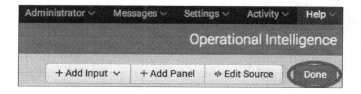

8. Click on the **Edit** button.

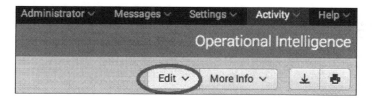

9. Click on the **Convert to HTML** menu item.

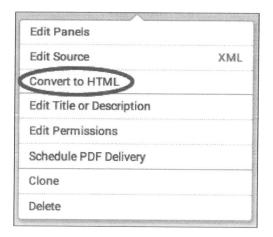

10. Click on the **Replace Current** option.

11. Click on **Convert Dashboard**.

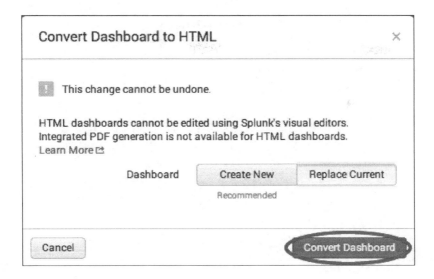

12. Click on the **Edit HTML** button.

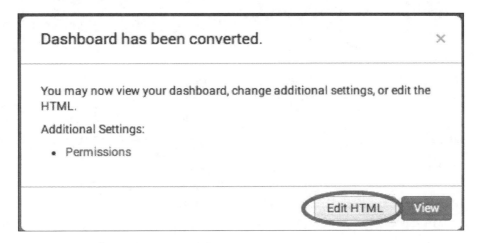

13. In the dashboard editor form, locate the HTML `<div>` tag with the `data-role="main"` value and update it to look like the following lines of code:

```
<div class="dashboard-body container-fluid main-section-
body" data-role="main">
    <div class="dashboard-header clearfix">
        <h2>Purchase Volumes</h2>
        <p class="description"></p>
    </div>
```

```
<div class="dashboard-row dashboard-row1">
    <div class="dashboard-cell" style="width: 100%;">
        <div class="dashboard-panel clearfix">
            <div class="panel-element-row">
                <div class="dashboard-element chart"
id="element1" style="width: 100%">
                    <div class="panel-head">
                        <h3>Volumes</h3>
                    </div>
                    <div class="panel-body">
                    <div id="cal-chart"></div>
                    </div>
                </div>
            </div>
        </div>
    </div>
</div>
```

14. Locate the `require.config` statement and add the additional path that will help Splunk find the toolkit components. Add the app path as follows (remember to add a comma to the preceding item after `0`):

```
require.config({
    baseUrl: "{{SPLUNKWEB_URL_PREFIX}}/static/js",
    waitSeconds: 0, // Disable require.js load timeout
    paths:
    {
        "app": "../app"
    }
});
```

15. Locate the `require` portion of the JavaScript and add this item to the array (remember to add a comma to the preceding array item):

`"app/operational_intelligence/components/calendarheatmap/calendarheatmap"`

16. Below the `function` statement, add `CalendarHeatmap` (remember to add a comma to the preceding array item):

```
PostProcessManager,
UrlTokenModel,
CalendarHeatmap
```

17. Locate the SEARCH MANAGERS section of the JavaScript and add the following code:

```
var search1 = new SearchManager({
    "id": "search1",
    "status_buckets": 0,
    "latest_time": "now",
    "search": " index=main sourcetype=log4j requestType=checkout |
timechart span=1h sum(total) as purchase_total",
    "cancelOnUnload": true,
    "earliest_time": "-7d",
    "app": utils.getCurrentApp(),
    "auto_cancel": 0,
    "preview": true
}, {tokens: true, tokenNamespace: "submitted"});
```

18. Locate the VIEWS: VISUALIZATION ELEMENTS section of the JavaScript and add the following lines of code:

```
var calendarheatmap = new CalendarHeatmap({
        'id' : 'fcal',
        'managerid' : 'search1',
        'domain' : 'day',
        'subDomain' : 'x_hour',
        'el' : $('#cal-chart')
}).render();
```

19. Click on **Save**, and you will be taken back to the dashboard.

20. You should see a dashboard rendering the amount of product purchases each hour for the past 7 days as a calendar heatmap visualization. The scroll arrows allow you to scroll to different days in the calendar.

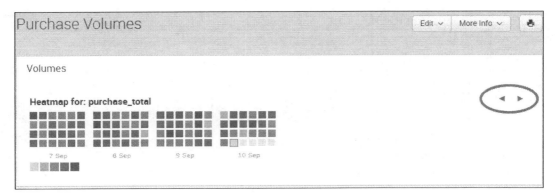

How it works...

The calendar heatmap visualization is a way to represent and render the magnitude of time-series data as a heatmap. In this case, we represented the amount of purchases per hour for each given day over the past 7 days. This visualization can be used to spot trends or patterns in purchasing either by time of day, day of the week, or week of the year.

As we saw in the *Adding a force-directed graph of web hits* recipe, the calendar heatmap is a prebuilt component that is available when you install the Splunk Web Framework Toolkit app.

The dashboard needs to be in HTML format, so you created an empty dashboard in SimpleXML and then converted it. You then added the HTML code that will hold the heatmap visualization and set the correct CSS classes to ensure that it is formatted with the right look and feel to match the Operational Intelligence app.

The majority of the dashboard functionality comes in the JavaScript section. You first added references to the libraries you copied into the Operational Intelligence app from the Web Framework Toolkit app so that the Operational Intelligence app can see them. Next, you added a search manager object that controls the searching functionality and returns the data to the heatmap object. Finally, you added an object that will hold our heatmap and tell it which HTML entity it will be put into.

 To learn more about D3.js and the types of visualizations that you can create with it, visit `http://d3js.org/`.

See also

▸   The *Adding a force-directed graph of web hits* recipe
▸   The *Remotely querying Splunk's REST API for unique page views* recipe
▸   The *Creating a Python application to return unique IP addresses* recipe

Remotely querying Splunk's REST API for unique page views

Web services have become the technology of choice for most of the applications that we use daily. By leveraging the connections that we use for regular web browsing, we can transfer data in a more programmatic fashion; this allows for easy integration between applications.

In this recipe, you will learn how to use Splunk's REST API to return unique IP addresses from the web server logs of our application.

Getting ready

To step through this recipe, you will need a running Splunk Enterprise server, with the sample data loaded from *Chapter 1, Play Time – Getting Data In*. You should be familiar with navigating the Splunk user interface and using the Splunk search language. This recipe will use the open source command-line tool, **curl**. There are also other command-line tools available, such as **wget**. The curl tool is usually installed by default on most Mac and Linux systems but can be downloaded for Windows systems as well.

 For more information on curl, visit `http://curl.haxx.se/`.

How to do it...

Follow the steps in this recipe to remotely query Splunk for unique page views using the REST API. Note that you will need to change `admin` and `changeme` throughout this recipe to the Splunk username and password you have configured:

1. Open a console or command-line window on your Splunk server.

2. Create an initial request to ensure that the authentication works correctly. If it is successful, it will return a list of Splunk apps installed in an XML format:

   ```
   curl  -k -u admin:changeme
   https://localhost:8089/servicesNS/admin
   ```

3. Update the REST endpoint in the request. This will return a fatal error as we have not defined a search:

   ```
   curl  -k -u admin:changeme
   https://localhost:8089/servicesNS/admin/search/search/jobs/
   export
   ```

4. Add the search to be executed to the request. This will return the results of the search in XML over the past 7 days, as we are including the `earliest` field value:

   ```
   curl  -k -u admin:changeme --data-urlencode search="search
   index=main sourcetype=access_combined earliest=-7d status=200 |
   dedup clientip uri_path | stats count by uri_path"
   https://localhost:8089/servicesNS/admin/search/search/jobs/
   export
   ```

 In all of the curl examples, the username `admin` and password `changeme` were used. This is the default username and password set in a new installation of Splunk, and it is recommended that you update it with a more secure password.

How it works...

In this recipe, you executed a Splunk search using the REST API to look for unique page views over the past 7 days. On every Splunk installation, Splunk opens port 8089 by default to listen for REST requests. The requests can be sent using command-line tools such as curl, as seen in our examples, or they can be called using the browser directly.

Splunk supports GET, POST, and DELETE requests. You use a GET request to retrieve or view data, a POST request to update data, and a DELETE request to remove data. Also, results can be returned in various formats such as XML, JSON, and CSV.

The type of operation you are looking to perform will change the value of the URL you are accessing. In this recipe, we are using an endpoint that allows for an export job, and as such, the URL included search/jobs/export.

As with all of Splunk, the access controls and permissions that you set up in Splunk are enforced in the REST API as well. This ensures that your users can't get around any security restrictions using tools other than the normal web interface. All requests to the REST API are also encrypted using SSL. Self-signed SSL certificates are created by default but can also be replaced with the ones signed by your own certificate authority.

 Even the Splunk Web GUI uses the Splunk REST API behind the scenes when performing operations such as searching. For more information on REST, check out the REST Wikipedia page at http://en.wikipedia. org/wiki/Representational_State_Transfer.

There's more...

The REST API in Splunk is very flexible, and there are a few tweaks we can make to improve or modify the behavior of the API calls.

Authenticating with a session token

Instead of having to pass the username and password on every request to the API, as we saw by setting the –u parameter, we can create a session token and then pass this on subsequent requests. The advantage of this is that it reduces the load on your Splunk server, as it does not require to authenticate every request.

First, create the session token by calling the `auth/login` endpoint:

```
curl -k https://localhost:8089/servicesNS/admin/search/auth/login/ -d"
username=admin&password=changeme"
```

This will return a token such as the following:

```
<response>
<sessionKey>XzcmjvXT4SKL6loDHx6dsGxFCrQNENwlWoKraskF_yQbvDyQ47zIl9
icR1VUzA6dX8tGbKiCMghnhKfbPslKuzSaV4eXLioKwo</sessionKey>
</response>
```

Then, use the value contained in the session key tags as an authentication header in the subsequent requests:

```
curl  -k --data-urlencode search="search
index=main sourcetype=access_combined status=200 latest=now
earliest=-15m | dedup clientip uri_path | stats count by uri_path"
-H "Authorization: Splunk
XzcmjvXT4SKL6loDHx6dsGxFCrQNENwlWoKraskF_yQbvDyQ47zIl9icR1VUzA6dX8tGb
KiCMghnhKfbPslKuzSaV4eXLioKwo"
https://localhost:8089/servicesNS/admin/search/search/jobs/export
```

See also

▶ The *Adding a calendar heatmap of product purchases* recipe

▶ The *Creating a Python application to return unique IP addresses* recipe

▶ The *Creating a custom search command to format product names* recipe

Creating a Python application to return unique IP addresses

The Splunk Python SDK was one of the first SDKs that Splunk developed and has since been used to integrate Splunk's ability to process and analyze large streams of data into custom applications. By leveraging the ability to integrate directly with your applications, you can see immediate results and fully leverage your operational intelligence capabilities.

In this recipe, you will learn how to use Splunk's Python SDK to create a custom Python application that will return unique IP addresses from the web server logs of our application.

Getting ready

To step through this recipe, you will need a running Splunk Enterprise server, with the sample data loaded from *Chapter 1, Play Time – Getting Data In*. You should be familiar with navigating the Splunk user interface and using the Splunk search language. Some basic knowledge of Python is recommended. The Splunk Python SDK should also be downloaded and available on your Splunk Enterprise server.

 The Splunk Python SDK can be downloaded from `http://dev.splunk.com`. For this book, v1.2.3 of the Splunk Python SDK was used.

How to do it...

Follow the steps in this recipe to create a Python application that returns unique IP addresses:

1. Open a console window on your Splunk server.

2. Execute the following command to export the Python SDK directory location as an environment variable. Update the value of PYTHONPATH with the actual path where you have installed the SDK:

   ```
   export PYTHONPATH=~/splunk-sdk-python
   ```

3. Create a new file called `uniqueip.py` and open it for editing.

4. To the `uniqueip.py` file, add the import statements that are needed to load the correct Splunk libraries that we will be using:

   ```
   import splunklib.client as client
   import splunklib.results as results
   ```

5. Add constants to hold the values of the Splunk server we are connecting to and the credentials we are connecting with. You will likely need to change the Splunk username and password credentials from the default ones:

   ```
   HOST     = "localhost"
   PORT     = 8089
   USERNAME = "admin"
   PASSWORD = "changeme"
   ```

6. Define the service instance we will be using to connect and communicate with our Splunk Enterprise server:

   ```
   service = client.connect(
       host=HOST,
       port=PORT,
       username=USERNAME,
       password=PASSWORD)
   ```

7. Define a dictionary of search arguments that will be used with our search that will modify its behavior:

```
kwargs = {"earliest_time": "-15m",
          "latest_time": "now",
          "search_mode": "normal",
          "exec_mode": "blocking"}
```

8. Add a variable to hold the search query we will be using to return our list of unique IP addresses. Any double quotes in the search query need to be escaped:

```
searchquery = "search index=main
sourcetype=\"access_combined\" | stats count by clientip"
```

9. Create the job request and print out to the console when it has been completed:

```
job = service.jobs.create(searchquery, **kwargs)
print "Job completed...printing results!\n"
```

10. Create a reference to the search results as follows:

```
search_results = job.results()
```

11. Add a ResultsReader object, iterate through the results, and print out the IP address and the associated count:

```
reader = results.ResultsReader(search_results)
for result in reader:
    print "Result: %s => %s" % (result['clientip'],result['count']
)
```

The completed program code should look as follows:

```
import splunklib.client as client
import splunklib.results as results


HOST      = "localhost"
PORT      = 8089
USERNAME = "admin"
PASSWORD = "changeme"

service = client.connect(
    host=HOST,
    port=PORT,
    username=USERNAME,
    password=PASSWORD)

kwargs = {"earliest_time": "-15m",
          "latest_time": "now",
          "search_mode": "normal",
```

```
                    "exec_mode": "blocking"}

    searchquery = "search index=main sourcetype=\"access_combined\" |
    stats count by clientip"

    job = service.jobs.create(searchquery, **kwargs)
    print "Job completed...printing results!\n"

    search_results = job.results()

    reader = results.ResultsReader(search_results)
    for result in reader:
        print "Result: %s => %s" % (result['clientip'],result['count']
    )
```

12. To execute your program, run:

```
python uniqueip.py
```

The output of the program should look like this:

```
Result: 106.207.151.69 => 1
Result: 107.220.112.174 => 12
Result: 12.181.33.129 => 12
Result: 120.76.179.40 => 1
Result: 128.180.195.184 => 10
```

The program output details the number of events in the web access logs by the client IP over the last 15-minute timeframe specified in the Python code.

> In all of the curl examples, the username admin and password changeme were used. This is the default username and password set in the new installation of Splunk and it is recommended that you update it with a more secure password.

How it works...

At the core of working with Splunk is the REST API. The REST API is used by Splunk to do everything from authenticating to searching to configuration management. As we have seen in the *Remotely querying Splunk's REST API for unique page views* recipe of this chapter, we can interact with the REST API very easily with simple command-line tools.

Organizations that maintain their own line of business applications and are looking to integrate the operational intelligence they can get out of Splunk can do so by leveraging the SDK for the language that their application is written in. Splunk has created SDKs for many of the mainstream programming languages.

The SDK is a wrapper around calls to the REST API and helps abstract the details by providing easy-to-use objects that can be interacted with. Most of the same REST endpoints available natively can be created as objects from the SDK.

As seen in the recipe, the majority of functionality that is used is assisting with the creation of a connection and management of the authentication, creation of a search job, and processing of the results. There are also objects that can be created to manage users and roles, getting data into Splunk, and working with saved searches.

There's more...

In this recipe, we began to scratch the surface of utilizing the Python SDK. We also saw how you can extend your own applications to leverage Splunk data. As with most of Splunk, there are many different ways to manipulate and view your data.

Paginating the results of your search

Leveraging the program created in this recipe, you can modify it as follows to paginate through your results:

```python
import splunklib.client as client
import splunklib.results as results

...

job = service.jobs.create(searchquery, **kwargs)
print "Job completed...printing results!\n"

total   = job["resultCount"]
offset  = 0;
count   = 10;

while (offset < int(total)):
    page_args = {"count": count,
                 "offset": offset}

    search_results = job.results(**page_args)
```

```
reader = results.ResultsReader(search_results)
for result in reader:
    print "Result: %s => %s" %
    (result['clientip'],result['count'])
offset += count
```

See also

▶ The *Remotely querying Splunk's REST API for unique page views* recipe

▶ The *Adding a calendar heatmap of product purchases* recipe

▶ The *Creating a custom search command to format product names* recipe

Creating a custom search command to format product names

Sometimes, you just need that extra bit of logic or custom processing of data that might be very unique to your line of business. You might also simply be in the position where you have picky executives who like to see their data formatted in a very specific manner.

In this recipe, you will learn how to use Splunk's Python SDK to create a custom search command that you can use to apply consistent formatting to product names or any other string field by capitalizing the first letter of each word in the string.

Getting ready

To step through this recipe, you will need a running Splunk Enterprise server, with the sample data loaded from *Chapter 1, Play Time – Getting Data In*. You should be familiar with navigating the Splunk user interface and using the Splunk search language. Some basic knowledge of Python is recommended. The Splunk Python SDK should also be downloaded and available on your Splunk Enterprise server.

The Splunk Python SDK can be downloaded from http://dev.splunk.com. For this book, v1.2.3 of the Splunk Python SDK was used.

How to do it...

Follow the steps in this recipe to create a custom search command to format product names:

1. Open a console terminal on your Splunk server.

2. Change to the directory where you downloaded the Splunk Python SDK.

3. Expand the ZIP file using an appropriate tool located on your Splunk server.

4. Create a `splunklib` directory inside the `$SPLUNK_HOME/etc/apps/operational_intelligence/bin` directory.

5. Copy the `splunk-sdk-python/splunklib/searchcommands` directory to `$SPLUNK_HOME/etc/apps/operational_intelligence/bin/splunklib`.

6. Create and add the following code to `commands.conf` located in the `$SPLUNK_HOME/etc/apps/operational_intelligence/local` directory:

```
[fixname]
filename = fixname.py
supports_getinfo = true
supports_rawargs = true
outputheader = true
requires_srinfo = true
```

7. In `$SPLUNK_HOME/etc/apps/operational_intelligence/bin`, create `fixname.py` and add the following code:

```
#!/usr/bin/env python
import sys
from splunklib.searchcommands import \
    dispatch, StreamingCommand, Configuration, Option, validators


@Configuration()
class FixNameCommand(StreamingCommand):
    """ Takes the first letter of each word in the field and
capitalizes it
    ##Syntax
    .. code-block::
        fixname fieldname=<field>
    ##Description
    Takes the first letter of each word in the field and
capitalizes it

    ##Example
    Uppercase the first letter of each word in the message field
in the _internal
    index

    .. code-block::
        index=_internal | head 20 | fixname fieldname=message
    """
```

```
fieldname = Option(
                doc='''
                **Syntax:** **fieldname=***<fieldname>*
                **Description:** Name of the field that will be
capitalized''',
                require=True, validate=validators.Fieldname())

    def stream(self, records):
                self.logger.debug('FixNameCommand: %s' % self)
# logs command line
                for record in records:
                                record[self.fieldname] =
record[self.fieldname].title()
                                yield record


dispatch(FixNameCommand, sys.argv, sys.stdin, sys.stdout, __
name__)
```

8. Ensure that the `fixname.py` script is marked as an executable by executing the following command:

    chmod a+x fixname.py

9. Restart Splunk.

10. Log in to Splunk.

11. Select the **Operational Intelligence** application.

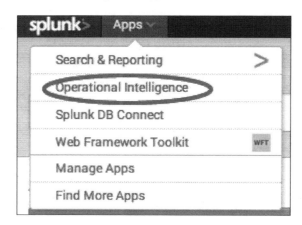

12. In the search bar, enter the following search over **Last 24 hours**:

```
index=main sourcetype=log4j | eval
ProductName=lower(ProductName) | fixname
fieldname=ProductName
```

You should see that despite forcing the `ProductName` field values to be all lowercase, the `fixname` command has now capitalized each value.

How it works...

The Splunk Python SDK can allow us to not only get information out of Splunk in an easy, programmatic way, but also manipulate the processing of events as they move through your search.

Originally, custom search commands could be created using Python and added to Splunk, but they were difficult to debug and had no logging mechanism. With the Python SDK, you can now create your own custom search commands in a quicker and easier way with better tools for troubleshooting.

Custom search commands come in three different flavors.

Command type	Description
Generating commands	This type of command generates new events that are inserted into the results. Examples include commands that read from lookup files, such as `inputcsv`.
Reporting commands	This type of command takes incoming events and generates a new set of outgoing events usually based on some sort of processing or analysis. Examples include commands that do statistics, such as `stats` and `top`.
Streaming commands	This type of command takes incoming events and modifies or filters the outgoing events. Examples include commands that add or replace fields or eliminate events based on some calculation, such as `eval`, `rename`, and `where`.

Let's explain how the `fixname.py` script works.

Script fragment	Description

`#!/usr/bin/env python`
 	
`import sys`
 	
`from splunklib.searchcommands import \`
`    dispatch, StreamingCommand,`
`    Configuration, Option,`
`    validators`
	Import the necessary modules and libraries. This includes the Splunk library that has to be copied into the `bin` directory of the Splunk app.

Script fragment	Description
`@Configuration()`	Here, we apply any configuration options that need to be specified to Splunk when the command is executed.
`class FixNameCommand` `(StreamingCommand):`	This line defines the class name of the command as well as any class inheritance that might be required. In this case, our `FixNameCommand` class is to inherit from, the `StreamingCommand` class.

``
""" Takes the first letter of each
word in the field and capitalizes
it
 	
    ##Syntax
 	
    .. code-block::
        fixname
fieldname=<field>
 	
    ##Description
 	
    Takes the first letter of each
    word in the field and
    capitalizes it
 	
    ##Example
 	
    Uppercase the first letter of
    each word in the message field
    in the _internal
    index
 	
    .. code-block::
        index=_internal
	head
	20 |
	        fixname
	fieldname=message
	
	    """
	``
		Here, we outline all of the help information that Splunk will present through the Splunk Web interface in the search bar.

Script fragment	Description
| ```
fieldname = Option(
    doc='''
    **Syntax:**

**fieldname=***<fieldname>*
    **Description:** Name of
    the field that will be
    capitalized''',
    require=True, validate=
    validators.Fieldname())
``` | This section defines the various options that the custom command will accept or is required to accept. The format as well as any validation that is required is also specified here. |
| ```
def stream(self, records):
    self.logger.debug
    ('FixNameCommand: %s'
    % self)   # logs
    command line
    for record in records:
        record[self.
fieldname]
        = record[self.
fieldname].title()
        yield record
``` | This section implements the `stream` function. The `stream` function is called when records are to be processed. In this example, we iterate through each of the records, and depending on the field that was defined in the options, we execute the `title` method on that value. |
| ```
dispatch(FixNameCommand, sys.
argv,
sys.stdin, sys.stdout,
__name__)
``` | Finally, we dispatch the command, passing in the required arguments. |

The `fixname` command is a straightforward command that leverages the `title` method of a `String` object in Python. When the `title` method is called, it will uppercase the string for which it is called for. It is a streaming command, as it is manipulating a field within an event as it moves through the command.

By leveraging the SDK, any number of commands can be developed that integrate with third-party systems or apply proprietary algorithms or logic to implement business rules that give organizations better visibility into their operations.

 For more information on how to create custom search commands, check out the documentation at `http://dev.splunk.com`.
```

See also

- ▸ The *Remotely querying Splunk's REST API for unique page views* recipe
- ▸ The *Creating a Python application to return unique IP addresses* recipe

Summary

The key takeaways from this chapter are as follows:

- ▸ Splunk provides methods to customize the user experience within an application through the use of navigation menus, CSS templates, and much more
- ▸ Use advanced visualizations to expose even more operational intelligence
- ▸ Use command-line tools to make simple integrations possible
- ▸ Leverage Splunk SDKs to create deep integration with your own applications
- ▸ Extend Splunk with custom search commands to add value directly into your searches

Index

M

map 78
map panel
  adding, SimpleXML used 152
marker gauge 78
maximum concurrent checkouts
  displaying 212-217
maximum number of concurrent sessions
    over time
  displaying 342-347
maximum pause
  defining 204
method requests
  by host 101
  timechart, creating 98-101
modular inputs
  using 22-26
monitor input type 13
multi-tier web requests
  average execution time, calculating 205-211

N

NAT (Network Address Translation) 91
network input
  adding, via CLI 18
  adding, via inputs.conf 18
network ports
  data, getting through 15-18
number of errors
  displaying, gauge used 92-95
number of method requests
  charting, by host 96, 97
  charting, by type 96, 97
number of purchases
  backfilling, by city 332-340
  summary index, generating search 339

O

object attributes
  Auto-Extracted 159
  Eval-Expression 159
  Geo IP 159
  Lookup 159
  Regular Expression 159

object constraint
  child object constraint 158
  event object constraint 158
  search object constraint 158
  transaction object constraint 158
object types
  child objects 158
  event objects 158
  search objects 158
  transaction objects 158
one-time indexing
  of data files, via Spunk CLI 14
OpenStreetMap service
  URL 151
Operational Intelligence application
  creating 117-119
  creating, from another application 119, 120
Operational Intelligence dashboard
  creating 79-81
  permissions, changing 82
outputlookup command
  <filename> 251
  <tablename> 251
  append 251
  create_empty 251
  createinapp 251
  max 251
outputs.conf
  receiving indexer, adding via 29
overlay
  adding, to Sessions Over Time chart 147

P

PDF delivery
  scheduling, of dashboard 152-155
permission
  changing, of saved reports 126
  URL 272
per-result alert 286
pie chart
  about 77
  using, to show most accessed
    web pages 82-86
pivot charting
  top error codes 194-196

T

table command 44, 48

tables
drilldown feature, disabling 136

tags
about 36
adding, via tags.conf 39
defining 37, 38
URL 37

tail command 44

Technical Add-Ons (TAs) 45

ticket
creating, for application errors 269-273

timechart
creating, of method requests 98-101
creating, of response times 98-101
creating, of views 98-101

timechart command 43

time modifiers 44

time range
changing, on search manager 367

time series data points
using, with scatter chart 104

top command 44

top error codes
pivot charting 194-196

top-referring websites
identifying 55-57
searching, stats command used 57

top viewed products
listing 64-66

total number of items purchased
predicting 226

total sales transactions
pivoting 178-182

transaction
events, defining 204
grouping 198
identifying 198
maximum pause, defining 204
span, defining 204

transaction command
about 44, 69
URL 205

transaction object constraint 158

transaction objects 158

transforming command 348

trigger conditions
about 287
custom 287
number of hosts 287
number of results 287
number of sources 287
per-result 287

triggered alerts
viewing, on Splunk's Alert manager 293, 294

U

unique IP addresses
returning, by creating Python
  application 377-381
search results, paginating 381

unique number of visitors
displaying 87-91

unique page views
REST API, querying remotely 374-376

Universal Forwarder (UF)
using, to gather data 26-29

V

value
based on ranges, coloring 92

views
by host 101
timechart, creating 98-101

visitors
geographical map, displaying 148-151
unique number of visitors, displaying 87-91

visualizations
about 76, 77
best practices 78, 79
data, enriching with 76, 77
URL 78

W

About Packt Publishing

Packt, pronounced 'packed', published its first book "*Mastering phpMyAdmin for Effective MySQL Management*" in April 2004 and subsequently continued to specialize in publishing highly focused books on specific technologies and solutions.

Our books and publications share the experiences of your fellow IT professionals in adapting and customizing today's systems, applications, and frameworks. Our solution based books give you the knowledge and power to customize the software and technologies you're using to get the job done. Packt books are more specific and less general than the IT books you have seen in the past. Our unique business model allows us to bring you more focused information, giving you more of what you need to know, and less of what you don't.

Packt is a modern, yet unique publishing company, which focuses on producing quality, cutting-edge books for communities of developers, administrators, and newbies alike. For more information, please visit our website: www.packtpub.com.

Writing for Packt

We welcome all inquiries from people who are interested in authoring. Book proposals should be sent to author@packtpub.com. If your book idea is still at an early stage and you would like to discuss it first before writing a formal book proposal, contact us; one of our commissioning editors will get in touch with you.

We're not just looking for published authors; if you have strong technical skills but no writing experience, our experienced editors can help you develop a writing career, or simply get some additional reward for your expertise.

Implementing Splunk: Big Data Reporting and Development for Operational Intelligence

ISBN: 978-1-84969-328-8   Paperback: 448 pages

Learn to transform your machine data into valuable IT and business insights with this comprehensive and practical tutorial

1. Learn how to search effectively, create fields, build dashboards, reports, and package apps, manage your indexes, integrate into the enterprise, and extend Splunk.

2. Start working with Splunk fast, with a tested set of practical examples and useful advice.

3. Step-by-step instructions and examples with a comprehensive coverage for Splunk veterans and newbies alike.

Pentaho for Big Data Analytics

ISBN: 978-1-78328-215-9   Paperback: 118 pages

Enhance your knowledge of Big Data and leverage the power of Pentaho to extract its treasures

1. A guide to using Pentaho Business Analytics for Big Data analysis.

2. Learn Pentaho's visualization and reporting tools with practical examples and tips.

3. Precise insights into churning Big Data into meaningful knowledge with Pentaho.

Please check **www.PacktPub.com** for information on our titles

43808742R00229

Made in the USA
Lexington, KY
14 August 2015